Praise for Dr. Stephen LaBerge's first ground-breaking book, *Lucid Dreaming*

Also by Stephen LaBerge
Published by Ballantine Books:

LUCID DREAMING

EXPLORING THE WORLD OF LUCID DREAMING

Stephen LaBerge, Ph.D.
and
Howard Rheingold

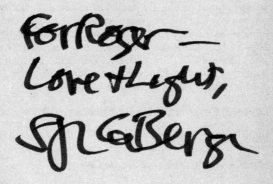

forRoger —
Love + light,

SnLaBerge

BALLANTINE BOOKS • NEW YORK

Grateful acknowledgment is made to the following for permission to reprint previously published material *Harcourt Brace Jovanovich*, Inc.: Figure from *Sensation and Perception*. Third Edition by Stanley Coren and Lawrence Ward. Copyright © 1989 by Harcourt Brace Jovanovich, Inc. Reprinted by permission of the publisher. *The Octagon Press Ltd.*: "The Men and the Butterfly" reproduced by permission from *Letters and Lectures of Idries Shah*. (The Octagon Press Ltd., London).

Library of Congress Catalog Card Number: 89-90884

ISBN 0-345-37410-X

Manufactured in the United States of America

First Hardcover Edition: August 1990
First Mass Market Edition: December 1991
Fourth Printing: September 1992

To Love and Light, with Gratitude,
                                    S.L.
For My Inspiration and Teacher,
my Mother, Geraldine Rheingold,
                                    H.R.

Contents

Exercises

Acknowledgments

We cannot say how much we owe to our predecessors; without the efforts of countless others, this work could not have been accomplished. Thanks to them all, known and unknown.

We especially wish to thank all the people who wrote to us about their experiences with lucid dreaming, especially those whose reports we used. It would have been impossible to obtain permissions from everyone, so we have used initials for attributions rather than full names.

Thanks also to Joanne Blokker, Charles Brandon, the Fetzer Institute, Dr. Oscar Janiger, the Monteverde Foundation, and Jonathan Parker of the Institute for Human Development for financial and other support which made this book possible. Drs. William Dement and Phil Zimbardo provided professional encouragement. Our agent, John Brockman, earned his percentage many times over. Laurie Cook, Dorothy LaBerge, Michael LaPointe, K. Romana Machado, and Judith Rheingold all read drafts of the book and made valuable suggestions. Cheryl Woodruff's perspicacious editing did much to make the book more human and intelligible.

Mushkil Gusha made the usual contribution. Finally, we gratefully acknowledge that Lynne Levitan deserves to be a coauthor for all the work she put into the book.

1

The World of
Lucid Dreaming

The Wonders of
Lucid Dreaming

I realized I was dreaming. I raised my arms and began to rise (actually, I was being lifted). I rose through black sky that blended to indigo, to deep purple, to lavender, to white, then to very bright light. All the time I was being lifted there was the most beautiful music I have ever heard. It seemed like voices rather than instruments. There are no words to describe the JOY I felt. I was very gently lowered back to earth. I had the feeling that I had come to a turning point in my life and I had chosen the right path. The dream, the joy I experienced, was kind of a reward, or so I felt. It was a long, slow slide back to wakefulness with the music echoing in my ears. The euphoria lasted several days; the memory, forever. (A.F., Bay City, Michigan)

I was standing in a field in an open area when my wife pointed in the direction of the sunset. I looked at it and thought, "How odd; I've never seen colors like that before." Then it dawned on me: "I must be dreaming!" Never had I experienced such clarity and perception— the colors were so beautiful and the sense of freedom so exhilarating that I started racing through this beautiful golden wheat field waving my hands in the air and yelling at the top of my voice, "I'm dreaming! I'm dreaming!" Suddenly, I started to lose the dream; it must have been the excitement. I instantly woke up. As it dawned on me what had just happened, I woke my wife and said, "I did it, I did it!" I was conscious within the dream state and I'll never be the same. Funny, isn't it? How a taste of it can affect one like that. It's the freedom, I guess; we see that we truly are in control of our own universe. (D.W., Elk River, Minnesota)

I am studying to become a professional musician (French horn), and I wished to remove my fear of performing in front of people. On several occasions I placed myself in a state of self-hypnosis/daydreaming by relaxing my entire body and mind before going to sleep. Then I focused on my desire to have a dream in which I was performing for a large audience by myself but was not nervous or suffering from any anxiety. On the third night of this experiment, I had a lucid dream in which I was performing a solo recital without accompaniment at Orchestra Hall in Chicago (a place where I have performed once before, but in a full orchestra). I felt no anxiety regarding the audience, and every note that I played made me feel even more confident. I played perfectly a piece that I had heard only once before (and never attempted to play), and the ovation I received added to my confidence. When I woke up, I made a quick note of the dream and the piece that I played. While practicing the next day, I sight-read the piece and played it nearly perfectly. Two weeks (and a few lucid dream performances) later, I performed Shos-

takovich's Fifth Symphony *with the orchestra. For the first time, nerves did not hamper my playing, and the performance went extremely well.* (J.S., Mt. Prospect, Illinois)

Strange, marvelous, and even impossible things regularly happen in dreams, but people usually don't realize that the explanation is that they are dreaming. *Usually* doesn't mean always and there is a highly significant exception to this generalization. Sometimes, dreamers *do* correctly realize the explanation for the bizarre happenings they are experiencing, and *lucid dreams*, like those recounted above, are the result.

Empowered by the knowledge that the world they are experiencing is a creation of their own imagination, lucid dreamers can consciously influence the outcome of their dreams. They can create and transform objects, people, situations, worlds, even themselves. By the standards of the familiar world of physical and social reality, they can do the impossible.

The world of lucid dreams provides a vaster stage than ordinary life for almost anything imaginable, from the frivolous to the sublime. You could, if you chose, revel at a saturnalian festival, soar to the stars, or travel to mysterious lands. You could join those who are testing lucid dreaming as a tool for problem solving, self-healing, and personal growth. Or you could explore the implications of teachings from ancient traditions and reports from modern psychologists that suggest that lucid dreams can help you find your deepest identity—who you really are.

Lucid dreaming has been known for centuries, but has until recently remained a rare and little-understood phenomenon. My own scientific and personal explorations, together with the findings of other dream researchers around the world, have just begun to shed light on this unusual state of consciousness. Recently, this new research field has captured the attention of the population outside the world of scientific dream research because studies have shown that given proper training, people can learn to have lucid dreams.

But why are people interested in learning to be conscious in their dreams? According to my own experience, and the testimony of thousands of other lucid dreamers, lucid dreams can be extraordinarily vivid, intense, pleasurable, and exhilarating. People frequently consider their lucid dreams as among the most wonderful experiences of their lives.

If this were all there were to it, lucid dreams would be delightful, but ultimately trivial entertainment. However, as many have already discovered, you can use lucid dreaming to improve the quality of your *waking* life. Thousands of people have written to me at Stanford telling how they are using the knowledge and experience they have acquired in lucid dreams to help them get more out of living.

Although the outlines of a practical art and science of lucid dreaming are just beginning to emerge and the systematic use of lucid dreaming as a tool for psychological self-exploration is still in its infancy, most people can safely use the available knowledge about lucid dreaming to conduct their own explorations. Probably the only people who should *not* experiment with lucid dreaming are those who are unable to distinguish between waking reality and constructions of their imagination. Learning lucid dreaming will not cause you to lose touch with the difference between waking and dreaming. On the contrary, lucid dreaming is for becoming *more aware*.

Why This New Book?

In *Lucid Dreaming*, I collected the available knowledge on the subject from both ancient and modern sources.

Since that book's publication, some ten thousand people have written to me describing their experiences and discoveries, and requesting more practical information about lucid dreaming. In response to those requests, I decided to collaborate on a new book with Howard Rheingold. Howard has written extensively on topics such as creativity, consciousness, and dreamwork.

Exploring the World of Lucid Dreaming is a self-teaching curriculum, a step-by-step method for learning to have and use lucid dreams. You can learn at your own pace, and to your own depth, how to explore your lucid dreams and use them to enrich your life. You will read a rich variety of examples of actual lucid dreams excerpted from letters to the Stanford program, like the three quoted at the beginning of this chapter. While the kind of "anecdotal evidence" offered by these nonprofessional dream explorers cannot replace the carefully controlled experimentation that is required for testing scientific theories, it does offer invaluable inspiration for continued exploration of the world of lucid dreaming.

Since *Lucid Dreaming*, my research team has continued its laboratory work at Stanford University, mapping mind/body relationships during the dream state and, in courses and workshops with volunteer oneironauts (pronounced oh-NIGH-ro-knots, meaning "explorers of the dream world"), studying techniques for inducing, prolonging, and using lucid dreams.[1] This book draws on a number of sources of knowledge about lucid dreaming, including the Stanford research, the teachings of Tibetan dream yogis, and the work of other scientists. The investigations of the German psychologist Paul Tholey, who has been studying lucid dreams for the past twenty years, have been particularly valuable in writing this book.

Our Approach

This book strives to present, in a step-by-step manner, everything you need to know in order to learn the skill of lucid dreaming. All the many techniques and exercises presented work for some people, but how effective each exercise will be for you depends on your individual psychology and physiology. Experiment with the exercises, test them for yourself, and see what works best for you.

The basic structure of the book is as follows: You will be guided through preparations for learning to have lucid dreams, provided with plainly spelled out techniques for learning lucid dreaming, and then shown how lucid dreaming can be applied to your life. If you practice diligently, the lucid dream induction techniques should significantly increase your frequency of lucid dreaming. Chapter 5 presents the relevant scientific background and theory to help you understand the basis for the applications. The remaining chapters are devoted to describing how you can use lucid dreaming to enhance your life, both waking and sleeping. Examples selected from our compendium of lucid dreams illustrate what others have achieved, to model for you some of the potentials of lucid dreaming.

As far as we know, this is the first time that detailed instructions on lucid dreaming have been widely available to the general public. However, you are not likely to learn lucid dreaming by quickly skimming through this book. Like most anything else worth learning, lucid dreaming requires effort. Motivation is an essential prerequisite; you have to really want to do it and make sufficient time to practice. If you persevere with the exercises and procedures, we are confident that you will increase your proficiency at lucid dreaming.

Outline of the Book

This chapter reviews reasons for learning to become lucid in your dreams and describes the contents of this book.

Chapter 2: "Preparation for Learning Lucid Dreaming" provides necessary background information on sleep and helps you overcome any reservations you might have about lucid dreaming that could inhibit your progress. Next, it helps you get acquainted with your dreams. You will learn how to begin a dream journal and how to increase your dream recall. You should be able to recall at least one dream per night before attempting lucid dream induction techniques. When you have a dream journal with several entries, you will be ready to build a catalog of dreamsigns. These are the characteristic features of dreams that you can use as signposts to lucidity.

Chapter 3: "Waking Up in the Dream World" discusses techniques for realizing you are dreaming from within the dream. The two major techniques presented are the reflection-intention technique, which is based on the practice of questioning whether you are awake or dreaming, and MILD, the technique I used to learn to have lucid dreams at will. MILD trains you to remember to notice when you are dreaming.

Chapter 4: "Falling Asleep Consciously" describes techniques for entering the lucid dream state directly from the waking state.

Chapter 5: "The Building of Dreams" provides a solid background on the origins and nature of the dreaming process and discusses lucid dreaming in the context of dreams in general.

Chapter 6: "Principles and Practice of Lucid Dreaming" shows you how to gain control over the dream: how to remain in a lucid dream, how to awaken when you wish, and how to manipulate and observe the dream world. In addition to explaining methods of exercising power over the dream, we discuss the benefits inherent in taking an open, flexible, and noncommanding role in lucid dreams.

Chapter 7: "Adventures and Explorations" shows how you can use lucid dreaming for wish fulfillment and the satisfaction of your desires. Examples and suggestions are provided to help you explore new worlds or enact exciting adventures in your dreams, and show how you can tie your dream adventures into your personal self-development.

Chapter 8: "Rehearsal for Living" explains how lucid dreaming can be a practical tool for preparing for your waking life. Lucid dreaming can be used as a "flight simulator" for life, a way in which you can test new ways of living, as well as particular skills. Practice in the dream state can contribute to enhanced experience, improved performance, and deepened understanding in waking life.

Chapter 9: "Creative Problem Solving" discusses lucid dreaming as a fruitful source of creativity for art, science, business, and personal life. Diverse examples show how people have used lucid dreaming to find a name for a soon-to-be-born child, to repair cars, and to understand abstract mathematical concepts.

Chapter 10: "Overcoming Nightmares" helps you use lucid dreaming to face and overcome fears and inhibitions that may be preventing you from getting the most out of your life. Lucid dreamers can overcome nightmares, and in so doing learn how to make the best of the worst situations imaginable.

Chapter 11: "The Healing Dream" shows how lucid dreamers can achieve more integrated, healthier personalities. Lucid dreams can help those who have unresolved conflicts from past or present relationships, or with deceased friends or family members. Also, in lucid dreams, we can learn mental flexibility. Because nothing can harm us in dreams, we can try to solve our problems in unusual or unheard of ways. This helps us to increase our repertoire of possible behaviors in the waking world, thereby decreasing the probability of getting stuck in situations we don't know how to cope with.

Chapter 12: "Life Is a Dream: Intimations of a Wider World" takes a step beyond the application of lucid dreaming to your everyday life, and shows how lucid dreams can be used to attain a more complete understanding of yourself and your relation to the world. In the dream you are who you "dream yourself to be," and understanding this can help you see to what extent your waking self is limited by your own conceptions of who you are. Examples of transcendental experiences in lucid dreams will show you a direction that you might wish to explore in your own inner worlds.

The book ends with an afterword ("The Adventure Continues") inviting you to join the Lucidity Institute, a membership society devoted to advancing knowledge on the nature and potentials of lucid dreaming.

Life is Short

Before we get into the specifics of how to have lucid dreams, let's take a closer look at the reasons for learning to awaken in your dreams. Do the potential benefits justify the time and effort required for mastering lucid dreaming? We think so, but read on and decide for yourself.

Proverbially, and undeniably, life is short. To make matters worse, we must spend between a quarter and a half of our lives asleep. Most of us are in the habit of virtually sleepwalking through our dreams. We sleep, mindlessly, through many thousands of opportunities to be fully aware and alive.

Is sleeping through your dreams the best use of your limited lifespan? Not only are you wasting part of your finite store of time to be alive, but you are missing adventures and lessons that could enrich the rest of your life. By awakening to your dreams, you will add to your experience of life and, if you use these added hours of lucidity to experiment and exercise your mind, you can also improve your enjoyment of your waking hours.

"Dreams are a reservoir of knowledge and experience," writes Tibetan Buddhist Tarthang Tulku, "yet they are often overlooked as a vehicle for exploring reality. In the dream state our bodies are at rest, yet we see and hear, move about, and are even able to learn. When we make good use of the dream state, it is almost as if our lives were doubled: instead of a hundred years, we live two hundred."[2]

We can carry not only knowledge but also moods from the lucid dream state to the waking state. When we awaken laughing with delight from a wonderful lucid dream, it isn't surprising that our waking mood has been brightened with feelings of joy. A young woman's first lucid dream, which she had after reading an article about lucid dreaming, provides a vivid example. Upon realizing she was dreaming, she "tried to remember the advice in the article," but the only thing that came to mind was a notion of her own: "ultimate experience." She felt herself taken over by a "blissful sensation of blending and melting with colors and light" that continued, "opening up into a total 'orgasm.'" Afterward, she "gently floated into waking consciousness" and was left with "a feeling of bubbling joy" that persisted for a week or more.[3]

This carryover of positive feeling into the waking state is an important aspect of lucid dreaming. Dreams, remembered or not, often color our mood upon awakening, sometimes for a good part of a day. Just as the negative aftereffect of "bad" dreams can cause you to feel as if you got up on the wrong side of the bed, the positive feelings of a pleasant dream can give you an emotional uplift, helping you to start the day with confidence and energy. This is all the more true of inspirational lucid dreams.

Perhaps you are still thinking, "My dream life is interesting enough as it is. Why should I make an effort to enhance my awareness of it?" If so, consider the traditional mystical teaching that holds that most of humanity is asleep. When Idries Shah, the preeminent Sufi teacher, was asked to name "a fundamental mistake of man's," he replied, "To think that he is alive, when he has merely fallen asleep in life's waiting room."[4]

Lucid dreaming can help us understand Shah's words. Once you have had the experience of realizing that you are dreaming and that your possibilities are far greater than you had thought, you can imagine what a similar realization would be like in your waking life. As Thoreau put it, "Our truest life is when we are in dreams awake."

The Experience of Lucid Dreaming

If you haven't yet had a lucid dream, you may find it difficult to imagine what it is like. Although you have to experience it to really know what it is like ("Those who taste, know"), it is possible to get an idea of the experience by comparing lucid dreaming to a presumably more familiar state of consciousness: the one you are in right now! The following experiential exercise will guide you through a tour of your everyday waking state of consciousness. Spend about one minute on each of the steps.

EXERCISE:
YOUR PRESENT STATE OF CONSCIOUSNESS

1. Look
Become aware of what you see: notice the richly varied and vivid impressions—shapes, colors, movement, dimensionality, the entire visible world.

2. Listen
Become aware of what you hear: register the various sounds taken in by your ears—a diverse range of intensities, pitches, and tonal qualities, perhaps including the commonplace miracle of speech or the wonder of music.

3. Feel
Become aware of what you touch: texture (smooth, rough, dry, sticky, or wet), weight (heavy, light, solid, or empty), pleasure, pain, heat and cold, and the rest. Also note how your body feels right now and compare that to the many other ways it feels at other times, tired or energetic, stiff or limber, painful or pleasant, and so on.

4. Taste
Become aware of what it is like to taste: taste a number of different foods and substances, or remember and vividly imagine their tastes.

5. Smell
Become aware of what you smell: the odor of warm bodies, earth, incense, smoke, perfume, coffee, onions, alcohol, and the sea. Remember and imagine as many of them as you can.

6. Breathing
Attend to your breathing. A moment ago you probably were not consciously aware of your breathing even though you have inhaled and exhaled fifty times while

doing this exercise. Hold your breath for a few seconds. Let it out. Now take a deep breath. Notice that being conscious of your breathing allows you to alter it deliberately.

7. Emotions
Become aware of your feelings. Remember the difference between anger and joy, serenity and excitement, and as many other emotions as you care to feel. How real do emotions feel?

8. Thoughts
Become aware of your thoughts. What have you been thinking while doing this exercise? What are you thinking right now? How real do thoughts seem?

9. "I"
Become aware of the fact that your world always includes *you*. As William James noted, it is *I* see, *I* hear, *I* feel, *I* think that is the basic fact of experience.[5] You are not what you see, hear, think, or feel; you *have* these experiences. Perhaps most essentially, you are *who is aware*. You are always at the center of your multidimensional universe of experience, but you are not always consciously aware of yourself. Briefly repeat the exercise with the following difference: At the same time you attend to each of the various aspects of your experience, be aware that it is *you* who is noticing these things ("*I* see the light . . .").

10. Awareness of awareness
Finally, become aware of your awareness. Normally, awareness focuses on objects outside ourselves, but it can itself be an object of awareness. In the light of ordinary experience, we seem to be distinct and limited centers of awareness, each alone in our inner worlds. In the light of eternity, mystics tell us, we are ultimately all one—the unlimited awareness that is the source of being. Here, experience cannot be adequately expressed by language.

Lucid Dreaming and Waking Life

How does your renewed appreciation of the richness of your ordinary waking state of consciousness relate to the experience of lucid dreaming? Much of what you just observed about your present experiential world applies as well to the dream world. If you were dreaming, you would experience a multisensory world as rich as the world you are experiencing right now. You would see, hear, feel, taste, think, and *be*, just as you are now.

The crucial difference is that the multisensory world you experience while dreaming originates internally rather than externally. While awake, most of what you perceive corresponds to actually existing people, objects, and events in the external world. Because the objects of waking perception actually exist independently of your mind, they remain relatively stable. For example, you can look at this sentence, shut the book for a moment, and reopen to the same page, and you will see the same sentence.

But, as you will see in chapter 3, the same is not true for dreaming. Because there is no stable external source of stimulation from which to build your experiential world, dreams are much more changeable than the physical world.

If you were in a lucid dream, your experience of the world would be even more different from waking life. First of all, you would know it was all a dream. Because of this, the world around you would tend to rearrange and transform even more than is usual in dreams. "Impossible" things could happen, and the dream scene itself, rather than disappearing once you know it to be "unreal," might increase in clarity and brilliance until you found yourself dumbfounded with wonder.

If fully lucid, you would realize that the entire dream world was your own creation, and with this awareness might come an exhilarating feeling of freedom. Nothing external, no laws of society or physics, would constrain your experience; you could do anything your mind could conceive. Thus inspired, you might fly to the heavens. You might dare to face someone or something that you have been avoiding; you might choose an erotic encounter with the most desirable partner you can imagine; you might visit a deceased loved one to whom you have been wanting to speak; you might seek self-knowledge and wisdom.

By cultivating awareness in your dreams, and learning to use them, you can add more consciousness, more life, to your life. In the process, you will increase your enjoyment of your nightly dream journeys and deepen your understanding of yourself. By waking in your dreams, you can waken to life.

2

Preparation for Learning
Lucid Dreaming

Learning How to Learn

Many people experience lucid dreams after reading or
hearing about lucid dreaming for the first time. This may
be akin to beginner's luck: they heard it could be done,
and so they did it. As a result of indulging your curiosity
about lucid dreaming by buying this book, you may already have had a lucid dream or two, but you probably
have not learned how to have lucid dreams whenever you
want. This chapter will provide you with background
knowledge and skills that you will need for practicing
the lucid dreaming techniques in the following chapters.

Before you set out to explore the world of lucid dreaming, you need to know some basic facts about your brain
and body in sleep. Then, it may help you to know about
the origins of common "mental blocks" that prevent
people from committing themselves to the task of becoming aware in their dreams.

Your lucid dream training will start with keeping a
dream journal and improving your dream recall. Your

journal will help you discover what your dreams are like. The next step will be to use your collection of dreams to find peculiarities (*dreamsigns*) that appear often enough in your dreams to be reliable signposts of the dream state. Your list of dreamsigns will help you succeed with the lucid dream induction techniques presented in chapters 3 and 4.

When you are familiar with your ordinary dreams, and have learned how to become more or less lucid at will, you will be ready to try out some of the applications described in the later chapters of this book. But first, it is important that you focus your mind on learning the preliminary skills and background information required for becoming a lucid dreamer. You cannot write poetry until you learn the alphabet.

Sleeping Brain, Dreaming Mind

People are mystified by the need for sleep. Why do we turn ourselves off for eight hours out of twenty-four? Some likely answers are to restore the body and mind, and to keep us out of trouble during the dark hours. But to call sleep a mystery begs an even larger question: What does it mean to be awake? A basic definition of being awake is *to be aware*. Aware of what? When we speak of sleep and wakefulness, we are referring to awareness of the outside world. Yet, while asleep and unaware for the most part of the outside world, one can still be aware (and thus ''awake'') in a world within the mind. There are degrees of wakefulness. Lucid dreamers are more aware of their real situation—they know they are dreaming; thus we can say they are ''awake in their dreams.'' Exponents of traditional methods for achieving higher consciousness speak of ''awakening,'' meaning increasing one's awareness of one's place in the cosmos.

But how does anyone or anything come to be ''aware''?

Awareness in biological organisms is a function of the brain. The sensory organs detect information (light, sound, heat, texture, odor) in the world and transmit it to the brain. The brain interprets the information and synthesizes it into a conception of what is happening in the outside world.

The brains with which we experience our worlds, whether dreaming or awake, are the product of biological evolution. During the past thousands of millions of years, living organisms have competed in Mother Nature's life-and-death game of "Eat or Be Eaten: Survival of the Fittest." The simplest one-celled organisms don't know until they bump into something whether it is predator or prey. If it is food, they engulf it. If it is a predator, they are eaten. This is obviously a dangerously ignorant way to try to stay alive.

Since knowing what is going on around you obviously has enormous survival value, creatures gradually evolved sense organs that allowed them to predict whether they should approach or avoid something in their environment without having to bump into it. Over billions of generations, organisms developed increasingly sophisticated nervous systems and correspondingly reliable and precise capacities for perceiving the environment and controlling their actions.

Our brain maintains an up-to-date model of what's going on in the world and predicts what may happen in the future. Prediction requires using previously acquired information to go beyond the information currently available. If you are a frog and a small dark object flies by, information built into your frog brain through evolution allows it to predict that the object is edible and—zip! you have eaten a fly. Or if a large shadow suddenly falls on your lily pad, information (also acquired through evolution) allows your frog brain to predict danger, and—plop! Frogs do not see the same world we do—the complex patterns of color, light, shade, and movement that we can identify as trees, flowers, birds, or ripples in water. The frog's world is probably composed of simple elements like "small flying object" (food), "large approaching object" (danger), "pleasant warmth" (sunlight), or "attractive sound" (frog of the other sex).

Although the human brain is far more complex than that of the frog, it works on the same basic principles. Your brain accomplishes its world-modeling task so well that you ordinarily aren't aware that it is modeling anything. You look with your eyes, and you see. The experience of visual perception seems as straightforward as looking out a window and simply seeing what is there. Nonetheless, seeing, hearing, feeling, or perceiving through any other sense is a process of mental modeling, a simulation of reality. The contents of your consciousness, that is, your current experiences, are *constructed* and depend on your present purposes, what you are doing and what relevant information is currently available.

The mind in sleep

If you are awake and engaged in some kind of activity (walking, reading, etc.), your brain is actively processing external sensory input from the environment, which, together with your memory, provides the raw material from which you construct a model of the world. While awake and active, the model accurately reflects your relationship to the external world.

If you are awake but physically inactive, the balance of input moves from the external to the internal. To a certain extent your thinking becomes independent of external stimuli, your mind wanders, you daydream. With part of your mind you are modeling worlds that might be, rather than the current actual environment. Still, you tend to maintain a reduced model of the external world and your attention can easily be drawn back to it, if, for example, some sign of danger appears.

In the case of sleep, so little sensory input is available from the outside world that you stop maintaining a conscious model of it. When your sleeping brain is activated enough to construct a world model in your consciousness, the model is mostly independent from what is happening in your environment—in other words, a dream. The sleeping brain isn't always creating a multidimensional world model. Sometimes it seems to be merely thinking, or doing very little. The differences in mental activity during sleep depend largely upon differences in the state of the sleeper's brain.

Sleep is not a uniform state of passive withdrawal from the world, as scientists thought until the twentieth century. There are two distinct kinds of sleep: a quiet phase and an active phase, which are distinguished by many differences in biochemistry, physiology, psychology, and behavior. Changes in brain waves (electrical activity measured at the scalp), eye movements, and muscle tone are used to define the two states. The quiet phase fits fairly well with the commonsense view of sleep as a state of restful inactivity—your mind does little while you breathe slowly and deeply; your metabolic rate is at a minimum, and growth hormones are released facilitating restorative processes. When awakened from this state, people feel disoriented and rarely remember dreaming. You can observe this state in your cat or dog, when it is quietly sleeping in a moderately relaxed posture (in the case of cats, the "sphinx" posture) and breathing slowly and regularly. Incidentally, this is the phase of sleep in which sleeptalking and sleepwalking occur.

The transition from quiet to active sleep is quite dramatic. During the active sleep phase, commonly called rapid eye movement or REM sleep, your eyes move rapidly about (under closed lids, of course), much as they would if you were awake. Your breathing becomes quick and irregular, your brain burns as much fuel as it does when you're awake, and you dream vividly. If you're male, you probably will have an erection; if you're female, increased vaginal blood flow. While all this activity is happening in your brain, your body remains almost completely still (except for small twitches), because it is temporarily paralyzed during REM sleep to prevent you from acting out your dreams.

The "sleep paralysis" of REM sleep doesn't always turn off immediately upon awakening; this is why you may have experienced waking up and not being able to move for a minute. Sleep paralysis can seem a terrifying experience, but actually it is quite harmless, and indeed, can even be useful for inducing lucid dreams (see chapter 4). You can get a good view of "paradoxical sleep," as REM sleep is called in Europe, when you see your cat or dog sleeping totally collapsed, breathing irregularly, twitching, showing eye movements, and in the case of dogs, tail wagging, whimpering, growling, and barking. This is when people justifiably say, "Look, Spotto is dreaming!"

The sleeper's night journey

Quiet sleep is itself divided into three substages. Stage 1 is a transitional state between drowsy wakefulness and light sleep, characterized by slow drifting eye movements and vivid, brief dreamlets called hypnagogic (from Greek, meaning "leading into sleep") imagery. Normally, you quickly pass through Stage 1 into Stage 2, which is bona fide sleep and is characterized by unique brain wave patterns called "sleep spindles" and "K-complexes." Mental activity at this point is sparse, mundane, and thoughtlike.

Typically after twenty to thirty minutes, you sink deeper into "delta sleep," so named after the regular large, slow brain waves that characterize this stage of quiet sleep. Very little dream content is reported from delta sleep. Interestingly, this state of deep and dreamless sleep is highly regarded in some Eastern mystical traditions as the state in which we establish contact with our innermost consciousness. According to Swami Rama, "It is when the inner world can be suffused with the full light of the highest universal consciousness. The ego state of waking consciousness drops away. Moreover, the personal aspects of the unknown mind are temporarily abandoned. The memories, the problems, the troubled dream images are left behind. All the limitations of the personal unconscious are drowned out in the full light of the highest consciousness."[1]

After gradually entering the deepest stage of delta sleep and lingering there for thirty or forty minutes, you come back up to Stage 2. Approximately seventy to ninety minutes after sleep onset, you enter REM sleep for the first time of the night. After five or ten minutes of REM, and possibly following a brief awakening in which you would likely remember a dream, you sink back into Stage 2 and possibly delta, coming up again for another REM period approximately every ninety minutes, and so on through the night.

While learning and practicing lucid dreaming, you should keep in mind two elaborations on this cycle: (1) the length of the REM periods increase as the night proceeds and (2) the intervals between REM periods decrease with time of night, from ninety minutes at the beginning of the night to perhaps only twenty to thirty minutes eight hours later. Finally, after five or six periods of dreaming sleep you wake up for perhaps the tenth or fifteenth time of the night (we awaken this many times on an average night, but we promptly forget it happened, just as you may forget a conversation with someone who calls you in the middle of the night).

Having completed your tour of a night's journey through sleep, you may wonder in which stage of sleep lucid dreaming occurs. How we found the answer to this question is a story that deserves retelling.

Communiqué from the dream world

What if you slept, and what if in your sleep you dreamed, and what if in your dream you went to heaven and there you plucked a strange and beautiful flower, and what if when you awoke you had the flower in your hand? Ah, what then? (Samuel Taylor Coleridge)

Throughout history, poets, philosophers, and other dreamers have been challenged by the fantastic idea of bringing something back from the dream world—something as substantial and real as Coleridge's flower—something to prove that the dream was as real as this life.

In the late 1970s, when I began my Ph.D. study on lucid dreams at Stanford, I found myself challenged by a seemingly even more hopeless task: proving that lucid dreaming is real. The experts at the time were convinced that dreaming with consciousness that you were dreaming was a contradiction in terms and therefore impossible. Such philosophical reasoning could not convince me, since I had experienced lucid dreams—impossible or not.

I had no doubt that lucid dreaming was a reality, but how could I prove it to anyone else? To do so I needed to bring back evidence from the dream world as proof that I had really known I was dreaming during sleep. Simply reporting I had been lucid in a dream after awakening wouldn't prove that the lucidity had occurred while I was actually asleep. I needed some way to mark the time of the lucid dream on a record showing that I had been asleep.

I knew that earlier studies had demonstrated that the direction of dreamers' physical eye movements during REM was sometimes exactly the same as the direction that they reported looking in their dreams. In one remarkable example reported by pioneer sleep and dream researcher Dr. William Dement, a dreamer was awakened from REM sleep after making a series of about two dozen regular left-right-left-right eye movements. He reported that he was dreaming about a table tennis game; just before awakening he had been watching a long volley with his dream gaze.

I also knew from my own experience that I could look in any direction I wished while in a lucid dream, so it occurred to me that I ought to be able to signal while I was having a lucid dream by moving my eyes in a prearranged, recognizable pattern. To test this idea, I spent the night at the Stanford Sleep Laboratory. I wore electrodes that measured my brain waves, eye movements, and muscle tone, which my colleague Dr. Lynn Nagel monitored on a polygraph while I slept.

During the night I had a lucid dream in which I moved my eyes left-right-left-right. The next morning, when we looked through the polygraph record, we found the eye movement signals in the middle of a REM period. At this writing, dozens of other lucid dreamers have also successfully signaled from lucid dreams, and these dreams have occurred almost exclusively during REM sleep.

This method of communication from the dream world has proven to be of inestimable value in the continued study of lucid dreams and dream physiology. The fact that lucid dreamers could remember to perform previously agreed upon actions in their dreams and that they could signal to the waking world made an entirely new approach to dream research possible.

By using trained lucid dreamers, we were able to develop the eye movement signaling technique into a powerful methodology. We have found that oneironauts can carry out all kinds of experimental tasks, functioning both as subjects and experimenters in the dream state. The oneironautical approach to dream research is illustrated by a series of studies conducted at the Stanford Sleep Research Center that have begun to map out mind/body relationships during dreaming.

Why dreams seem real:
Mind/brain/body relationships during dreaming

One of the earliest experiments conducted by my research team tested the traditional notion that the experience of dream time is somehow different from time in the waking world. We approached the problem of dream time by asking subjects to make an eye movement signal in their lucid dreams, estimate a ten-second interval (by counting one thousand and one, one thousand and two, etc.), and then make another eye movement signal. In all cases, we found time estimates made in lucid dreams were within a few seconds of estimates made in the waking state and likewise quite close to the actual time between signals. From this we have concluded that in lucid dreams, estimated dream time is very nearly equal to clock time; that is, it takes just as long to do something in a dream as it does to actually do it.

You may be wondering, then, how you could have a dream that seems to last for years or lifetimes. I believe this effect is achieved in dreams by the same stage trick that causes the illusion of the passage of time in the movies or theater. If, on screen, stage, or dream, we see someone turning out the light as the clock strikes midnight, and after a few moments of darkness, we see him turning off an alarm as the bright morning sun shines through the window, we'll accept (pretend, without being aware that we are pretending) that many hours have passed even though we ''know'' it was only a few seconds.

The method of having lucid dreamers signal from the dream world by means of eye movements has demonstrated a strong relationship between the gazes of dreamers in the dream and their actual eye movements under closed lids. Researchers interested in this question, but not using lucid dreamers to study it, have had to rely on the chance occurrence of highly recognizable eye movement patterns readily matchable to subjects' reported dream activities. As a result, they usually have obtained only weak correspondences between dreamed and actual eye movements. The implication of the strong tie between the movements of the dream eyes and the movements of the actual eyes is that we use the same visual system to look around in the dream world as we do to see the waking world.

One of the most dramatic demonstrations of the correspondence between physiology and dream activity came from studies of lucid dream sex. In 1983 we undertook a pilot study to determine the extent to which subjectively experienced sexual activity during REM lucid dreaming would be reflected in physiological responses.

Since women report more orgasms in dreams than men do, we began with a female subject. We recorded many different aspects of her physiology that would normally be affected by sexual arousal, including respiration, heart rate, vaginal muscle tone, and vaginal pulse amplitude. The experiment called for her to make specific eye movement signals at the following points: when she realized she was dreaming, when she began sexual activity (in the dream), and when she experienced orgasm.

She reported a lucid dream in which she carried out the experimental task exactly as agreed upon. Our analysis revealed significant correspondences between the dream activities she reported and all but one of the physiological measures. During the fifteen-second section of her physiological record which she signaled as the moment of orgasm, her vaginal muscle activity, vaginal pulse amplitude, and respiration rate reached their highest values of the night, and they also were considerably elevated in comparison to the rest of the REM period. Contrary to expectation, heart rate increased only slightly.

Since then, we have carried out similar experiments with two male lucid dreamers. In both cases, respiration showed striking increases in rate. Again, there were no significant elevations of the heart rate. Interestingly, although both oneironauts reported vividly realistic orgasms in their lucid dreams, neither actually ejaculated, in contrast to the "wet dreams" commonly experienced by adolescent males, which frequently are not associated with erotic dreams.

Dreamed action produces real effects on the brain and body

The experiments just reviewed supported the conclusion that the events you experience while asleep and dreaming produce effects on your brain (and, to a lesser extent, your body) much the same as if you were to experience the corresponding events while awake. Additional studies uphold this conclusion. When lucid dreamers hold their breaths or breathe fast in a dream, they really do hold their breaths or pant. Furthermore, the differences in brain activity caused by singing versus counting in the waking state (singing tends to engage the right hemisphere and counting, the left) are nearly duplicated in the lucid dream. In short, to our brains, dreaming of doing something is equivalent to actually doing it. This finding explains why dreams seem so real. To the brain, they *are* real.

We are continuing to study the connection between dreamed actions and physiology, with the goal of producing a detailed map of mind/body interactions during dreaming sleep for all measurable physiological systems. Such a map could prove to be of great value for experimental dream psychology and for psychosomatic medicine. Indeed, since dream activities produce real physiological effects, lucid dreaming may be useful for facilitating the functioning of the immune system (more on this in chapter 11). In any case, the physiological effects caused by dreaming show that we cannot dismiss dreams as idle children of the imagination. Although the tendency of our culture has been to ignore dreams, dream experiences are as real to us as waking life. If we seek to improve our lives, we would do well to include our dream lives in our efforts.

Social Values and Lucid Dreaming

I have received numerous letters from people with an interest in lucid dreaming who feel restricted because, as one writer put it, "I can't talk to anyone about this; they all think I'm nuts and look at me oddly if I even try to explain what I do in my dreams." Our culture offers little social support to those interested in exploring mental states. This resistance probably has its roots in the behaviorist perspective in psychology, which treated all animals, including humans, as "black boxes" whose actions were entirely dependent on external inputs. The contents of the "mind" of an animal were considered unmeasurable and hence out of the bounds of scientific study.

Since the late 1960s, however, science has once again begun to explore the realm of conscious experience. The study of lucid dreaming is an example. However, cultural understanding normally lags behind scientific understanding. Darwin's scientific theories of the evolution of biological organisms are a century old, but the cultural turmoil they caused by upsetting the status quo of accepted thought is still affecting our society. Hence, we are not surprised to find that some people, scientists included, remain resistant to the new (to the West) capabilities of the human mind that scientific research is discovering and demonstrating.

To help you realize that lucid dreams can have a significant and valuable effect on your life, this book includes many personal accounts from lucid dreamers. If you happen to live in a place where you feel you cannot share your dream life, these examples should give you some feeling of connection with others who are exploring their dreams. In addition, in the afterword you will find an invitation to share your experiences with us.

Concerns About Lucid Dreaming: Questions and Answers

Q. Might lucid dreaming be dangerous for some people?
A. The overwhelming majority of lucid dreams are positive, rewarding experiences, much more so than ordinary dreams (to say nothing of nightmares). Nevertheless, there probably will be some people who find the experience of lucid dreaming frightening and, in some cases, extremely disturbing. For this reason we cannot recommend lucid dreaming to everyone. On the other hand, we are confident that for people no more than "normally neurotic," lucid dreaming is completely harmless. Different people will use lucid dreaming for different purposes; it makes little sense to warn the typical explorer of the dream world away from lucid dreaming because some might use it in a less than optimal manner.

If, after reading the first six chapters of this book, you still have serious reservations about lucid dreaming, then we recommend that you not continue. "To thine own self be true." Just make sure that it is really *your* self to which you are being true. Don't allow others to impose their personal fears on you.

Q. I am afraid that if I learn to induce lucid dreams, all my dreams will become lucid. Then what will I do?
A. The philosopher P. D. Ouspensky experienced conflicting emotions regarding "half-dream states," as he called lucid dreams: "The first sensation they produced

was one of astonishment. I expected to find one thing and found another. The next was a feeling of extraordinary joy which the 'half-dream states,' and the possibility of seeing and understanding things in quite a new way, gave me. And the third was a certain fear of them, because I very soon noticed that if I let them take their own course they would begin to grow and expand and encroach both upon sleep and upon the waking state."[2]

I experienced exactly the same fear when I first began attempting to induce lucid dreams. My efforts were soon met with impressive success; after a few months, I was having more and more lucid dreams at what suddenly seemed an alarmingly rapid rate of increase. I became afraid that I wouldn't be able to control the process: "What if *all* my dreams become lucid? I'm not wise enough to consciously direct all of my dreams. What if I make mistakes?" And so on.

However, I found that the moment I entertained this worrisome line of thinking, I stopped having lucid dreams. Upon calm reflection, I realized that without my consent there was really very little chance that all my dreams would become lucid. As both Ouspensky and I had forgotten, lucid dreaming takes effort. Lucid dreams occur only rarely unless you go to sleep with the deliberate and definite intention to become conscious, or lucid, in your dreams. Thus, I understood that I would be able to regulate (and limit, if necessary) the frequency of my lucid dreams. In fact, after a decade of experience with more than a thousand lucid dreams, I rarely have more than a few per month unless I have a conscious desire to have more.

Q. Since I believe that dreams are messages from the unconscious mind, I am afraid that consciously controlling my dreams would interfere with this important process and deprive me of the benefits of dream interpretation.

A. As chapter 5 will explain, dreams are not letters from the unconscious mind, but experiences created through the interactions of the unconscious and conscious mind. In dreams, more unconscious knowledge is available to our conscious experience. However, the dream is not at all the exclusive realm of the unconscious mind. If it were, people would never remember their dreams, because we do not have waking access to what is not conscious.

The person, or dream ego, that we experience being in the dream is the same as our waking consciousness. It constantly influences the events of the dream through its expectations and biases, just as it does in waking life. The essential difference in the lucid dream is that the ego is aware that the experience is a dream. This allows the ego much more freedom of choice and creative responsibility to find the best way to act in the dream.

I don't think that you should always be conscious that you are dreaming any more than I think that you should always be conscious of what you are doing in waking life. Sometimes self-consciousness can interfere with effective performance; if you are in a situation (dream or waking) in which your habits are working smoothly, you don't need to direct your action consciously. However, if your habits are taking you in the wrong direction (whether dreaming or waking), you should be able to "wake up" to what you are doing wrong and consciously redirect your approach.

As for the benefits of dream interpretation, lucid dreams can be examined as fruitfully as nonlucid ones. Indeed, lucid dreamers sometimes interpret their dreams while they are happening. Becoming lucid is likely to alter what would have otherwise happened, but the dream can still be interpreted.

Q. Sometimes in lucid dreams I encounter situations of otherworldliness, accompanied by feelings of the pres-

*ence of great power or energy. At these times my con-
sciousness expands far beyond anything I have experienced in waking life, so that the experience seems
much more real than the reality I know, and I become
terrified. I cannot continue these dreams for fear that I
will never awaken from them, since the experience seems
so far out of the realm of waking existence. What would
happen if I was unable to awaken myself from these lucid
dreams? Would I die or go mad?*

A. Despite the seemingly horrific nature of this concern,
it amounts to little more than fear of the unknown. There
is no evidence that anything you do in a dream could
affect your basic brain physiology in a way that is harmful. And, as intense as a dream may be, it can't last any
longer than the natural course of REM periods—at most
an hour or so. Of course, since explorations of the world
of dreams have really just begun, there are bound to be
regions as yet uncharted. But you should not fear to pioneer them. The feeling of intense anxiety that accompanies the sudden onset of strange experiences in dreams
is a natural part of the orientation response: it is adaptive
in the waking world for a creature in a new situation or
territory to look first for danger. However, the fear is not
necessarily relevant to what is happening. You need not
fear physical harm in your dreams. When you find yourself in the midst of a new experience, let go of your fear
and just see what happens. (Chapter 10 covers the theory
and practice of facing fears in dreams.)

*Q. They say that if you die in your dream, you really will
die. Is this true?*

A. If it were true, how would anybody know? There is
direct evidence to the contrary: many people have died
in their dreams with no ill effects, according to the reports they gave after waking up—alive. Moreover, dreams
of death can become dreams of rebirth if you let them,
as is illustrated by one of my own dreams. After a mys-

terious weakness quickly spread through my whole body, I realized I was about to die of exhaustion and only had time for one final action. Without hesitation, I decided that I wanted my last act to be an expression of perfect acceptance. As I let out my last breath in that spirit, a rainbow flowed out of my heart, and I awoke ecstatic.[3]

Q. If I use my lucidity in a dream to manipulate and dominate the other dream characters, and magically alter the dream environment, won't I be making a habit of behavior that is not likely to benefit me in waking life?
A. Chapter 6 discusses an approach to lucid dreams that will help you establish ways of behaving that will be useful to you in waking life. This is to control your own actions and reactions in the dream, and not the other characters and elements of the dream. However, this does not mean that we believe it harmful if you choose to enjoy yourself by playing King or Queen of Dreamland. In fact, if you normally feel out of control of your life, or are an unassertive person, you well may benefit from the empowered feeling engendered by taking control of the dream.

Q. Won't all these efforts and exercises for becoming lucid lead to loss of sleep? And won't I feel more tired after being awake in my dreams? Is it worth sacrificing my alertness in the daytime just to have more lucid dreams?
A. Dreaming lucidly is usually just as restful as dreaming nonlucidly. Since lucid dreams tend to be positive experiences, you may actually feel invigorated after them. How tired you feel after a dream depends on what you did in the dream—if you battled endlessly and nonlucidly with frustrating situations, you probably will feel more tired than if you realized in the dream that it was a dream and that none of your mundane concerns were relevant.

You should work on learning lucid dreaming when you have time and energy to devote to the task. The exercises for increasing dream recall and inducing lucid dreams probably will require that you spend more time awake during the night than usual, and possibly that you sleep longer hours. If you are too busy to allot more time to sleeping or to sacrifice any of the little sleep you are getting, it's probably not a good idea for you to work on lucid dreaming right now. Doing so will add to your current stress, and you probably won't get very good results. Lucid dreaming, at least at first, requires good sleep and mental energy for concentration. Once you learn the techniques, you should be able to get to a point at which you can have lucid dreams any time you wish just by reminding yourself that you can do so.

Q. I am afraid that I may not have what it takes to have lucid dreams. What if, after doing all of the exercises you suggest and devoting a lot of time to it, I still can't learn to have lucid dreams? If I put all that time into it, and don't get any results, I will feel like a failure.
A. One of the greatest stumbling blocks in learning almost any skill is *trying too hard*. This is especially the case with lucid dreaming, which requires that you sleep well and have a balanced state of mind. If you find you are losing sleep while struggling to have lucid dreams without result, let go of your efforts for a while. Relax and forget about lucid dreaming for a few days or a few weeks. Sometimes you will find that after you let go, lucid dreams will appear.

Q. Lucid dreams are so exciting and feel so good that real life pales by comparison. Isn't it possible to get addicted to them and not wish to do anything else?
A. It may be possible for the die-hard escapist whose life is otherwise dull to become obsessed with lucid dreaming. Whether or not this deserves to be called addiction is another question. In any case, some advice for those who find the idea of "sleeping their life away" for the

sake of lucid dreaming is to consider applying what they have learned in lucid dreams to their waking lives. If lucid dreams seem so much more real and exciting, then this should inspire you to make your life more like your dreams—more vivid, intense, pleasurable, and rewarding. In both worlds your behavior strongly influences your experience.

Q. I am currently undergoing psychotherapy. Is it okay for me to try lucid dreaming? Can it assist in my therapy?
A. If you are in psychotherapy and want to experiment with lucid dreaming, talk it over with your therapist. Not every therapist will be well informed about lucid dreaming and its implications for therapy, so make sure your therapist understands what you are talking about and is familiar with the current information. Chapters 8, 10, and 11 of this book offer ideas of how lucid dreaming may be instrumental in psychotherapy. If your therapist doesn't think that lucid dreaming would be a good idea for you at this time, follow his or her advice. If you disagree, you should either trust the judgment of your current therapist on this issue or find another therapist, ideally one who knows how to help you to work with your lucid dreams therapeutically.

Getting to Know Your Dreams

How to recall your dreams

It has been said that "everything is dependent upon remembering," and this is certainly true of lucid dreaming.[4] Learning to remember your dreams is necessary if you want to learn how to dream lucidly. Until you have excellent dream recall, you won't stand much chance of having many lucid dreams. There are two reasons for this. First, without recall, even if you do have a lucid dream, you won't remember it. Indeed, we all probably have lost numerous lucid dreams among the many thousands of dreams we have forgotten in the normal course of our lives. Second, good dream recall is crucial because to become lucid you have to recognize that your dream *is* a dream, while it is happening. Since they are your dreams that you are trying to recognize, you have to become familiar with what they are like.

You know what a dream is, in general terms. But dream stories are not always easy to distinguish from accounts of events that actually happened. Dreams in general seem like life, with certain notable exceptions. These exceptions are violations of your expectations about the behavior of the world. So, you need to get to know what your dreams are like, and in particular, what is dreamlike about them. You can accomplish this by collecting your dreams and analyzing them for dreamlike elements.

Before it will be worth your time to work on lucid dream induction methods, you should be able to recall at least one dream every night. The following suggestions will help you attain this goal.

The first step to good dream recall is getting plenty of sleep. If you are rested, you will find it easier to focus on your goal of recalling dreams, and you won't mind taking the time during the night to record them. Another reason to sleep longer is that dream periods get longer and closer together as the night proceeds. The first dream of the night is the shortest, perhaps only ten minutes in length, while after eight hours of sleep, dream periods can be forty-five minutes to an hour long.

You may have more than one dream during a REM (dream) period, separated by short arousals that are most often forgotten. It is generally accepted among sleep researchers that dreams are not recalled unless the sleeper awakens directly from the dream, rather than after going on to other stages of sleep.

If you find that you sleep too deeply to awaken from

your dreams, try setting an alarm clock to awaken you at a time when you are likely to be dreaming. Since REM periods occur at approximately ninety-minute intervals, good times will be multiples of ninety minutes from your bedtime. Aim for the later REM periods by setting the alarm to go off at four and a half, six, or seven and a half hours after you go to sleep.

Another important prerequisite to recalling dreams is motivation. For many people it is enough to intend to remember their dreams and remind themselves of this intention just before bed. Additionally, it may help to tell yourself you will have interesting, meaningful dreams. Keeping a dream journal by your bed and recording your dreams as soon as you awaken will help strengthen your resolve. As you record more dreams, you will remember more. Suggestions for keeping a dream journal are given below.

You should get into the habit of asking yourself this question the moment you awaken: "What was I dreaming?" Do this first or you'll forget some or all of your dream, due to interference from other thoughts. Don't move from the position in which you awaken, as any body movement may make your dream harder to remember. Also, don't think of the day's concerns, because this too can erase your dream recall. If you remember nothing, keep trying for several minutes, without moving or thinking of anything else. Usually, pieces and fragments of the dream will come to you. If you still can't remember any dream, you should ask yourself: "What was I just thinking?" and "How was I just feeling?" Examining your thoughts and feelings often can provide the necessary clues to allow you to retrieve the entire dream.

Cling to any clues of what you might have been experiencing, and try to rebuild a story from them. When you recall a scene, ask yourself what happened before that, and before that, reliving the dream in reverse. It doesn't take long to build enough skill at this to trigger a detailed replay of an entire dream simply by focusing your attention on a fragment of memory. If you can't recall anything, try imagining a dream you might have had—note your present feelings, list your current concerns to yourself, and ask yourself, "Did I dream about that?" If after a few minutes all you remember is a mood, describe it in your journal (see below). Even if you don't remember anything in bed, events or scenes of the day may remind you of something you dreamed the night before. Be ready to notice this when it happens, and record whatever you remember.

In developing dream recall, as with any other skill, progress is sometimes slow. Don't be discouraged if you don't succeed at first. Virtually everyone improves through practice. *As soon as you recall your dreams at least once per night, you're ready to try lucid dreaming.* It probably won't take long to reach this stage of readiness. And a significant percentage of people who get this far will already be experiencing lucid dreams.

Keeping a dream journal

Get a notebook or diary for writing down your dreams. The notebook should be attractive to you and exclusively dedicated for the purpose of recording dreams. Place it by your bedside to remind yourself of your intention to write down dreams. Record your dreams immediately after you awaken from them. You can either write out the entire dream upon awakening from it or take down brief notes to expand later.

Don't wait until you get up in the morning to make notes on your dreams. If you do, even if the details of a dream seemed exceptionally clear when you awakened in the night, by morning you may find you remember nothing about it. We seem to have built-in dream erasers in our minds which make dream experiences more difficult to recall than waking ones. So, be sure to write down at least a few key words about the dream immediately upon awakening from it.

You don't have to be a talented writer. Your dream journal is a tool, and you are the only person who is going to read it. Describe the way images and characters look and sound and smell, and don't forget to describe the way you felt in the dream—emotional reactions are important clues in the dream world. Record anything unusual, the kinds of things that would never occur in waking life: flying pigs, or the ability to breathe underwater, or enigmatic symbols. You also can sketch particular images in your journal. The drawing, like the writing, does not have to be fine art. It's just a way for you to make an intuitive and memorable connection with an image that might help you attain lucidity in future dreams.

Put the date at the top of the page. Record your dream under the date, carrying over for as many pages as required. Leave a blank page following each dream description for exercises you will do later.

If you remember only a fragment of a dream, record it, no matter how unimportant it might seem at the time. And if you recall a whole dream, title your journal entry with a short, catchy title that captures the subject or mood of the dream. "The Guardian of the Spring" or "Riot in the Classroom" are examples of good descriptive titles.

When you begin to accumulate some raw material in your dream journal, you can look back at your dreams and ask yourself questions about them. The use of dream symbols for self-analysis is not the purpose of this book, but many different techniques are available for working with dream journals.[5]

There are many different methodologies for interpreting dreams. Lucid dreaming is a state of awareness, not a theory, and as such it can be applied equally to many different kinds of dreamwork. No matter which kind of analysis you might perform on the contents of your dream journals, you will find that lucid dreaming skills can increase your understanding of the way in which your mind creates symbols. This in turn can empower your effort toward integration of the different parts of your personality (see chapter 11). Furthermore, reading over your journal will help you become familiar with what is dreamlike about your dreams so you can recognize them while they are still happening—and become lucid.

Dreamsigns: Doors to Lucidity

I was standing on the pavement outside my London home. The sun was rising and the waters of the Bay were sparkling in the morning light. I could see the tall trees at the corner of the road and the top of the old grey tower beyond the Forty Steps. In the magic of the early sunshine the scene was beautiful enough even then.

Now the pavement was not of the ordinary type, but consisted of small, bluish-grey rectangular stones, with their long sides at right-angles to the white curb. I was about to enter the house when, on glancing casually at these stones, my attention became riveted by a passing strange phenomenon, so extraordinary that I could not believe my eyes—they had seemingly all changed their position in the night, and the long sides were now parallel to the curb!

Then the solution flashed upon me: though this glorious summer morning seemed as real as real could be, I was dreaming! With the realization of this fact, the quality of the dream changed in a manner very difficult to convey to one who has not had this experience. Instantly, the vividness of life increased a hundred-fold. Never had sea and sky and trees shone with such glamourous beauty; even the commonplace houses seemed alive and mystically beautiful. Never had I felt so absolutely well, so clear-brained, so inexpressibly "free"! The sensation was

*exquisite beyond words; but it lasted only a few minutes
and I awoke.*[6]

Thanks to a strange little detail—the apparently changed
position of the cobblestones—a single out-of-place feature in an otherwise convincingly realistic scene, this
dreamer was able to realize that he was dreaming. I have
named such characteristically dreamlike features "dreamsigns." Almost every dream has dreamsigns, and it is
likely that we all have our own personal ones.

Once you know how to look for them, dreamsigns can
be like neon lights, flashing a message in the darkness:
"This is a dream! This is a dream!" You can use your
journal as a rich source of information on how your own
dreams signal their dreamlike nature. Then you can learn
to recognize your most frequent or characteristic dreamsigns—the specific ways your dream world tends to differ
from your waking world.

When people realize they are dreaming, it is often because they reflect on unusual or bizarre occurrences in
their dreams. By training yourself to recognize dreamsigns, you will enhance your ability to use this natural
method of becoming lucid.

People don't become lucid more often in the presence
of dreamsigns because of a normal tendency to rationalize and confabulate—they make up stories to explain
what is going on, or they think, "There must be some
explanation." Indeed, there must be, but too rarely does
such a half-awake dreamer realize what it actually is. If,
on the other hand, the dreamsign occurs in the dream of
someone who has learned to recognize it, the result is a
lucid dream.

*In a dangerous part of San Francisco, for some reason I
start crawling on the sidewalk. I start to reflect: This is
strange; why can't I walk? Can other people walk upright
here? Is it just me who has to crawl? I see a man in a*

suit walking under a streetlight. Now my curiosity is replaced by fear. I think, crawling around like this may be interesting but it is not safe. Then I think, I never do this—I always walk around San Francisco upright! This only happens in dreams. Finally, it dawns on me: I must be dreaming! (S.G., Berkeley, California)

I once awoke from a dream in which my contact lens, having dropped out of my eye, was multiplying like some sort of super-protozoan, and I resolved that in future dreams like this I would notice the mutant lens as a dreamsign. And indeed, I have become lucid in at least a dozen dreams by recognizing this particular oddity. Each of us has his or her own individual dreamsigns, though some are familiar to most of us, like the case of going to work in your pajamas. The illustrative inventory of dreamsigns below can help you look for your personal dreamsigns, but remember that your dreamsigns will be as unique as you are.

The dreamsign inventory lists types of dreamsigns organized according to the way people naturally seem to categorize their experiences in dreams. There are four primary categories. The first one, inner awareness, refers to things that dreamers (egos) perceive as happening within themselves, such as thoughts and feelings. The other three categories (action, form, and context) classify elements of the dream environment. The action category includes the activities and motions of everything in the dream world—the dream ego, other characters, and objects. Form refers to the shapes of things, people, and places, which are often bizarre and frequently transform in dreams. The final category is context. Sometimes in dreams the combination of elements—people, places, actions, or things, is odd, although there is nothing inherently strange about any item by itself. Such strange situations are context dreamsigns. Also included in the context category are events like finding yourself in a place you are unlikely to be, meeting other characters in unusual places, finding objects out of place, or playing an unaccustomed role.

Each category is divided into subdivisions and illustrated with examples from real dreams. Read the inventory carefully so that you understand how to identify dreamsigns. Then, the next exercise will guide you through the process of collecting your own. The lucid dream induction techniques in the following chapters will make use of the dreamsign targets that you come up with in this exercise.

The Dreamsign Inventory

INNER AWARENESS

You have a peculiar thought, a strong emotion, feel an unusual sensation, or have altered perceptions. The thought can be one that is unusual, that could occur only in a dream, or that "magically" affects the dream world. The emotion can be inappropriate or oddly overwhelming. Sensations can include the feeling of paralysis, or of leaving your body, as well as unusual physical feelings and unexpectedly sudden or intense sexual arousal. Perceptions may be unusually clear or fuzzy, or you may be able to see or hear something you wouldn't be able to in waking life.

EXAMPLES:
Thoughts
- "I'm trying to figure out where the house and furnishings are from, and I realize this is an odd thing to be thinking about."
- "When I thought I didn't want to crash, the car swerved back on the road."
- "When I found the door locked, I 'wished' it open."

Emotions
- "I am filled with extreme anxiety and remorse."

- "I was rhapsodized over G."
- "I am so unbelievably angry at my sister that I throw something a woman gave her into the sea."

Sensations

- "I seem to lift 'out of body,' am caught in the covers, but shake free."
- "A strong wave of sexual arousal comes over me."
- "It feels like there's a giant hand squeezing my head."

Perceptions

- "Somehow I could see perfectly without my glasses."
- "Everything looks as though I have taken LSD."
- "I somehow can hear two men talking even though they are far away."

ACTION

You, another dream character, or a dream thing (including inanimate objects and animals) do something unusual or impossible in waking life. The action must occur in the dream environment, that is, not be a thought or feeling in the dreamer's mind. Malfunctioning devices are examples of object action dreamsigns.

EXAMPLES:

Ego action

- "I'm riding home on a unicycle."
- "I was underwater, yet I was breathing."
- "Doing pull-ups got easier and easier."

Character action

- "The staff throws slime worms at the audience."
- "D kisses me passionately in front of his wife."
- "The hairdresser refers to a blueprint to cut my hair."

Object action

- "The bologna lights up."
- "A large flashlight floats past."
- "The car accelerates dangerously, and the brakes don't work."

FORM

Your shape, the shape of a dream character, or that of a dream object is oddly formed, deformed, or transforms. Unusual clothing and hair count as anomalies of form. Also, the place you are in (the setting) in the dream may be different than it would be in waking life.

EXAMPLES:

Ego form
- "I am a man." (dreamed by a woman)
- "I am embodied in a stack of porcelain plates."
- "I am Mozart."

Character form
- "Her face changes as I look at her."
- "A giant with a *Creature from the Black Lagoon* type of head walks by."
- "Contrary to reality, G's hair is cut short."

Setting form
- "The edge of the beach is like a pier with benches."
- "The drafting room was the wrong shape."
- "I get lost because the streets are not as I remember them."

Object form
- "I see a tiny purple kitten."
- "One of the purses transforms completely."
- "My car keys read Toyama instead of Toyota."

CONTEXT

The place or situation in the dream is strange. You may be somewhere that you are unlikely to be in waking life, or involved in a strange social situation. Also, you or another dream character could be playing an unaccustomed role. Objects or characters may be out of place, or the dream could occur in the past or future.

EXAMPLES:

Ego role
- ''We're fugitives from the law.''
- ''It was a James Bond type of dream, with me in the starring role.''
- ''I'm a commando behind enemy lines in World War II.''

Character role
- ''My friend is assigned to be my husband.''
- ''My father is behaving like R, my lover.''
- ''Reagan, Bush, and Nixon are flying jets.''

Character place
- ''My coworkers and former high school friends are together.''
- ''Madonna was seated on a chair in my room.''
- ''My brother, who is dead, was in the kitchen with me.''

Object place
- ''My bed was in the street.''
- ''There was a phone in my room.''
- ''The wall had cream cheese and vegetables in it.''

Setting place
- ''I'm in a colony on Mars.''
- ''I'm in an amusement park.''
- ''I'm on the ocean, by myself, at night.''

Setting time
- ''I am in grade school.''
- ''I'm at my twenty-fifth high school reunion.''
- ''I'm with my horse in his prime.''

Situation
- ''I'm in an odd ceremony.''
- ''A commercial is being filmed at my house.''
- ''Two families have been brought together to get to know each other.''

EXERCISE:
CATALOGING YOUR DREAMSIGNS

1. Keep a dream journal
Keep a journal in which you record all of your dreams. When you have collected at least a dozen dreams, proceed to the next step.

2. Catalog your dreamsigns
While continuing to collect dreams, mark the dreamsigns in your dream reports. Underline them, and list them after each dream description.

3. Classify each dreamsign using the dreamsign inventory
Next to each dreamsign on your list, write the name of its category from the dreamsign inventory. For instance, if you dreamed of a person with the head of a cat, this would be a form dreamsign.

4. Pick target dreamsign categories
Count how many times each dreamsign category (inner awareness, action, form, or context) occurs and rank them by frequency. Whichever occurs most often will be your target dreamsign category in the next step. If there is a tie between categories, pick the one that appeals to you.

5. Practice looking for dreamsigns while you are awake
Make a habit of examining your daily life for events that fit under your dreamsign category. For instance, if your target category is action, study how you, other people, animals, objects, and machines act and move. Become thoroughly familiar with the way things usually are in waking life. This will prepare you to notice when something unusual happens in a dream.

Goal Setting for Success

Lucid dreaming is a kind of mental performance, and you can enlist the aid of psychological techniques developed for enhancing performance to improve your lucid dreaming skills. Sports psychologists have conducted a considerable amount of research on improving performance. One of the most powerful tools to emerge from their work is the theory and practice of goal setting.[7]

Goal setting works. Researchers who reviewed more than 100 studies concluded that "the beneficial effect of goal setting on task performance is one of the most robust and replicable findings in the psychological literature."[8] Furthermore, the research has revealed many details about the right way to go about setting goals.

Here, adapted from one researcher's findings on goal setting are some tips about the right way to approach learning the skill of lucid dreaming.[9]

EXERCISE:
GOAL SETTING FOR SUCCESS

1. Set explicit, specific, and numerical goals
Goals are personal, and are related to both your potential and your demonstrated abilities. Depending on your level of achievement, you might want to remember one dream every night or two dreams every night, or to have at least one lucid dream within the next week or month. When I started my dissertation research, I set myself a goal to increase the number of lucid dreams I had each month. This made it easy for me to evaluate my performance in terms of specific goals.

(exercise continues)

---

2. Set difficult but realistic goals

For many people, to have a lucid dream is a difficult but realistic goal. For more advanced oneironauts, a more appropriate goal might be to learn how to fly or to face scary characters. Your performance will increase in proportion to the ambition of your goals, as long as you keep them within the range of your ability.

3. Set short-range as well as long-range goals

Set short-term goals, like remembering a certain number of dreams or performing a certain number of stated tests per day (see chapter 3). Also, plan longer-range goals, such as having at least one lucid dream per month. Set dates by which you would like to achieve a certain level of proficiency, for example, "I want to have four lucid dreams by June 1."

4. Record and evaluate your progress

When you reach a goal you have set, such as having twelve lucid dreams in one month, record this achievement. When you reach a goal, set a new one. Or, if you are getting frustrated because you are far from attaining your goals, set yourself less demanding and more realistic aims. Keep notes and statistics in your dream journal. A chart may provide a more visible record of your progress.

How to Schedule Your Efforts for Best Results

Many lucid dreamers have reported that their lucid dreams happen most frequently after dawn, in the late morning hours of sleep. A partial explanation for this is that there is more REM sleep in the second half of the night than in the first. Additionally, analysis of the time of occurrence of lucid dreams in the laboratory showed that the relative likelihood of lucid dreaming continuously increases with each successive REM period.[10]

To illustrate what this means, let's say that ordinarily you sleep for eight hours. In the course of the night, you probably will have six REM periods, with the last half occurring in the last quarter of the night. According to our research, the probability of your having a lucid dream during these last two hours of sleep is more than twice as great as the probability of your having a lucid dream in the previous six hours. This also means that, if you were to cut two hours from your ordinary sleep time, you would halve your chances of lucid dreaming. Likewise, if you normally get only six hours of sleep, you could double your chances of lucid dreaming by extending your sleep by two hours.

The conclusion is obvious: If you want to encourage the occurrence of lucid dreams, extend your sleep. If you are serious about lucid dreaming, and can find the extra time, you should arrange at least one morning a week in which you can stay in bed for several hours longer than usual.

Even though most people enjoy sleeping late, we don't all have the time to do it. If you find that you just cannot afford to spend more time in bed, there is a simple secret to increasing your frequency of lucid dreaming that requires no more time than the usual number of hours you sleep.

The secret is to rearrange your sleep time. If you normally sleep from midnight to 6:00 A.M., then get up at 4:00 A.M. and stay awake for two hours, doing whatever you need to do. Go back to bed and catch up on your remaining sleep from 6:00 to 8:00 A.M. During the two hours of delayed sleep you will have much more REM than you would have had sleeping at the usual time (4:00 to 6:00), and you will enjoy an increased likelihood of lucid dreaming, with no time lost to sleep.

Some lucid dreaming enthusiasts make rearranged sleep a regular part of their lucid dream induction ritual. For example, Alan Worsley reports that when he wants to induce lucid dreams, he goes to bed at 1:30 A.M. and sleeps a little less than six hours, from about 2:00 until 7:45, when the alarm clock awakens him. He then gets up and eats breakfast, drinks tea, reads the newspaper, mail, etc., staying awake for two or three hours. At 9:00 or 9:30 he writes down in detail his plans and intentions regarding specific experiments or activities he wants to carry out in his lucid dreams and then goes back to bed, usually falling asleep by 10:00 or 10:30. He then sleeps for several hours, during which he frequently has lucid dreams, sometimes extended series of them lasting up to an hour.[11]

Redistributing sleep can be a remarkably powerful way to facilitate lucid dreaming. Be sure to try it. For the small amount of effort, you will be more than amply rewarded. Here is an exercise to get you started.

EXERCISE: SCHEDULING TIME FOR LUCID DREAMING

1. Set your alarm
Before going to bed, set your alarm to awaken you two to three hours earlier than usual, and go to sleep at your normal time.

2. Get out of bed promptly in the morning
When your alarm goes off, get out of bed immediately. You are going to stay awake for two or three hours. Go about your business until about a half hour before returning to bed.

3. Focus on your intentions for your lucid dreams
For the half hour before you return to sleep think about what you want to accomplish in your lucid dream: where you want to go, who want to see, or what you want to do. You can use this time to incubate a dream about a

(exercise continues)

particular topic (see chapter 6). If you are working on any of the applications in later chapters of this book, this is a good time to practice the exercises for the applications.

4. *Return to bed and practice an induction technique*
After two or three hours have passed since you awakened, make sure your sleeping place will be quiet and undisturbed for the next couple of hours. Go to bed, and practice the induction technique that works best for you. Techniques are provided in the next two chapters.

5. *Give yourself at least two hours to sleep*
Set your alarm or have someone awaken you if you like, but be sure to give yourself two hours to dream. You are likely to have at least one long REM period in this time, perhaps two.

The morning hours are ideal for lucid dreaming for another reason. Although it takes us an hour to an hour and a half to get to REM sleep at the start of the night, after several hours of sleep we often can enter into REM only a few minutes after having been awake. Sometimes we can awaken from a dream and reenter it moments later. These facts make possible another type of lucid dream—the wake-initiated lucid dream, which is discussed in chapter 4.

Final Preparations:
Learning to Relax Deeply

Before you are ready to practice techniques for inducing lucid dreams, you need to be able to put yourself into a state of attentive relaxation, with alert mind and deeply relaxed body. The two exercises described below will show you how. They are important for helping you to clear your mind of the day's worries so that you can focus on lucid dream induction. Lucid dreaming requires *concentration*, which is nearly impossible to achieve with a distracted mind and tense body. Before going on to the next chapter, master these essential techniques.

EXERCISE:
PROGRESSIVE RELAXATION

1. Lie down on a firm surface
If you can't lie down, sit in a comfortable chair. Close your eyes.

2. Attend to your breathing
Pay attention to your breathing and allow it to deepen. Take a few complete breaths by moving your diaphragm down slightly while inhaling, pushing the abdomen out and drawing air into the lungs from the bottom up. Allow yourself to sigh deeply on the exhale, letting tension escape as you do so.

3. Progressively tense and relax each muscle group
Tense and then relax all the muscle groups in your body, one at a time. Begin with your dominant arm. Bend your hand backward at the wrist, as if you are trying to place the back of the hand on your forearm. Hold it tight for

(exercise continues)

---

five to ten seconds. Pay attention to the tension. Release the tension and relax. Note the difference. Tense and relax again. Pause for twenty to thirty seconds as you take a deep abdominal breath, then exhale slowly. Repeat the procedure for the other hand. Then repeat the tension-relaxation-tension-relaxation sequence for your forearms, upper arms, forehead, jaws, neck, shoulders, abdomen, back, buttocks, legs, and feet. Pause between each major muscle group, take a deep breath, and release more tension in a sigh.

4. Let go of all tension
After you have worked through all muscle groups, let them go limp. Wherever you feel tension, perform an additional tense-and-relax sequence. Cultivate the image of tension flowing out of your body like an invisible fluid. Every time you tense and relax, remind yourself that the relaxation is greater than the tension that preceded it.

(Adapted from Jacobsen.[12]*)*

EXERCISE: 61-POINT RELAXATION

1. Study the figure
Figure 2.1 illustrates 61 points on the body. To do this exercise, you need to memorize the sequence of points. (This is not difficult, because the points are arranged in a simple pattern.) They begin at the forehead, travel down and up your right arm, then across to your left arm, down your torso, down and up your right and left legs, then back up your torso to the forehead.

2. Focus your attention on one point at a time
Begin at your forehead. Focus your attention between your eyebrows and think of the number one. Keep your attention fixed at Point 1 for several seconds until you

(exercise continues)

feel that your awareness of the location is clear and distinct. Think of your self being located at this point. Before moving on to the next point, you should feel a sense of warmth and heaviness at this spot.

3. Move through each point in sequence
In the same manner, successively focus your attention on each of the first thirty-one points. Proceed slowly, and imagine your self being located at each point as you reach it. Feel the sense of warmth and heaviness before moving on. Do not allow your mind to wander. At first you may find this difficult to do; you will discover that at times you suddenly will forget that you are doing the exercise and start daydreaming or thinking about something else. If you lose your place, return to the beginning or the last numbered point you attended to, and continue. Practice with thirty-one points until you can attend to them all in sequence without daydreaming or losing track.

4. Extend your practice to include all sixty-one points
When you can attend to thirty-one points in sequence, repeat Steps 1 and 2 with all sixty-one points. Practice this until you can do all points without losing your focus. Now you are ready to use this exercise with lucid dream induction techniques.

(Adapted from Rama.[13])

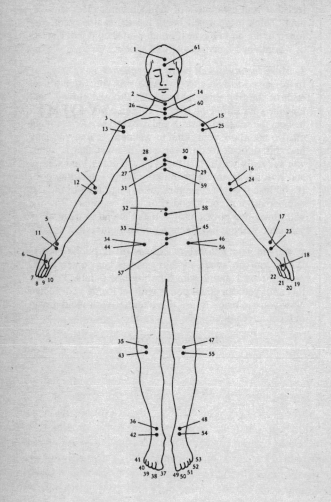

Figure 2.1. 61 points of relaxation[14]
(Adapted from *Exercise Without Movement* by Swami Rama
[Himalyan Institute, Honesdale, PA].)

3

~~~~~~~~

Waking Up
in the Dream World

Lucid Dreaming is Easier
Than You May Think

Before beginning the exercises in this chapter you should
recall at least one dream per night. You also should have
recorded a dozen or more dreams in your journal, from
which you will have extracted a number of personal
dreamsigns. You are now ready to learn techniques designed to help you have your first lucid dream, if you
haven't had one yet. With some effort these same techniques can help you to learn to have lucid dreams at will.

Before going further, I'd like to offer a piece of advice
which may prevent some frustration. Sometimes people
develop mental blocks that effectively prevent them from
intentionally inducing lucid dreams. Typically, they think
of lucid dreaming as a very difficult state to achieve. Believing this seems to make it so. However, I've learned
how to have lucid dreams at will, so I know that it can
be done, and I also know that it's easy—once you know

how. My experience with teaching hundreds of people how to have lucid dreams suggests that almost everyone who diligently practices these techniques succeeds. No one can say how long it will take you to learn to have lucid dreams; this depends on your dream recall, motivation, how much you practice, and a factor we can call "talent for lucid dreaming." Even though I was highly motivated and was having three or four lucid dreams per week, it took me two and a half years to reach the point at which I could have a lucid dream anytime I wanted. But then, I had to invent my own methods. You have the great advantage of being able to work with techniques that have been tested and refined by other lucid dreamers.

Don't be discouraged if you don't succeed right away. And don't give up! Virtually everyone who stays with it improves through practice. Lucid dreaming is easier than you may think.

Find the technique that works best for you

The next two chapters will present a wide variety of techniques for stimulating lucid dreams. The emphasis is on techniques that work best for most people. However, there are variations as to which method will be most useful for you, due to individual differences in physiology, personality, and life-style. For example, the techniques described in chapter 4 are most readily (but not exclusively) cultivated by people who fall asleep rapidly. Therefore, we have striven for completeness and have described most of the known lucid dream induction techniques. You should try any that appeal to you. Once you understand the principles and practice of lucid dream induction, you may choose to develop your own method by combining features of the techniques we have described. In any case, experiment, observe, and persevere: you will find a way.

If practicing mental exercises is a new idea to you, you may be uncertain about your ability to use them successfully. In the appendix is an exercise, called "Strengthening Your Will," designed to help you learn how to achieve things through mental effort. Practicing this exercise will improve your success with all of the induction techniques in this book.

Critical State Testing

Building a bridge between the two worlds

Pause now to ask yourself the following question: "Am I dreaming or awake, right now?" Be serious. Really try to answer the question to the best of your ability and be ready to justify your answer.

Now that you have an answer, ask yourself another question: "How often do I ask myself whether I am dreaming or awake during the course of an average day?" Unless you are a philosophy major or are already practicing lucid dreaming induction techniques, the answer is probably never. If you never ask this question while awake, how often do you suppose you will ask it while you are dreaming? Again, because the things you habitually think about and do in dreams are the same things you habitually think about and do while awake, the answer will probably be never.

The implications of this should be clear. You can use the relationship between habits in waking and dreaming life to help you induce lucid dreams. One way to become lucid is to ask yourself whether or not you are dreaming *while you are dreaming*. In order to do this, you should make a habit of asking the question while awake.

The critical faculty

A part of your mind has the job of "reality testing," that is, determining whether stimuli are of internal or external origin. Oliver Fox called this critical reflective system "the critical faculty" and he regarded it as typically "asleep" in ordinary dreams. He also believed this faculty to be fundamental to the attainment of lucidity. In order to become lucid in a dream, wrote Fox:

. . . we must arouse the critical faculty which seems to a great extent inoperative in dreams, and here, too, degrees of activity become manifest. Let us suppose, for example, that in my dream I am in a café. At a table near mine is a lady who would be very attractive—only, she has four eyes. Here are some illustrations of these degrees of activity of the critical faculty:

(1) In the dream it is practically dormant, but on waking I have the feeling that there was something peculiar about this lady. Suddenly, I get it—"Why, of course, she had four eyes!"

(2) In the dream I exhibit mild surprise and say, "How curious that girl has four eyes! It spoils her." But only in the same way that I might remark, "What a pity she had broken her nose! I wonder how she did it."

(3) The critical faculty is more awake and the four eyes are regarded as abnormal; but the phenomenon is not fully appreciated. I exclaim, "Good Lord!" and then reassure myself by adding, "There must be a freak show or a circus in the town." Thus I hover on the brink of realization, but do not quite get there.

(4) My critical faculty is now fully awake and refuses to be satisfied by this explanation. I continue my train of thought, "But there never was

such a freak! An adult woman with four eyes—it's impossible. I am dreaming.''[1]

The challenge, then, is how to activate the critical faculty before bed so that it remains sufficiently primed to function properly when it is needed to explain some strange occurrence in a dream.

Paul Tholey has recently derived several techniques for inducing lucid dreams from over a decade of research involving more than two hundred subjects. Tholey claims that an effective method for achieving lucidity (especially for beginners) is to develop a "critical-reflective attitude" toward your state of consciousness. This is done by asking yourself whether or not you are dreaming while you are awake. He stresses the importance of asking the "critical question" ("Am I dreaming or not?") as frequently as possible, at least five to ten times a day, and in every situation that seems dreamlike. The importance of asking the question in dreamlike situations is that in lucid dreams the critical question is usually asked in situations similar to those in which it was asked during the day. Asking the question at bedtime and while falling asleep is also favorable. We have incorporated these hints into the following adaptation of Tholey's reflection technique.

CRITICAL STATE TESTING TECHNIQUE

1. Plan when to test your state

Pick five to ten different occasions during the day to test your state. These should be circumstances that are similar in some ways to your dreams. Any time you come in contact with something that resembles a dreamsign, test your state. Whenever anything surprising or unlikely occurs or anytime you experience unusually powerful

(exercise continues)

emotions, or anything dream like, test your state. If you have recurrent dreams, any situations related to the recurrent content are ideal. For example, if you have recurrent anxiety dreams featuring your fear of heights, you should do a state test when you cross a bridge or visit a room near the top of a tall building.

For example, Joe Dreamer decides to test his state whenever

1. He steps into an elevator (source of many of his anxiety dreams).
2. He speaks to his boss.
3. He sees an attractive woman.
4. He reads a typographical error.
5. He goes to the bathroom. (He's noticed that bathrooms are often quite strange in his dreams.)

2. Test your state

Ask yourself the critical question as often as possible (at least the five to ten specific times you selected in Step 1): "Am I dreaming or awake?" Don't just automatically ask the question and mindlessly reply, "Obviously, I'm awake," or you will do the same thing when you actually are dreaming. Look around for any oddities or inconsistencies that might indicate you are dreaming. Think back to the events of the last several minutes. Do you have any trouble remembering what just happened? If so, you may be dreaming. For guidance on correctly answering the critical question, please see the suggestions in the following section.

(Adapted from Tholey's reflection technique.[2]*)*

Tips on state testing

As most people know from firsthand experience, dreamers don't always reason clearly. While wondering whether or not they're dreaming, they sometimes mistakenly decide that they are awake. This could happen to you if you try to test reality in the wrong way. For example, you might conclude in a dream that you couldn't be dreaming because everything seems so solid and vividly real. Or you might pinch yourself, according to the classical test. This rarely—and never in my experience—awakens you from your dream, but instead produces the convincing sensation of a pinch!

When dreamers share their realization or suspicion that they are dreaming with other dream figures, they frequently encounter protests and arguments to the contrary, as in the following example:

One lucid dream was about a former residence I lived at when I was in high school. The house had a garden, which was the nicest feature of the yard. A very close friend of mine was there. As I sat looking at the house with my present-day consciousness I realized that the house, although it seemed intact, had actually been razed about seven years ago. Yet there it was in front of me, as clear as day. Right away I knew I was in the dream space and turned to my friend and asked him to wake up, that we were in a dream and if only he would realize that, we would be able to go anywhere or do whatever we wanted. Well, he wouldn't listen to me and he kept saying that it was real and that I had been reading too many Carlos Castaneda books. He told me that instead I should read the Gospel. (P.K., Columbus, North Carolina)

The moral here is not to take anyone else's word for it: test your own reality! Trying to fly is a more reliable test used by many lucid dreamers. The easiest way to do this is to hop into the air and attempt to prolong your time off the ground. If you stay airborne for even a split second longer than normal, you can be sure you're dreaming.

Use the same test each time you do a state check. In my experience, the best test is the following: find some writing and read it once (if you can), look away, then reread it, checking to see if it stays the same. Every time

I have tried this in my own lucid dreams the writing has mutated in some way. The words may no longer make sense or the letters may turn into hieroglyphics.

An equally effective state test, if you normally wear a digital watch, is to look at its face twice; in a dream, it will never behave correctly (that is, with the numbers changing in the expected manner) and usually won't show anything that makes sense at all (maybe it is displaying *Dream Standard Time*). Incidentally, this test works only with digital and not with old-style analog watches, which can sometimes tell dream time quite believably. Once when I decided to do a state test I looked at my watch and found it had been converted to a fairly realistic analog watch. But I didn't remember trading in my digital watch for the Mickey Mouse watch that was on my wrist, so I figured I must be dreaming. Be careful with this test; you might find yourself coming up with some absurd rationalization for why you can't read the correct time, such as "maybe the battery is wearing down" or "the light is too dim to see the face."

In general, if you want to distinguish dreaming from waking, you need to remember that although dreams can seem as vividly real as waking life, they are much more changeable. In most instances, all you have to do is look around critically, and in a dream you will notice unusual transmutations.

State testing is a way to find out the truth of your situation when you suspect you might be dreaming. As such, you usually will employ it as the final step in becoming lucid. With practice, you will find yourself spending less time testing dreamsigns, and instead pass more frequently from suspecting you're dreaming to *knowing* you're dreaming. You may discover that anytime you feel the genuine need to test reality, *this in itself is proof enough that you're dreaming*, since while awake we almost never seriously wonder if we're really awake.[3] This is the last word in state testing: Anytime you find yourself seriously suspecting that you just might be dreaming, you probably are!

Intention Techniques

The idea of cultivating a state of mind while awake for the purpose of carrying it into the dream state as a means of inducing lucid dreams has been used by Tibetan Buddhists for more than a thousand years. The origin of these techniques is shrouded in the mists of the past. They are said to derive from the teachings of a master called Lawapa of Urgyen in Afghanistan and were introduced into Tibet in the eighth century by Padmasambhava, the founder of Tibetan Buddhism.[4]

The Tibetan teachings were passed down from generation to generation to present times, when we have *The Yoga of the Dream State*, a manuscript first compiled in the sixteenth century and translated in 1935, which outlines several methods for "comprehending the nature of the dream state" (that is, inducing lucid dreams).[5] Most of the Tibetan techniques were evidently tailored to the skills of practiced meditators. They involve such things as complex visualizations of Sanskrit letters in many-petaled lotuses while carrying out special breathing and concentration exercises. In the future, when thousands of people achieve high expertise in the oneironautical skills discussed in this book, perhaps we will be advanced enough to learn more from our Tibetan predecessors. For now, the essence of the Tibetan techniques is distilled for you in this and the next chapter.

POWER OF RESOLUTION TECHNIQUE

For beginning lucid dreamers, the most relevant Tibetan technique is called "comprehending it by the power of resolution," which consists of "resolving to maintain unbroken continuity of consciousness" throughout both the waking and dream states. It involves both a day and a night practice.

1. Day practice
During the day, "under all conditions" think continuously that "all things are of the substance of dreams" (that is, that your experience is a construction of your mind) and resolve that you will realize their true nature.

2. Night practice
At night, when about to go to sleep, "firmly resolve" that you will comprehend the dream state—that is, realize that it is not real, but a dream. (Optional exercise: Pray to your guru that you will be able to comprehend the dream state. This option will probably need to be modified for most people. If you have a guru, go ahead and pray. If you don't have a guru but do pray, then pray as usual. You can also substitute a symbolic figure associated in your mind with lucid dreaming. If you neither pray nor have a guru, either skip the instruction or ask help from the wisest part of yourself.)

Commentary
Because we dream of things that have concerned us recently, it is likely that if you spend enough time thinking during the day that "everything is of the substance of dreams," then eventually you will entertain that thought while you are dreaming.

(Adapted from Evans-Wentz.[6]*)*

Case history

Twenty years ago I attended Tarthang Tulku's workshop on Tibetan Buddhism at the Esalen Institute in Big Sur, California. Rinpoche ("precious jewel"), as we called the teacher, had been forced to leave Tibet when the Chinese Communists had invaded, and had "just gotten off the boat" from India. He therefore spoke precious little English. The bits of his speech that weren't already broken were frequently broken with laughter. I had been expecting esoteric explanations of advanced theory, but what I got was something incalculably more valuable.

Rinpoche would indicate the world around us with a casual sweep of the hand and portentously announce: "This . . . dream!" Then he would laugh some more and pointing at me or some other person or object, rather mysteriously it seemed, he would insist: "This dream!" followed by more laughter. Rinpoche managed to get the idea across to us (how, I don't really know; I wouldn't rule out telepathy, considering how very few words were exchanged) that we were to attempt to think of all our experiences as dreams and to try to maintain unbroken continuity of consciousness between the two states of sleep and waking. I didn't think I was doing very well with the exercise, but on my way back to San Francisco after the weekend, I unexpectedly found my world was in some way expanded.

A few nights later, I had the first lucid dream I remember since the serial adventure dreams I had when I was five years old. In the dream:

It was snowing gently. I was alone on the rooftop of the world, climbing K2. As I made my way upward through the steeply drifting snow, I was astonished to notice my arms were bare: I was wearing a short-sleeved shirt, hardly proper dress for climbing the second highest mountain in the world! I realized at once that the expla-

nation was that I was dreaming! I was so delighted that I jumped off the mountain and began to fly away, but the dream faded and I awoke.

I interpreted the dream as suggesting that I wasn't yet prepared for the rigors of Tibetan dream yoga. But it was also a starting point, and I continued to have lucid dreams occasionally for eight years before I began to cultivate lucid dreaming in earnest. Incidentally, my impulsive behavior when I became lucid is typical of beginners. If I were to have such a dream now, I would not precipitously jump off the mountain. Instead, I would fly to the top of the mountain and find out if I was climbing it for any reason besides ''because it was there.''

Intention for Westerners

Few Westerners are likely to feel at home with the Eastern idea of a guru, but the idea of intention should be familiar enough. Although most people report occasional spontaneous lucid dreams, lucid dreaming rarely occurs without our intending it. Consequently, if we want to have lucid dreams more frequently, we must begin by cultivating the intention to recognize when we are dreaming. If you are not initially successful in your efforts, take heart from the Tibetan exhortation that it takes no fewer than twenty-one efforts each morning to ''comprehend the nature of the dream state.''

Paul Tholey has experimented extensively with a variation on the ancient Tibetan technique of inducing lucid dreams through the power of resolution.[7] Here is my adaptation of Tholey's method.

INTENTION TECHNIQUE

1. Resolve to recognize dreaming
In the early morning hours, or during an awakening in the latter part of your sleep period, clearly and confidently affirm your intention to remember to recognize the dream state.

2. Visualize yourself recognizing dreaming
Imagine as vividly as possible that you are in dream situations which would typically cause you to realize that you are dreaming. Incorporate several of your most frequently occurring or favorite dreamsigns in your visualizations.

3. Imagine carrying out an intended dream action
In addition to mentally practicing recognizing dreamsigns, resolve to carry out some particular chosen action in the dream. A good choice would be an action that is itself a dreamsign. For example, see yourself flying in your dream and recognizing that you are dreaming. While doing this be sure to firmly resolve to recognize the next time you are dreaming.

Commentary
The reason for setting an intention to do a particular action in the dream is that dreamers sometimes remember to do the action without first having become lucid. Then upon reflection, they remember: "This is what I wanted to do in my dream. Therefore, I must be dreaming!" The intended action should be a dreamsign, because you're more likely to become lucid if you find yourself doing your dream action.

Tholey's Combined Technique

Tholey has claimed that critical state testing has the single most effective technique for inducing lucid dreams out of the several he has discussed.[8] His combined technique is based on critical state testing, and includes elements of his intention and autosuggestion techniques. He doesn't make it clear whether or not the combined technique is superior to the reflection technique, but we believe that it is likely to be more effective. Tholey conjectures, apparently referring to the combined technique,

> . . . that whoever consistently follows the advice given can learn to dream lucidly. Subjects who have never previously experienced a lucid dream will have the first one after a median time of 4 to 5 [weeks], with great interindividual deviation. Under the most favorable circumstances the subject will experience his first lucid dream during the very first night, under unfavorable circumstances only after several months. Practice in attaining the critical-reflective frame of mind is only necessary in the beginning phase, which may last a number of months. Later on, lucid dreams will occur even if the subject has not asked himself the critical question during the day. The frequency of lucid dreams then depends to a large extent on the will of the subject. Most subjects who consistently follow the above advice experience at least one lucid dream every night.[9]

I have modified Tholey's combined technique in view of my own experience.

REFLECTION-INTENTION TECHNIQUE

1. Plan when you intend to test your state
Choose in advance certain occasions when you intend to remember to test your state. For example, you might

(exercise continues)

decide to ask, "Am I dreaming?" when you arrive home from work, at the beginning of each conversation you have, every hour on the hour, and so on. Choose a frequency of state testing that feels comfortable. Use imagery to help you remember to ask the question. For instance, if you intend to ask it when you arrive at home, see yourself opening the door and remembering your intention.

Practice the exercise a dozen times or more during the day at your selected times and also whenever you find yourself in a situation which is in any way dreamlike, for example, whenever something surprising or odd happens or you experience inappropriately strong emotions or find your mind (and especially memory) strangely unresponsive.

2. Test your state
Ask yourself, "Am I dreaming or awake?" Look around you for any oddities or inconsistencies that might indicate you are dreaming. Think back to the events of the last several minutes. Do you have any trouble remembering what just happened? If so, you may be dreaming. Read some text twice. Don't conclude that you are awake unless you have solid proof (for example, the writing stays the same every time you look at it).

3. Imagine yourself dreaming
After having satisfied yourself that you're awake, tell yourself, "Okay, I'm not dreaming, now. But if I were, what would it be like?" Imagine as vividly as possible that you are dreaming. Intently imagine that what you are perceiving (hearing, feeling, smelling, or seeing) is a dream: the people, trees, sunshine, sky and earth, and yourself—all a dream. Observe your environment carefully for your target dreamsigns from chapter 2. Imagine what it would be like if a dreamsign from your target category were present.

(exercise continues)

As soon as you are able to vividly experience yourself as if in a dream, tell yourself, "The next time I'm dreaming, I will remember to recognize that I'm dreaming."

4. Imagine doing what you intend to do in your lucid dream

Decide in advance what you would like to do in your next lucid dream. You may wish to fly or talk to dream characters or try one of the applications suggested later in this book.

Now, continue the fantasy begun in Step 2 and imagine that after having become lucid in your present environment, you now fulfill your wish: Experience yourself doing whatever you have chosen to do. Firmly resolve that you will remember to recognize that you are dreaming and to do what you intend in your next lucid dream.

(Adapted from Tholey.[10])

Commentary

At first you may find it strange to question the very foundations of the reality you are experiencing, but you undoubtedly will find that taking a critical look at the nature of reality a few times a day is an enjoyable habit to cultivate. In our workshops we have distributed business cards with the words AM I DREAMING? printed on them. You can write this question on the back of a business card and stick it in your pocket. Take it out and read it, and perform a reality test by looking away from the card and then looking at it again very quickly. If the words scramble, you are dreaming.

Once you establish a systematically critical attitude in your waking life, sooner or later you will decide to try a state test when you are actually dreaming. And then you will be awake in your dream.

Mnemonic Induction of Lucid Dreams (MILD)

Ten years ago, I developed an effective method of lucid dream induction while investigating the feasibility of learning to have lucid dreams at will for my Ph.D. dissertation work.[11]

Before trying induction procedures, I remembered less than one lucid dream per month. While using autosuggestion during the first sixteen months of my study (the technique is presented below), I recalled an average of five lucid dreams per month with a range of one to thirteen. (The month in which I had thirteen lucid dreams using autosuggestion happened while I was doing my first laboratory studies of lucid dreaming, which incidentally illustrates the powerful effect of motivation on the frequency of lucid dreaming.) However, during the period I was using autosuggestion to induce lucid dreams, I had no understanding of how I was doing it! All I knew was that I was telling myself before bed: "Tonight, I will have a lucid dream." But how? I had no idea. And having no idea meant that there was little I could do to make it happen. Without understanding the process involved, I stood little chance of learning to have lucid dreams at will.

Nevertheless, I gradually observed a psychological factor that correlated with the occurrence of my lucid dreams: the presleep intention to *remember* to recognize I was dreaming. Once I knew how I was trying to induce lucid dreams, it became much easier to focus my efforts. This clarification of intention was followed by an immediate increase in the monthly frequency of my lucid dreams. Further practice and refinements led to a method whereby I could reliably induce lucid dreams. With this new method, I had as many as four lucid dreams in one night, and as many as twenty-six in one month. I now could have a lucid dream on any night I chose and had accomplished my goal of showing that it is possible to bring access to the lucid dream state under volitional control. For people who were willing and able to learn my method, it was now possible to enter the world of lucid dreaming almost at will.

Once I knew that I was trying to remember to do something (that is, become lucid) at a later time (that is, when next I'm dreaming), I was able to devise a technique to help me accomplish that. How can we manage to remember to do something in a dream? Perhaps we should start with a simpler question: How do we remember to do things in ordinary life?

In everyday life we remember most things we have to do by using some sort of external mnemonic or memory aid (a grocery list, phone pad, string around the finger, memo by the door, etc.). But how do we remember future intentions (this is called *prospective memory*) without relying on external reminders? Motivation plays an important role. You are less likely to forget to do something that you really want to do.

When you set yourself the goal to remember to do something, you have made the goal one of your current concerns and thereby have activated a goal-seeking brain system that will stay partially activated until you have achieved it. If the goal is very important to you, the system stays highly activated and you keep checking to see if it's time to do it, until it *is* time.[12] It never becomes fully unconscious. But the more typical case is when, for example, you decide to buy some tacks the next time you go to the store. This is hardly important enough to keep on the front page of your mind, so you go to the store and forget about your intention. That is, unless while at the store you just happen to notice a box of tacks, or even a hammer which brings up tacks by association.

This reveals the other major factor involved in remembering to do things: association. When facing the challenge of remembering to do something, we can increase the likelihood of success by (1) being strongly motivated to remember and (2) forming mental associations between what we want to remember to do and the future circumstances in which we intend to do it. These associations are greatly strengthened by the mnemonic (memory aid) of visualizing yourself doing what you intend to remember.

Thinking of lucid dream induction as a problem of prospective memory, I developed a technique designed to increase my chances of remembering my intention to be lucid: the Mnemonic Induction of Lucid Dreams procedure, (MILD).[13] I have revised the procedure for this book in light of my experience, both using the technique myself to produce lucid dreams and teaching it to hundreds of others. Please take note of the prerequisites discussed below.

MILD prerequisites

To successfully induce lucid dreams with MILD, you need to have certain capacities. First of all, if you can't reliably remember to carry out future intentions while *awake*, there is little chance that you will remember to do anything while *asleep*. So before attempting MILD, you need to prove to yourself that you can indeed remember to do things while awake. If you are like most people, you are used to relying on external reminders and therefore need practice in remembering intentions using only your own mental power. The following is an exercise to help you acquire the necessary skill to perform the MILD technique.

EXERCISE:
PROSPECTIVE MEMORY TRAINING

1. Read the day's targets
This exercise is designed to be practiced over an entire week. Below is a set of four target events for each day of the week. When you get up in the morning, read only the targets for that day. (Do not read the targets before the proper day.) Memorize the day's targets.

2. Look for your targets during the day
Your goal is to notice the next occurrence of each event, at which time you will perform a state test: "Am I dreaming?" So, if your target is, "The next time I hear a dog bark," when you hear this next, note it and do a state test. You are aiming to notice the target once—the next time it happens.

3. Keep track of how many target events you hit
At the end of the day, write down how many of the four targets you succeeded in noticing (you can make a space in your dream journal to record your progress with this exercise). If you realize during the day that you missed your first chance to notice one of your targets, then you have failed to hit that target, even though you may notice its occurrence later in the day. If you are certain that one or more of the targets did not occur at all during the day, say so with a note in your dream journal.

4. Continue the exercise for at least one week
Practice the exercise until you have tried all of the daily targets given below. If at the end of the week, you are still missing most of the targets, continue until you can hit most of them. Make up your own list of targets, keep track of your success rate, and observe how your memory develops.

(exercise continues)

Daily Targets

SUNDAY:
The next time I see a pet or animal
The next time I look at my face in a mirror
The next time I turn on a light
The next time I see a flower

MONDAY:
The next time I write anything down
The next time I feel pain
The next time I hear someone say my name
The next time I drink something

TUESDAY:
The next time I see a traffic light
The next time I hear music
The next time I throw something in the garbage
The next time I hear laughter

WEDNESDAY:
The next time I turn on a television or radio
The next time I see a vegetable
The next time I see a red car
The next time I handle money

THURSDAY:
The next time I read something other than this list
The next time I check the time
The next time I notice myself daydreaming
The next time I hear the telephone ringing

FRIDAY:
The next time I open a door
The next time I see a bird
The next time I use the toilet after noon
The next time I see the stars

SATURDAY:
The next time I put a key in a lock
The next time I see an advertisement
The next time I eat anything after breakfast
The next time I see a bicycle

MILD TECHNIQUE

1. Set up dream recall

Before going to bed resolve to wake up and recall dreams during each dream period throughout the night (or the first dream period after dawn, or after 6 A.M. or whenever you find convenient).

2. Recall your dream

When you awaken from a dream period, no matter what time it is, try to recall as many details as possible from your dream. If you find yourself so drowsy that you are drifting back to sleep, do something to arouse yourself.

3. Focus your intent

While returning to sleep, concentrate singlemindedly on your intention to remember to recognize that you're dreaming. Tell yourself: "Next time I'm dreaming, I want to remember I'm dreaming." Really try to feel that you mean it. Narrow your thoughts to this idea alone. If you find yourself thinking about anything else, just let go of these thoughts and bring your mind back to your intention to remember.

4. See yourself becoming lucid

At the same time, imagine that you are back in the dream from which you have just awakened, but this time you recognize that it is a dream. Find a dreamsign in the experience; when you see it say to yourself: "I'm dreaming!" and continue your fantasy. For example, you might decide that when you are lucid you want to fly. In that case, imagine yourself taking off and flying as soon as you come to the point in your fantasy that you "realize" you are dreaming.

5. Repeat

Repeat Steps 3 and 4 until your intention is set, then let

(exercise continues)

yourself fall asleep. If, while falling asleep, you find yourself thinking of anything else, repeat the procedure so that the last thing in your mind before falling asleep is your intention to remember to recognize the next time you are dreaming.

Commentary

If all goes well, you'll fall asleep and find yourself in a dream, at which point you'll remember to notice that you are dreaming.

If it takes you a long time to fall asleep while practicing this method, don't worry. The longer you're awake, the more likely you are to have a lucid dream when you eventually return to sleep. This is because the longer you are awake, the more times you will repeat the MILD procedure, reinforcing your intention to have a lucid dream. Furthermore, the wakefulness may activate your brain, making lucidity easier to attain.

In fact, if you are a very deep sleeper, you should get up after memorizing your dream and engage in ten to fifteen minutes of any activity requiring full wakefulness. Turn on the light and read a book. Get out of bed and go into another room. One of the best things to do is to write out your dream and read it over, noting all dreamsigns, in preparation for the MILD visualization.

Many people meet with success after only one or two nights of MILD; others take longer. Continued practice of MILD can lead to greater proficiency at lucid dreaming. Many of our advanced oneironauts have used it to cultivate the ability to have several lucid dreams any night they choose.

Autosuggestion and Hypnosis Techniques

Autosuggestion

Patricia Garfield has claimed that "using a method of self-suggestion, she obtained a classical learning curve, increasing the frequency of prolonged lucid dreams from a baseline of zero to a high of three per week."[14] She reported using autosuggestion for five or six years, producing an average of four or five lucid dreams per month.[15] As described above, I found very similar results with this type of technique: during the first sixteen months of my dissertation study in which I was using autosuggestion to induce lucid dreams, I reported an average of 5.4 lucid dreams per month.[16]

Tholey also reports experimenting with autosuggestion techniques, but unfortunately, he provides few details aside from mentioning that the effectiveness of suggestive formulae can be improved by employing special relaxation techniques.[17] He recommends that autosuggestions be given immediately before sleep, while in a relaxed state, and cautions that an effort of will must be avoided.

The distinction between effortful intention and noneffortful suggestion is interesting and perhaps explains some of my early experiences with trying to induce lucid dreams on demand. The first several times I tried to have lucid dreams in the laboratory, I was using autosuggestion and I found that trying too hard (effortful intention) was counterproductive. This was frustrating for me because I was required to have a lucid dream that very night, while sleeping in the laboratory. It was not enough to have the several lucid dreams a week that autosuggestion produced; I needed to have them on the nights I was in the laboratory. However, after I developed the MILD technique, I found I could try hard and always succeed. This was because MILD involves effortful intention. With autosuggestion I had had a lucid dream on only one out of six nights in the lab; with MILD I had one or more lucid dreams on twenty out of twenty-one nights spent in the sleep laboratory.

It should be clear from this that (for me, at least) autosuggestion is less effective than some other lucid dream induction techniques, such as MILD. However, due to its noneffortful nature, it may offer modest advantages for anyone willing to accept a relatively low yield of lucid dreams in exchange for a relatively undemanding and effortless method. For people who are highly susceptible to hypnosis, on the other hand, suggestion techniques may offer an effective solution to the lucid dream induction problem, as we shall see when we discuss posthypnotic suggestion.

AUTOSUGGESTION TECHNIQUE

1. Relax completely
While lying in bed, gently close your eyes and relax your head, neck, back, arms, and legs. Completely let go of all muscular and mental tension, and breathe slowly and restfully. Enjoy the feeling of relaxation and let go of your thoughts, worries, concerns, and plans. If you have just awakened from sleep, you are probably already sufficiently relaxed. Otherwise, you may use the progressive relaxation exercise (page 53).

2. Tell yourself that you will have a lucid dream
While remaining deeply relaxed, suggest to yourself that you are going to have a lucid dream, either later the same night or on some other night in the near future. Avoid putting intentional effort into your suggestion. Do not strongly insist with statements like "Tonight I will have a lucid dream!" You might find that if you don't succeed after a night or two following such misplaced certainty, you will rapidly lose faith in yourself. Instead, attempt to put yourself in the frame of mind of genuinely expecting that you will have a lucid dream tonight or sometime soon. Let yourself think expectantly about the lucid dream you are about to have. Look forward to it, but be willing to let it happen all in good time.

Posthypnotic suggestion

If autosuggestion can increase your lucid dream frequency, then this effect may be greatly enhanced by using hypnosis with a posthypnotic suggestion (PHS). Indeed, Charles Tart speculated that PHS may offer "the most powerful technique for content control of dreams via presleep suggestion."[18] Lucidity may be viewed as a kind of dream content, perhaps also subject to influence by PHS. I experimented on three occasions with using PHS to have lucid dreams and was successful twice.[19] I am only moderately hypnotizable. For highly hypnotizable subjects, PHS might be a very productive technique and certainly deserves study.

The only other information available on the topic of the induction of lucid dreams by PHS comes from a ground-breaking Ph.D. dissertation by clinical psychologist Joseph Dane. Here we will focus on only one of the intriguing aspects of this study. Two groups of fifteen college women, none of whom had ever had lucid dreams, were hypnotized several times and then monitored in the laboratory for one night each. One group (the PHS group) developed a personal dream symbol from the dream imagery they pictured in the hypnotic state. Another group (the control) was hypnotized but did not look for a personal dream symbol. Upon being rehypnotized, the women in the PHS group visualized their symbols while asking for help in producing a lucid dream later that night. In the course of a night in the sleep laboratory, they reported lucid dreams that were longer and personally more relevant and involving than those of the control group. Follow-up indicated that the women in the PHS group continued to have more lucid dreams than those in the control group.[20]

Psychotechnology: Electronic Lucid Dream Induction

The lucid dream induction techniques discussed in this chapter involve learning to bring your waking intention to become lucid into the dream. MILD, for example, is based on the ability to remember to do things in the future: "When I am dreaming, I will remember to notice that I am dreaming." Still, it can be difficult enough to remember to do things when we are awake, let alone when we are sleeping!

In recent years, my research at Stanford has focused on helping dreamers to remember their intentions. I reasoned that if dreamers could somehow be reminded when they were dreaming by a cue from the external world, then at least half of their task in becoming lucid would be done. All the individuals would have to do is remember what the cue means.

Getting a cue into a dream is not as difficult as it might sound. Although we are not conscious of the world around us while asleep and dreaming, our brains continue to monitor the environment through our senses. We are not entirely vulnerable as we sleep—we tend to awaken when we perceive novel and therefore potentially threatening events. Because of this continuous unconscious monitoring, occasionally pieces of the action around us enter our dreams (become incorporated). My research team at Stanford has been searching for the type of cue (stimulus) that would most readily be incorporated into dreams.

We began our experimentation on cuing lucid dreams with perhaps the most obvious sort of reminder: a tape-recorded message stating "This is a dream!"[21] We monitored brain waves, eye movements, and other physiological measures from four subjects as they slept in the laboratory. When the subjects were in REM sleep, the tape was played at a gradually increasing volume through speakers above their beds. The subjects in this study were already proficient at lucid dreaming, and the success rate for inducing lucid dreams was accordingly high. The tape was played a total of fifteen times and produced five lucid dreams. Three of the lucid dreams were initiated when the dreamers heard the phrase "This is a dream" in their dreams. The other two lucid dreams occurred while the tape was playing, but the subjects did not report hearing it in the dream.

The ten times the tape failed to induce lucidity illustrate two major challenges in cuing lucid dreams: the dreamer may either awaken or fail to recognize the meaning of the cue. Eight times the tape simply awakened the subjects.

Even if the cue is incorporated and the dreamer remains asleep, this alone does not guarantee success. On two occasions the message entered the dreamer's world, but the dreamer lacked the presence of mind to realize what it meant. In one particularly amusing case, the subject complained that someone in the dream was insistently telling him, "You're dreaming," but he paid no attention to the advice! From this and our subsequent efforts to stimulate lucid dreams with cues, we concluded that we can help people to realize when they are dreaming by giving them reminders from the outside world. But would-be lucid dreamers must still contribute to the effort by preparing their minds to recognize the cues and remember what they mean. Thereafter, we began to use early versions of the mental techniques in this book in conjunction with external cuing.

Our next cuing experiment was conducted as an honors thesis by Robert Rich, an undergraduate psychology student. Because an earlier study had shown that tactile stimuli were incorporated into dreams more frequently than visual or auditory stimuli,[22] we decided to test a related stimulus as a cue to induce lucid dreams. We used a vibration applied through the mattress when the subject was in REM sleep.[23]

In this study the subjects extensively practiced mental preparation exercises. During the day preceding the lab recording, they wore vibrators on their ankles that were set with a timer to turn on several times during the day. Whenever the subjects felt the vibration, they practiced an exercise combining state testing with a reminder to themselves that when they felt the vibration in their dreams they would recognize they were dreaming.

Eleven of the eighteen subjects had lucid dreams during the one or two nights they spent in the laboratory. They had a total of seventeen lucid dreams, eleven of which occurred in association with the vibration. One of the ways subjects perceived the vibration was as chaos in the dream world:

I started floating in the bed and the electrodes were pulling and then the walls started to move back and forth. Then Stephen appeared in the corner. He said, "If weird things start happening, you know you're dreaming. . . ."

This subject realized that weird things *were* happening, became lucid, and flew off to see the stars. We were on our way to finding an effective way to stimulate lucidity. Vibration, though a relatively effective cue, posed a number of technical difficulties, so we continued to investigate other types of stimuli.

We next tested light, since light rarely alerts humans to danger in their environment while they are asleep. Thus, it might be readily incorporated into dreams without leading to awakening. In one study we monitored the physiology of forty-four subjects as they slept wearing modified swim goggles fitted with arrays of red lights.[24] A few minutes after REM onset, when the subjects were likely to be involved in a dream, we briefly switched on the lights in the goggles. In later experiments we used a computer connected to the goggles to detect REM sleep and switch on the light cue. This was the first prototype of what later became the DreamLight™,[25] which is described in the next section.

In this study with light, twenty-four of the forty-four subjects had lucid dreams during the nights they slept in the lab (most subjects spent only one night). Collectively, the subjects spent fifty-eight nights in the lab and reported a total of fifty lucid dreams. As one might expect, those who tended to have lucid dreams more frequently had an easier time using the light to become lucid. Of the twenty-five subjects who normally had at least one lucid dream per month, seventeen (68 percent) had one or more lucid dreams in the lab, compared with five of the nineteen (26 percent) who reported having less than one lucid dream per month. However, of the three subjects in the study who had never before had a lucid dream, two had their first triggered by the light cue.

Other research has shown that people who recall dreams at least once a night report having at least one lucid dream a month.[26] Therefore, it seems likely that for people who meet the prerequisite of excellent dream recall, light cues are likely to be very helpful for inducing lucid dreams.

The flashing red lights from the goggles were incorporated into dreams in a remarkable variety of ways. The dreamers had to be fully alert for any sudden or peculiar changes in the lighting of their dreams. Here is one example of a light-induced lucid dream:

A woman handed me some metal or white object that threw light on my face, and I knew it was the cue. She was a beautiful blond woman and I realized she was my dream character and I hugged her tightly, gratefully, with great love for her, and I felt her dissolving into me. . . .

Our research results made it plain that we could help people to have lucid dreams in the laboratory by using sensory cues. However, we wanted people to be able to use this method at home, without having to take the sleep lab with them. We began working on the DreamLight, a portable lucid dream induction device. Besides being an effective cue to help people realize when they are dreaming, light fit well into a design for a sleep mask that contained both REM detecting sensors and flashing lights for cuing the dreamer.

Seeing the light: The story of the DreamLight™

In *Lucid Dreaming* I wrote, "I believe it is probably only a matter of time before someone perfects and markets an effective lucid-dream induction device; this is currently one of the top priorities of my own research . . . the technological aid might make it easier for the beginner to get started, perhaps saving him or her years of frustrated, misdirected effort."[27] Shortly after this book was published, I began to work on designing such a device. The experiments described above had shown that cuing lucid dreams with stimuli works in the laboratory.

In September 1985 I received a letter from Darrel Dixon, an engineer in Salt Lake City, indicating his interest in developing a lucid dream induction device and offering his assistance. I provided him with a design, and soon he had produced our first prototype. This was a pair of black boxes which worked as an interface between an eye movement detection system and a portable computer. Sensors in a mask worn by the sleeper detected eye movements and the computer monitored the level of eye movement activity. When this level was high enough, the computer sent the signal through the apparatus to switch on flashing lights in the mask. This early setup resembled a prop for a 1950s sci-fi film, with metal boxes covered with knobs, multifarious cables, a mask built from swim goggles, and flashing red lights. Nevertheless, it worked!

On her second night using the device, one subject had the following dream:

I'm sitting in the car outside a store. The lights in the goggles go on. I feel them on my face. I wait for them to turn off before doing a reality check. I reach up to take the goggles off . . . then the goggles aren't there anymore and, still sitting in the van, I decide to test reality by reading a dollar bill. A word is wrong, so I conclude I am dreaming! I get out and fly. It feels wonderful. The streets are bright and sunny, crisp and clear. I fly up over a building, and the sun gets in my eyes—it is the light! It washes out the imagery, so I spin my body. I end up inside the store with friends, no longer lucid, and tell them about my experience.

In the last several years the Stanford research group has conducted several laboratory studies using the DreamLight. And participants in two courses on lucid dreaming have had the chance to experiment with the DreamLight at home.

In the study on home use of the DreamLight we examined several different factors influencing success with lucid dreaming, including various types and degrees of mental preparation. In accordance with our findings in previous studies of cuing lucid dreams, we found that mental preparation is extremely important to successful lucid dream induction.

The DreamLight used at home proved to be an effective aid in stimulating lucid dreams, but not more so than practicing MILD. However, when the use of the DreamLight was combined with practicing MILD, the two appeared to interact synergistically to produce the highest frequency of lucid dreams of all possible combinations. Our first group test of the DreamLight showed that people who practiced MILD while using the

DreamLight had five times as many lucid dreams as those not using any lucid dream induction technique.[28]

Mental preparation is important when using the DreamLight, because if your mind isn't focused properly on the idea of recognizing a dream when you are in one, even when you see the light cue in your dream, you may not realize what it means. There is little chance of developing a device that will *make* you have lucid dreams—you must bring something of yourself to the effort.

The variety of experiences of the light

One of the challenges to users of the DreamLight is to prepare themselves to recognize whatever form the light cue may take within the dream. At times, the light from the DreamLight mask looks the same in the dream as it does when you're awake. However, 80 percent of the time the light takes on aspects of the dream world, becoming so seamlessly woven into the fabric of the dream that to recognize it the dreamer must be fully alert to the possibility of a message from the other world. If the dreamer is too immersed in the dream, when the signal comes through the results can be amusing and illustrative of our tendency to rationalize rather than think logically. For example, one subject reported the following:

On a trip—we are descending a mountain. Twice, covering my whole field of vision I see glorious, brilliant patterns in reds, radiating from a central point—I call them "Sufi fireworks" and think that they must have been produced to prevent us from seeing something. I feel I know something about the significance of this journey that my companions do not.

Psychologist Jayne Gackenbach has suggested that people fail to recognize the light when it appears in a dream because they have some sort of psychological "resistance'' to the notion of becoming lucid on cue.[29] However, incorporations of the light are much like dreamsigns. We all fail several times nightly to realize that we are dreaming, despite the inevitable occurrence of impossibly anomalous events that could only occur in dreams. This is not because we have psychological blocks against becoming lucid, but because we have not sufficiently prepared ourselves to recognize dreamsigns. When prepared to notice events that could be caused by the flashing lights of the DreamLight, dreamers can be remarkably astute in noticing the light and using it to become lucid:

I am in a tour group sitting in a theater watching a film when the screen goes dark and then red in an abstract geometric pattern and I realize that it is the DreamLight and I am dreaming.

The light stimulus appears in dreams in many ways. DreamLight users have reported five distinct types of incorporation:

- *Unchanged incorporations*—The light appears in the dream as it does when the DreamLight wearer is awake. For example: ''I saw a flashing light like the stimulus when I'm awake.''
- *Incorporations as dream imagery*—The light becomes part of the dream imagery. For example: ''I noticed the room lights flashing.''
- *Incorporations as light superimposed on dream scene*— The light enters the dream as uniform illumination that does not seem to come from a source in the dream imagery. For example: ''Two flashes of light filled my field of vision.''
- *Incorporation as a pattern superimposed on scene*— The light causes the dreamer to see brilliant patterns, sometimes geometric or ''psychedelic.'' For example:

"I see a beautiful pattern in gold and yellow with di-
amonds within one another."

- *Incorporation as pulsation in the dream scene*—Instead
of seeing the light, the dreamer seems to see only the
fluctuation caused by the flashing. For example: "I noticed a vague flickering in the environment."

Are light-induced lucid dreams different from spontaneous ones?

Light-induced lucid dreams are likely to differ from spontaneous lucid dreams in one obvious way—light! Whether they
differ in other ways will need to be researched. Nevertheless,
Gackenbach has suggested recently that "inducing lucidity
artificially may also adversely influence the quality of the lucid
dream" and result in experiences "that are not psychologi-
cally as evolved as those that arise naturally."[30] With all due
respect to my colleague, her conclusions seem entirely unjus-
tified. They were based on an extremely questionable interpretation of a small amount of data from a single subject. That
data was from a pilot study reporting that eighteen light-
induced lucid dreams had less flying and more sex than a
sample of eighteen spontaneous lucid dreams from the same
subject.[31] Gackenbach claimed that compared with dream sex,
flying is "more archetypical and represents a higher form of
dream lucidity." The only evidence she cited for this notion
was that dream content from a straight-laced group of mid-
western meditators had twenty times as many references to
flying as to sex. The point is moot anyway, because reanalysis
of the original data showed that the subject had as much sex
in light-induced as in spontaneous lucid dreams. As for flying,
several of the subject's spontaneous lucid dreams were initiated when she realized she was flying. After adjusting for this
confounding factor, there is no significant difference in rates
of flying in light-induced and spontaneous lucid dreams.

A more reasonable hypothesis regarding possible differences between spontaneous and light-induced lucid dreams

would be that dreamers might be less rational, less lucid, in the latter. We might expect to find this, at least in the first scenes of the lucid dream, because to become lucid spontaneously, dreamers might require a more coherent state of mind than they would need to become lucid on cue. We will need to conduct more research to prove or disprove this hypothesis. However, the reports of DreamLight users indicate that light-induced lucid dreams can be as intense, exciting, and thoughtful as spontaneous ones. This is illustrated by the following dreams reported by two intrepid oneironauts, Daryl Hewitt and Lynne Levitan, who have assisted us greatly in developing the DreamLight by testing each new model we design:

In my dream the light mask flashed. I recognized it as such, knew that I was dreaming, and gave the eye movement signal. The setting was the sleep lab. I wanted to get outside, and after a short time I found a locked glass door. I tried to pass through like a ghost, but finally just threw my body against it and broke through. I found an open area among the trees and joyfully leaped into the air and floated. I soared into the sky. It was a glorious experience. I flew over mountains only to see other mountains looming still higher, lost in clouds. Sometimes I swooped into deep valleys, through forests. Gradually it became dark, and the heavens filled with stars. I floated up very high in the sky, above the mountains. I could see the Milky Way and the moon. I chose a larger star and began spinning, holding the intention of reappearing near it. As I spun I cartwheeled through the sky ecstatically. I was so excited I could feel my heart pounding. The light flashed again, and I made the eye movement signal indicating that I was still lucid. I awoke a minute or two later. (D.H., San Francisco, California)

I dreamt of returning to the site of an earlier dream—a strange park area that had become a version of Paradise. I have returned to see if the place, now a market, had some interesting food. Just when I arrive, I see the lights flash. I spin to stay in the dream. My friend L appears. I ask him to help me look for the things I want. I am lucid, but motivated to see what the dream acts like. I find various strange noodle things. I know everything in this market is "special" because this is "Paradise." Satisfied about the noodles, I look at a sign, stare at it and watch it change, wondering if it could tell me anything. It is mostly jumbling nonsense, but for a moment pauses to say "Golden Acres." This doesn't mean much to me, but seems pleasant. I say to L, let's go on and look for the other thing I wanted. We walk through the store. I think of giving up control for "guidance" and immediately feel an intensification of the dream and of the sensation of being "awake." I reflect that ordinarily in lucid dreams I control, manipulate, and think a lot, and that this thinking and commanding seems to block my perception of something I might call "the inner light." I go outside. It is dark. I begin to ascend. The stars are beautiful. L is below. I invite him to fly with me. He agrees and is about to when the light flashes again, and I awaken. (L.L., Redwood City, California)

The Future of Lucidity Technology

So far we have succeeded in devising an apparatus that, when used in combination with mental concentration, can improve one's chances of having a lucid dream fivefold or more. This sounds good, but we cannot yet say that by using the DreamLight you *will* be able to have lucid dreams. Thus, we continue our work.

With further research into the initiation of lucidity in dreams, and the states of brain and body that accompany lucidity onset, we should be able to greatly enhance our ability to stimulate lucid dreams. And, of course, we want to pass that knowledge on to you, the oneironauts. If you want to know more about the DreamLight, and stay up-to-date on our progress, see the invitation in the afterword.

4

~~~~~~~

Falling Asleep
Consciously

Wake-Initiated Lucid Dreams (WILDS)

In the last chapter we talked about strategies for inducing
lucid dreams by carrying an idea from the waking world
into the dream, such as an intention to comprehend the
dream state, a habit of critical state testing, or the recognition of a dreamsign. These strategies are intended to
stimulate a dreamer to become lucid within a dream.

This chapter presents a completely different set of approaches to the world of lucid dreaming based on the idea
of *falling asleep consciously*. This involves retaining consciousness while wakefulness is lost and allows direct
entry into the lucid dream state without any loss of reflective consciousness. The basic idea has many variations. While falling asleep, you can focus on hypnagogic
(sleep onset) imagery, deliberate visualizations, your
breath or heartbeat, the sensations in your body, your

sense of self, and so on. If you keep the mind sufficiently active while the tendency to enter REM sleep is strong, you feel your body fall asleep, but *you*, that is to say, your consciousness, remains awake. The next thing you know, you will find yourself in the dream world, fully lucid.

These two different strategies for inducing lucidity result in two distinct types of lucid dreams. Experiences in which people consciously enter dreaming sleep are referred to as *wake-initiated lucid dreams* (WILDs), in contrast to *dream-initiated lucid dreams* (DILDs), in which people become lucid after having fallen asleep unconsciously.[1] The two kinds of lucid dreams differ in a number of ways. WILDs always happen in association with brief awakenings (sometimes only one or two seconds long) from and immediate return to REM sleep. The sleeper has a subjective impression of having been awake. This is not true of DILDs. Although both kinds of lucid dream are more likely to occur later in the night, the proportion of WILDs also increases with time of night. In other words, WILDs are most likely to occur in the late morning hours or in afternoon naps. This is strikingly evident in my own record of lucid dreams. Of thirty-three lucid dreams from the first REM period of the night, only one (3 percent) was a WILD, compared with thirteen out of thirty-two (41 percent) lucid dreams from afternoon naps.[2]

Generally speaking, WILDs are less frequent than DILDs; in a laboratory study of seventy-six lucid dreams, 72 percent were DILDs compared with 28 percent WILDs.[3] The proportion of WILDs observed in the laboratory seems, by my experience, to be considerably higher than the proportion of WILDs reported at home.

To take a specific example, WILDs account for only 5 to 10 percent of my home record of lucid dreams, but for fully 40 percent of my first fifteen lucid dreams in the laboratory.[4] I believe there are two reasons for this highly significant difference: whenever I spent the night in the sleep laboratory, I was highly conscious of every time I awakened and I made extraordinary efforts not to move more than necessary in order to minimize interference with the physiological recordings.

Thus, my awakenings from REM in the lab were more likely to lead to conscious returns to REM than awakenings at home when I was sleeping with neither heightened consciousness of my environment and self nor any particular intent not to move. This suggests that WILD induction techniques might be highly effective under the proper conditions.

Paul Tholey notes that, while techniques for direct entry to the dream state require considerable practice in the beginning, they offer correspondingly great rewards.[5] When mastered, these techniques (like MILD) can confer the capacity to induce lucid dreams virtually at will.

Attention on Hypnagogic Imagery

The most common strategy for inducing WILDs is to fall asleep while focusing on the hypnagogic imagery that accompanies sleep onset. Initially, you are likely to see relatively simple images, flashes of light, geometric patterns, and the like. Gradually more complicated forms appear: faces, people, and finally entire scenes.[6] The following account of what the Russian philosopher P. D. Ouspensky called "half-dream states" provides a vivid example of what hypnagogic imagery can be like:

I am falling asleep. Golden dots, sparks and tiny stars appear and disappear before my eyes. These sparks and stars gradually merge into a golden net with diagonal meshes which moves slowly and regularly in rhythm with the beating of my heart, which I feel quite distinctly. The next moment the golden net is transformed into rows of brass helmets belonging to Roman soldiers marching along the street below. I hear their measured tread and watch them from the window of a high house in Galata, in Constantinople, in a narrow lane, one end of which leads to the old wharf and the Golden Horn with its ships and steamers and the minarets of Stamboul behind them. I hear their heavy measured tread, and see the sun shining on their helmets. Then suddenly I detach myself from the window-sill on which I am lying, and in the same reclining position fly slowly over the lane, over the houses, and then over the Golden Horn in the direction of Stamboul. I smell the sea, feel the wind, the warm sun. This flying gives me a wonderfully pleasant sensation, and I cannot help opening my eyes.[7]

Ouspensky's half-dream states developed out of a habit of observing the contents of his mind while falling asleep or in half-sleep after awakening from a dream. He notes that they were much easier to observe in the morning after awakening than before sleep at the beginning of the night and did not occur at all "without definite efforts."[8]

Dr. Nathan Rapport, an American psychiatrist, cultivated an approach to lucid dreaming very similar to Ouspensky's: "While in bed awaiting sleep, the experimenter interrupts his thoughts every few minutes with an effort to recall the mental item vanishing before each intrusion by that inquisitive attention."[9] This habit is continued into sleep itself, with results like the following:

Brilliant lights flashed, and a myriad of sparkles twinkled from a magnificent cut-glass chandelier. Interesting as any stage extravaganza were the many quaintly detailed figurines upon a mantel against the distant, paneled wall adorned in rococo. At the right a merry group of beauties and gallants in the most elegant attire of Victorian England idled away a pleasant occasion. This scene continued for [a] period of which I was not aware, before I discovered that it was not

*reality, but a mental picture and that I was viewing it. In-
stantly it became an incommunicably beautiful vision. It was
with the greatest stealth that my vaguely awakened mind began to peep: for I knew that these glorious shows end abruptly
because of such intrusions.*

*I thought, "Have I here one of those mind pictures that
are without motion?" As if in reply, one of the young ladies
gracefully waltzed about the room. She returned to the group
and immobility, with a smile lighting her pretty face, which
was turned over her shoulder toward me. The entire color
scheme was unobtrusive despite the kaleidoscopic sparkles of
the chandelier, the exquisite blues and creamy pinks of the
rich settings and costumes. I felt that only my interest in dreams
brought my notice to the tints—delicate, yet all alive as if with
inner illumination.*[10]

HYPNAGOGIC IMAGERY TECHNIQUE

1. Relax completely
While lying in bed, gently close your eyes and relax your
head, neck, back, arms, and legs. Completely let go of
all muscular and mental tension, and breathe slowly and
restfully. Enjoy the feeling of relaxation and let go of
your thoughts, worries, and concerns. If you have just
awakened from sleep, you are probably sufficiently relaxed. Otherwise, you may use either the progressive relaxation exercise (page 53) or the 61-point relaxation
exercise (page 54) to relax more deeply. Let everything
wind down, slower and slower, more and more relaxed,
until your mind becomes as serene as the calmest sea.

2. Observe the visual images
Gently focus your attention on the visual images that will
gradually appear before your mind's eye. Watch how the
images begin and end. Try to observe the images as delicately as possible, allowing them to be passively re-

(exercise continues)

flected in your mind as they unfold. Do not attempt to hold
onto the images, but instead just watch without attachment or
desire for action. While doing this, try to take the perspective
of a detached observer as much as possible. At first you will
see a sequence of disconnected, fleeting patterns and images.
The images will gradually develop into scenes that become
more and more complex, finally joining into extended sequences.

3. Enter the dream

When the imagery becomes a moving, vivid scenario, you
should allow yourself to be passively drawn into the dream
world. Do not try to actively enter the dream scene, but instead
continue to take a detached interest in the imagery. Let your
involvement with what is happening draw you into the dream.
But be careful of too much involvement and too little attention.
Don't forget that you are dreaming now!

Commentary

Probably the most difficult part of this technique to master is
entering the dream at Step 3. The challenge is to develop a
delicate vigilance, an unobtrusive observer perspective, from
which you let yourself be drawn into the dream. As Paul Tholey has emphasized, "It is not desirable to want actively to
enter into the scenery, since such an intention as a rule causes
the scenery to disappear."[11] A passive volition similar to that
described in the section on autosuggestion in the previous
chapter is required: in Tholey's words, "Instead of actively
wanting to enter into the scenery, the subject should attempt
to let himself be carried into it passively."[12] A Tibetan teacher
advises a similar frame of mind: "While delicately observing
the mind, lead it gently into the dream state, as though you
were leading a child by the hand."[13]

      Another risk is that, once you have entered into the dream,
the world can seem so realistic that it is easy to lose lucidity,
as happened in the beginning of Rapport's WILD described
above. As insurance in case this happens, Tholey recommends
that you resolve to carry out a particular action in the dream,
so that if you momentarily lose lucidity, you may remember
your intention to carry out the action and thereby regain lucidity.

Attention on Visualization

Another approach to the induction of WILDs, much favored by the Tibetan tradition, involves deliberate visualization of a symbol while focusing on hypnagogic imagery. The symbolic nature of the imagery probably helps awareness to persist through the process of sleep onset. We will present three variations on this technique, two from an ancient manual of teachings dating from eighth-century Tibet and a third from a modern teacher of Tibetan Buddhism.

As you will see in the following exercises, yogic visualizations relating to sleep are frequently situated in the throat. Yogic psychophysiology holds that our bodies contain "subtle centers of awareness" called *chakras*. Seven in number, they are located throughout the body, from the base of the spine to the top of the head. One of these, the throat chakra, is said to regulate sleep and wakefulness. The degree of activation of the throat chakra is reputed to determine whether wakefulness, sleep, or dreaming occurs.[14] There is an intriguing similarity between the functions ancient Eastern psychologists have attributed to the throat chakra and the role modern Western physiologists have established for the nearby brainstem in the regulation of states of sleep and consciousness.[15] I would not dismiss without investigation the claims of a group of such obviously disciplined and careful observers of the human body and mind as the yogis, merely because they failed to follow modern scientific methodology—a system of standards that hadn't been invented when yoga was developed. Instead, I look forward to scientific investigations of more of these extraordinary ideas from the ancient East.

The Tibetan waking lucid dream induction techniques provided in this chapter involve a special deep-breathing method (called "pot-shaped" breathing because you extend your abdomen like a round pot). The following ex-

ercise shows you how to practice "pot-shaped" breathing.

EXERCISE:
RELAXED ("POT-SHAPED") BREATHING

1. Get comfortable
Because it is often too easy to fall asleep while lying
down, you may wish to perform the relaxation, meditation, and concentration exercises presented in this book
in a comfortable sitting position. The first time you practice this exercise, however, you should lie on your back
on a firm surface. Loosen your clothing at neck and
waist. Close your eyes. Rest your hands lightly on your
abdomen so that your thumbs rest on the bottom of your
rib cage and your middle fingers meet over your navel.

2. Study your breathing
Take a long, slow inhalation, and follow it with a long, slow
exhalation. Then return to a breathing pattern that is just a
little slower and deeper than normal, and notice your mid-
section. Direct your attention to your hands, and you will
see that your diaphragm and belly muscles contribute a great
deal to both the intake and expulsion of breath from your
lungs. Feel the motions of your abdomen and notice how
different groups of muscles expand and contract as you rhyth-
mically fill, then empty your lungs. Concentrate on the point
where your inhalation begins, at the juncture of your abdomen and the bottom of the chest, filling your lungs from the
bottom up. Simply pay attention to the way your body feels
as you breathe.

3. Breathe slowly and deeply
Allow your breath to find a calm but normal rhythm.
Don't force it, but allow your diaphragm and solar plexus
to contribute more to the "pot-shaped" phase of your
breathing—your abdomen should extend out roundly as
you inhale, like a pot. Think of yourself as inhaling

(exercise continues)

nourishing energy in the form of light, then sending the light through your body with your exhalation. Feel this "light" (a.k.a. oxygen) flow from your lungs through your arteries and capillaries to bring nutrients and energy to every cell in your body.

(Adapted from Hanh.[16])

POWER OF VISUALIZATION: WHITE DOT TECHNIQUE

1. Before bed
A. Firmly resolve to recognize when you are dreaming.
B. Visualize in your throat (Point 2 in the 61-point relaxation exercise, page 54) the syllable *ah*, red in color and vividly radiant (see Commentary below).
C. Mentally concentrate on the radiance of the *ah*. Imagine that the radiance illuminates and makes visible all things of the world showing them to be essentially unreal and of the nature of a dream.

2. At dawn
A. Practice pot-shaped breathing seven times (see relaxed ["pot-shaped"] breathing exercise above).
B. Resolve eleven times to comprehend the nature of the dream state.
C. Concentrate your mind upon a dot, colored bony white, situated between your eyebrows (Point 1 in the 61-point relaxation exercise).
D. Continue to focus on the dot until you find that you are dreaming.

Commentary
According to yogic doctrine, each chakra has a special sound or "seed syllable" associated with it. The seed syllable for the throat chakra is *ah*, viewed as a symbolic embodiment of Creative Sound, the power to bring a

(exercise continues)

world (conceptual or otherwise) into being. This concept has a certain similarity to the Gospel of St. John: "In the beginning was the Word. . . ."

The *Yoga of the Dream State* advises that if you fail to recognize dreaming by means of the white dot technique, then try the black dot technique, which immediately follows.

(Adapted from Evans-Wentz.[17])

POWER OF VISUALIZATION: BLACK DOT TECHNIQUE

1. Before bed
A. Meditate on the white dot between your eyebrows (Point 1 in the 61-point relaxation exercise, page 54).

2. At dawn
A. Practice pot-shaped breathing 21 times (see exercise above).
B. Make 21 resolutions to recognize the dream.
C. Then, concentrate your mind on a pill-sized black dot, as if "situated at the base of the generative organ" (Point 33 in the 61-point relaxation exercise).
D. Continue to focus on the black dot until you find that you are dreaming.

(Adapted from Evans-Wentz.[18])

Dream lotus background

The third visualization technique comes from Tarthang Tulku, a Tibetan teacher living and working in the United States. He first introduced me to Tibetan dream yoga in 1970, as recounted in chapter 3. This method is similar to the preceding two techniques in that it employs a throat center visualization, in this case a flame within a lotus blossom. The similarity is no accident; Padmasambhava, the eighth-century teacher who first brought the dream yoga techniques to Tibet, also founded the Nyingma order which Tarthang Tulku currently heads.

The flame, Tulku explains, represents awareness: the same awareness with which we experience both our waking life and dreams.[19] It therefore represents the potential for a continuity of awareness between wakefulness and sleep, the preservation of consciousness through sleep onset that we are trying to achieve.

In Buddhist iconography, the lotus represents the process of spiritual unfoldment. The lotus grows out of the darkness of the mud and above the surface of the swampy water, where it transcends earth and water, unfolding its many-petaled blossom to receive the pure light. Those who attain to spiritual understanding also grow out of the world and beyond it: their roots are in the dark depths of the material world, but their "heads" (understandings) are raised into the fullness of light.[20] As you practice the following exercise, bear in mind the symbolic meaning of the visualization.

DREAM LOTUS AND FLAME TECHNIQUE

1. Relax completely
While lying in bed, gently close your eyes and relax your head, neck, back, arms, and legs. Completely let go of all muscular and mental tension, and breathe slowly and restfully. Enjoy the feeling of relaxation and let go of your thoughts, worries, and concerns. If you have just awakened from sleep, you are probably sufficiently relaxed. Otherwise, you may use either the progressive

(exercise continues)

relaxation exercise (page 53) or the 61-point relaxation exercise (page 54).

2. Visualize the flame in the lotus

As soon as you feel fully relaxed, visualize in your throat (Point 1 in the 61-point relaxation exercise) a beautiful lotus flower with soft, light-pink petals curling slightly inward. In the center of the lotus, imagine a flame incandescent with reddish-orange light. See the flame as clearly as possible: it is brighter at the edges than at the center. Gently focus on the top of the flame, and continue to visualize it as long as possible.

3. Observe your imagery

Observe how the image of the flame in the lotus interacts with other images that arise in your mind. Do not try to think about, interpret, or concern yourself with any of these images, but, under all circumstances, continue to maintain your visualization.

4. Blend with the image, and with the dream

Contemplate the flame in the lotus until you feel the image and your awareness of it merge together. When this happens, you are no longer conscious of trying to focus on the image, but simply *see* it. Gradually, with practice, you will find that you are dreaming.

Commentary

Unless you are lucky enough to have naturally vivid imagery, you may find the preceding visualization difficult to achieve with any clarity and detail. If you do find it difficult, you should practice two supplementary exercises (see appendix) before attempting to master this technique. The first, the candle concentration exercise, involves concentrating on an actual candle flame. It will strengthen your ability to concentrate and provide a vivid sensory memory of a flame as a basis for the visualization. The second, visualization training, will help cultivate your ability to produce vivid and detailed imagery.

(exercise continues)

After you have mastered these two exercises, the dream
lotus and flame technique should be easier for you.

(Adapted from Tulku.[21]*)*

Attention on Other Mental Tasks

You can also use any cognitive process that requires minimal
but conscious effort to focus your mind while falling asleep.
Thus, in what is now a familiar story, your body falls asleep
while the cognitive process carries your conscious mind along
with it into sleep. The basic approach requires that you lie in
bed relaxed, but vigilant, and perform a repetitive mental
task. You focus your attention on the task while your perception of the environment diminishes and gradually vanishes
altogether as you fall asleep. As long as you continue to perform the mental task, your mind will remain awake. Ten years
ago, as part of my doctoral dissertation research, I developed
the following technique for producing WILDs with this strategy.[22]

COUNT YOURSELF TO SLEEP TECHNIQUE

1. Relax completely
While lying in bed, gently close your eyes and relax your
head, neck, back, arms, and legs. Completely let go of
all muscular and mental tension, and breathe slowly and
restfully. Enjoy the feeling of relaxation and let go of
your thoughts, worries, and concerns. If you have just
awakened from sleep, you are probably sufficiently relaxed. Otherwise, you may use either the progressive relaxation exercise (page 53) or the 61-point relaxation
exercise (page 54).

(exercise continues)

2. Count to yourself while falling asleep

As you are drifting off to sleep, count to yourself, "1, I'm dreaming; 2, I'm dreaming, . . . ," and so on, maintaining a degree of vigilance. You may start over after reaching 100 if you wish.

3. Realize you are dreaming

After continuing the counting and reminding process for some time, you will find that at some point, you'll be saying to yourself, "I'm dreaming . . . ," and you'll notice that you *are* dreaming!

Commentary

The "I'm dreaming" phrase helps to remind you of what you intend to do, but it isn't strictly necessary. Simply focusing your attention on counting probably would allow you to retain sufficient alertness to recognize dream images for what they are.

You can make rapid progress with this technique if you have someone watch over you while you fall asleep. Your assistant's job is to wake you up whenever you show any sign of having fallen asleep, and to ask you what number you reached and what you were dreaming.

The watcher's task may sound difficult, but in fact it's quite easy to tell when you have fallen asleep. There are several observable signs of sleep onset: with dim light, you can observe the movement of the eyes under the closed lids. Slow pendular movements of the eyes from side to side are a reliable sign of sleep onset, as are minor movements or twitches of the lips, face, hands, feet, and other muscles. A third sign of sleep onset is irregular breathing.

As you practice the exercise, your watcher should wake you from time to time and ask for your count and dream report. At first you will find that you will have reached, perhaps, "50, I'm dreaming . . ." and no further, because at that point you started to dream and forgot to count. Resolve then to try harder to retain consciousness

(exercise continues)

and continue with the exercise. After a few dozen awakenings over the course of an hour or so, the feedback
will start to help. Sooner or later, you'll be telling yourself, "100, I'm dreaming . . ." and find that it is really
finally true!

(Adapted from LaBerge.[23]*)*

Attention on Body or Self

If you focus on your body while falling asleep, you will
sometimes notice a condition in which it seems to un-
dergo extreme distortions, or begins to shake with mysterious vibrations, or becomes completely paralyzed. All
of these unusual bodily states are related to the process
of sleep onset and particularly REM sleep onset.

During REM sleep, as you will recall from chapter 2,
all the voluntary muscles of your body are almost completely paralyzed, except for the muscles that move your
eyes and those with which you breathe. REM sleep is a
psychophysiological state involving the cooperative activity of a number of distinct special-purpose brain systems. For example, independent neural systems cause
muscular paralysis, blockade of sensory input, and cor-
tical activation. When these three systems are working
together, your brain will be in the state of REM sleep,
and you will probably be dreaming.

Sometimes the REM systems don't turn on or off at the
same time. For example, you may awaken partially from
REM sleep, before the paralysis system turns off, so that
your body is still paralyzed even though you are otherwise awake. Sleep paralysis, as this condition is called,
can occur while people are falling asleep (rarely) or waking up (more frequently). If you don't know what's happening, your first experience with sleep paralysis can be
terrifying. People typically struggle in a fruitless effort

to move or to fully wake up. In fact, such emotional panic reactions are completely counterproductive; they are likely to stimulate the limbic (emotional) areas of the brain and cause the REM state to persist.

The fact is, sleep paralysis is harmless. Sometimes when it happens to you, you feel as if you are suffocating or in the presence of a nameless evil. But this is just the way your half-dreaming brain interprets these abnormal conditions: something terrible must be happening! The medieval stories of incubus attacks (malevolent spirits believed to descend upon and have sex with sleeping women) probably derived from fantastically overinterpreted experiences of sleep paralysis. The next time you experience sleep paralysis, simply remember to relax. Tell yourself that you are in the same state now as you are several hours every night during REM sleep. It will do you no harm and will pass in a few minutes.

Sleep paralysis is not only nothing to be frightened of, it can be something to be sought after and cultivated. Whenever you experience sleep paralysis you are on the threshold of REM sleep. You have, as it were, one foot in the dream state and one in the waking state. Just step over and you're in the world of lucid dreams. In the following exercises we present several techniques for taking that step.

THE TWIN BODIES TECHNIQUE

1. Relax completely

After awakening from a dream, lie on your back or right side with your eyes gently closed. Tighten and then relax your face and head, neck, back, arms, and legs. Completely let go of all muscular and mental tension, and breathe slowly and

(exercise continues)

calmly. Enjoy the feeling of relaxation and affirm your intention to consciously enter the dream state; let go of all other thoughts, worries, and concerns.

2. Focus on your body

Now focus your attention on your physical body. Use the 61-point relaxation exercise (page 54) to pass your attention from one part of your body to the next, recurrently going through all points. As you do, notice how your body feels at each point along the way. Watch for signs of strange sensations, vibrations, and distortions of your body image. These are the harbingers of REM sleep paralysis. Eventually you will experience sensations like those described above which will rapidly develop into complete paralysis of your physical body. At this stage you are ready to leave your paralyzed body behind and to enter the dream world in your dream body.

3. Leave your body and enter the dream

As soon as you feel that your physical body is in a profound state of sleep paralysis, you are ready to go. Remember that your currently paralyzed physical body has a magical, moveable twin, that is, your dream body, and that you can just as easily experience yourself as being in one body as the other. Indeed, except for occasional lucid periods, you rarely even notice that every night your dream body plays the role of its "twin," your physical body. Now imagine yourself embodied in your airy dream body and imagine what it would feel like to float or roll out of your earthbound twin. Let yourself peel free of the immobile physical body. Jump, fall, or crawl out of bed. Sit up or sink through the floor. Fly through the ceiling, or just get up. Now you're in the world of lucid dreaming.

Commentary

As soon as you "step out of bed," you should recognize that you are truly a stranger in a strange land. Remember that you are in a dream body and that everything around you is a dream thing too. That includes the bed you just got out of: it's a dream bed. And the "sleeping body"

(exercise continues)

you also just got out of, although you were thinking of it a moment ago as a physical body; now it's a dream body too. Everything you see is your dream.

If you believe that you are floating around the physical world in your "astral" body, then I ask you to make a critical observation or two and perform a few state tests. Here are three examples: (1) try reading the same passage from a book twice; (2) look at a digital watch, look away, then look back a few seconds later; (3) try finding and reading this paragraph, and draw your own conclusions!

(Adapted from Tholey[24] and Rama.[25])

Two bodies or one?

As Tholey points out, the "experience of a second body is an unnecessary assumption based on a naive epistemology."[26] As I explained in *Lucid Dreaming*, "out-of-body experiences" often give us the compelling impression that we have two distinct and separate bodies: the physical, earthly body and a more ethereal, astral one. In fact, a person experiences only one body, and this isn't the physical body, but the *body image*—the brain's representation of the physical body. The body image is what we experience anytime we feel embodied, whether in our physical, dream, or astral out-of-bodies.[27] So, since the idea of a second body is unnecessary, you may choose to try the following adaptation of Tholey's one body technique, which carries one less body in its metaphysical baggage compartment.

THE ONE BODY TECHNIQUE

1. Relax completely

After awakening from a dream, lie on your back or right side with your eyes gently closed. Tighten and then relax your face and head, neck, back, arms, and legs. Completely let go of all muscular and mental tension, and breathe slowly and calmly. Enjoy the feeling of relaxation and affirm your intention to consciously enter the dream state; let go of all other thoughts, worries, and concerns.

2. Focus on your body

Now focus your attention on your body. Use the 61-point relaxation exercise (page 54) to pass your attention from one part of your body to the next, recurrently going through all points. As you do, notice how your body feels at each point along the way. Watch for signs of strange sensations, vibrations, and distortions of your body image. These are the harbingers of REM sleep paralysis. Eventually you will experience sensations like those described above which will rapidly develop into complete paralysis of your body. At this stage you are ready to leave your paralyzed body behind, and to enter the dream world.

3. Leave your body and enter the dream

As soon as you feel that your physical body is in a profound state of sleep paralysis, you are ready to go. Remember that the body image you are currently experiencing as a paralyzed physical body cannot move (in mental space) because sensory information is telling your brain that your physical body is motionless. When sensory input is cut off (when you go deeper into REM sleep), there will be no information (except memory) indicating that your body is still in the position it was before. Now you are free to feel movement of your body image or dream body without any contradiction from your sensory systems. Your body image can move without

(exercise continues)

reference to the actual position of your physical body, as it does naturally in dreams.

Moreover, if you are experiencing sleep paralysis, you can be sure that inhibition of sensory input cannot be far off. Simply imagine that your body image can move again. Imagine you are somewhere other than sleeping in bed: anywhere else, in any other position or situation.

Once you experience that your dream body is out of bed, you will no longer feel the sensations from the paralysis of your physical body.

Commentary

The same caveats apply for the one body technique as for the twin bodies procedure: As soon as you "step out of bed," you should recognize that you are dreaming. Remember that you are moving in your dream body and that everything around you is a dream thing too. Everything you see is your dream.

(Adapted from Tholey[28] and Rama.[29])

One body or none?

Of course, even the one body (image) we were left with in the last technique is the product of naive metaphysical realism. Your body image is your brain's model of your physical body. Your body image acts as if it *is* your physical body while you're awake. This is because your body provides your brain with sensory information about its position and condition; from this sensory information your brain constructs a model of the current status and arrangement of your physical body. Finally, *you* experience your brain's model of your body (that is, the body image) as if it were your body.

This all makes good sense if you are trying to keep track of what your physical body is up to: your brain needs to keep a carefully updated model that correctly represents how things stand with your physical body, so that you can act without tripping over your own feet.

Let's consider a very different state of affairs—REM sleep. In this case, your physical body is providing virtually no useful sensory information about its condition to your brain. As a result, the brain cannot properly update the configuration of its body model to match that of the physical body. The brain, in a sense, has lost the sleeping body. So the body image travels through dreamland blissfully unaware that if the brain were in sensory contact with the physical body, the dream body wouldn't be going anywhere!

Now, let's take a radical look at the brain's body model. If it isn't representing the position, activity, or condition of the physical body, why should it need to maintain a model of the appearance, functionality, topology, or form of the physical body? As Tholey puts it, "The experiencing of one's own body in a dream is merely a phenomenon transferred from the waking state and is essentially expendable."[30] This allows us to throw overboard even more metaphysical baggage and really travel light: we've gone from the twin bodies technique to the one body technique; the last step is the no body technique.

THE NO BODY TECHNIQUE

1. Relax completely
After awakening from a dream, lie on your back or right side with your eyes gently closed. Tighten and then relax your face and head, neck, back, arms, and legs. Completely let go of all muscular and mental tension, and breathe slowly and calmly. Enjoy the feeling of relaxation and affirm your intention to consciously enter the dream state; let go of all other thoughts, worries, and concerns. If you have just awakened from sleep, you are probably sufficiently relaxed. Otherwise, you may use either the progressive relaxation exercise (page 53) or the 61-point relaxation exercise (page 54). Let everything

(exercise continues)

wind down, slower and slower, more and more relaxed, until your mind becomes as serene as the calmest sea.

2. Think that you will soon no longer feel your body
While falling asleep, concentrate on the thought that when you fall asleep your body will become imperceptible.

3. Float freely about the dream as an ego-point
As soon as you can no longer feel your body, imagine that you are a point of awareness from which you perceive, feel, think, and act in the dream world. Freely float about the dream world like a mote upon a sunbeam.

Commentary
Some people will probably feel that life as a disembodied spark leaves something to be desired. If so, never fear, there are plenty of vacant dream bodies available for immediate occupancy. Tholey describes a combination procedure called the image-ego-point technique which differs from the no body technique in only one way: you must also concentrate on hypnagogic imagery. He elaborates: "If a visual dream scenery has become established, then it is possible to travel into this scenery. The ego-point can under certain circumstances enter into the body of another dream figure and take over its 'motor system.'"[31]

(Adapted from Tholey's "Ego-point Technique"[32])

Where Do You Go From Here?

The last two chapters have described and explained the techniques for inducing lucid dreams. Try all the techniques, then focus on the ones that work best for you. Practice them frequently and you should find your proficiency growing. The more lucid dreams you have, the easier it will become to have them. Once you are able to enter the lucid dream world, the question will arise: Now that you are here, where do you go and what do you do next?

The next two chapters will prepare you for applying lucid dreams by providing background and techniques for prolonging lucid dreams, and by showing you how to work with dream imagery.

5

~~~~~~~~

The Building of Dreams

Dreams are Models of the World

This chapter presents a general framework for understanding the dreaming process. Since your dreaming head will be in the clouds, you should embark on your explorations with your feet on the ground.

The basic task of the brain, as you read in chapter 2, is to predict and control the results of your actions in the world. To accomplish this task, it constructs a model of the world. The brain bases its best guess of what is going on in the world on the information it is currently receiving from the senses. When asleep, the brain acquires little information from the senses. Therefore, the information most readily available is what is already inside our heads—memories, expectations, fears, desires, and so on. I believe that dreams are a result of our brains using this internal information to create a simulation of the world.

According to this theory, dreaming is the result of the same perceptual and mental process that we use to understand the world when awake. Therefore, to understand dreaming, we need to know about the process of waking perception and to consider how the functioning of the mind is modified by sleep.

The Construction of Perception

Perceptual experiences are constructed by a complicated and primarily unconscious evaluation of sensory information. This process includes many factors beyond simple sensory input. These factors fall into two major classes: expectation and motivation.

Expectation and perception

Perception (what we see, hear, feel, etc.) depends to a great extent on expectation. In a certain sense, what we perceive is what we most expect. Expectation takes many forms; one of the most important is context. To see how powerfully context influences perception, time how long it takes you to read aloud the following two sentences:

> Form as to arranged and the randomly quickly are example accurately words easier meaningful much a therefore words sentence these in and than read same preceding the.

> These words form a meaningful sentence and are therefore much easier to read quickly and accurately than the same words randomly arranged as in the preceding example.

It probably took you longer to read the first sentence. This is because in the second sentence you perceived that the organization of words had meaning; each word fell into a reasonable context, which helped you to see, un-

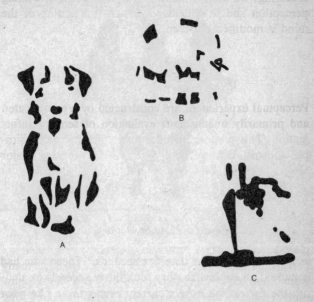

Figure 5.1. Incomplete figures

derstand, and read each word. While you read the first sentence, you had no help from the context of the words, so it took you longer to process them.

It also is easier to perceive the familiar than the unfamiliar. Study Figure 5.1 until you have identified all three elements. How long did it take you to identify each of the three figures? You probably identified the dog first, then the ship, and finally the elephant. This corresponds to the relative familiarity of the three images. The familiar, of course, is the expected.

Another important influence on perception is recent experience. Steinfeld found that subjects who had been told a story about an ocean cruise identified Figure 5.1c

Figure 5.2. An inkblot or . . . ?

as a steamship in less than five seconds.[1] Those who had been told an irrelevant story took thirty seconds to identify the figure. We expect current events to be like what has recently happened.

Personal interests, occupations, and personality can strongly influence people's experience. This fact is used in tests like the Rorschach inkblot test that use interpretations of ambiguous figures for personality assessment. In a classic study of imagination, Bartlett noted that subjects asked to interpret inkblots frequently reveal much information about their personal interests and occupation. For example, the same inkblot reminded a woman of a "bonnet with feathers," a minister of "Nebuchadnezzar's fiery furnace," and a physiologist of "an exposure of the basal lumbar region of the digestive system."[2] See Figure 5.2: what does the inkblot look like to you?

A bias of perception resulting from people's professions can also be seen with stimuli less ambiguous than inkblots. Clifford and Bull showed police officers and civilians several hours of films of a city street. Their instructions were to watch for certain fugitives (identified by mugshots) and for certain interchanges (legal vs. criminal, etc.). Although the two groups actually detected the same number of people and actions, the police reported more alleged thefts than did the civilians.[3] Police obviously expect to see crime, and they do. Expectation biases perception in the direction of how you think things really are.

Motivation and perception

Another important factor that influences perception is motivation. Our motivations are our reason for doing things. There are many different kinds of motivation, ranging from the most basic drives like hunger, thirst, and sex, to psychological needs like affection, recognition, and self-esteem, and finally to the highest motives, such as altruism and what Abraham Maslow called self-actualization, the need to fulfill one's unique potential. It is likely that all of these levels of motivation can affect perceptual processes.

The influence of the lower levels of motivation is easiest to study. For example, in one experiment, children were asked to estimate the size of coins. When shown the same coin, poor children saw it as bigger than rich children did. In another experiment, when schoolchildren were shown ambiguous figures before and after meals, they were twice as likely to interpret the figures as referring to food when hungry than after eating. As the proverb puts it, "What bread looks like depends upon whether you are hungry or not."

Strong emotions motivate behavior and influence perception. You probably know from experience that angry people are all too ready to see others as hostile. The fearful will tend to see what they fear, even if it means mistaking a bush for a bear. On a more positive note, lovers will tend to mistake strangers for their beloveds.

In general, motivations drive people to act to achieve goals or the satisfaction of some specific need. Having a motive or emotion biases your perception toward seeing things as you wish them to be.

Schemas: Building Blocks of the Mind

If perception involves analyzing and evaluating sensory information, then the brain must use some kind of matching process to determine what we are perceiving. Suppose, for example, you are presented with a somewhat ambiguous pattern of light. What are you seeing? Is it a bush or a bear? A rock or a pear? To identify it as any of these things, you must already have mental models of bushes, bears, rocks, pears, or whatever, to which you can compare the information from your senses. The best match is what you see.

The same process applies as well to more abstract levels of the mind, including language, reasoning, and memory. For example, you cannot judge whether in a given situation someone has spoken tactfully or truthfully unless you have mental models of tact and truth. These mental models, called ''schemas'' or ''frames'' or ''scripts,'' comprise the building blocks of perception and thought.

New schemas are created by adapting or combining old schemas, some of which we inherit genetically. They capture essential regularities about how the world has worked in the past and how we assume it will work in the future. A schema is a model of, or theory about, some part of the world. It is ''a kind of informal, private unarticulated theory about the nature of events, objects, or situations which we face. The total set of schemas we have available for interpreting our world,'' writes the

Stanford psychologist David Rumelhart, "in a sense constitutes our private theory of the nature of reality."[4]

Schemas help organize experience by grouping together typical sets of features or attributes of objects, people, or situations. These sets of assumptions allow us to go beyond the partial information available to our senses and perceive a whole.

EXERCISE:
HOW SCHEMAS TAKE US BEYOND THE INFORMATION GIVEN

1. Read the story
To see how schemas guide understanding, read the following story and imagine it happening before reading any further:

> Nasrudin walked into a shop and asked, "Have you ever seen me before?" "Never in my life," answered the shopkeeper. "In that case," replied Nasrudin, "how did you know it was me?"

2. List everything you know for certain about what happened
After having observed the story in your mind's eye, make a list of everything you know with absolute certainty about what happened. In other words, base your list only on the information explicitly given in the story; as Dragnet's Joe Friday was fond of saying, "Just the facts, ma'am." You may refer back to the story at any time. Take as long as necessary to compete the list (five minutes or so). To get you started, finish the following list on your own: (1) Nasrudin walked into a shop. (2) Nasrudin asked a question. (3) The shopkeeper answered the question. (4) . . . and so on.

(exercise continues)

3. List everything you can plausibly infer about what happened

Now list everything you can plausibly assume or infer about what happened in the story. Be aware of the basis for each of your assumptions. You may refer back to the story at any time. You should be kept busy for at least five or ten minutes without running out of plausible assumptions. You may stop at any time, but be sure that you have listed at least a dozen inferences. Here's a start: (a) Nasrudin is a man. (2) The shopkeeper was not blind. (3) Nasrudin walked on two legs. (4) The shopkeeper was not lying.

Commentary

Your list of inferences should be much longer than your list of directly observed facts. You probably listed all the facts you could think of but gave up listing inferences when you realized you could go on forever. We assume a great deal about the world, much more than we observe about it directly.

Notice how much you automatically assumed about the story. Your shop schema leads you to assume that the shopkeeper is in the business of selling something (probably goods, but possibly services); that the shop was illuminated either by sunlight or some sort of lamp; that the shop likely had walls, a ceiling, one or more doors and possibly windows, and certainly a floor; that the shop had a means of approach (street or path) and was probably situated in a business section of town. Your social behavior schemas allow you to assume that Nasrudin probably walked through a door rather than a window; that he addressed his question to the shopkeeper rather than to someone else; that the shopkeeper and Nasrudin had never met; that they were both speaking the same language during their interchange; and so on. General reality orientation schemas result in the assumption that the laws of physics were operating as usual: that gravity was present; that the door probably squeaked; that Nasrudin is not the shopkeeper (and that he wasn't therefore talking to himself); that Nasrudin is not a talking dog; and finally, because I think you can see by now that inferences are only limited by creativity and stamina, that Nasrudin was serious at the same time as he was joking.

Schemas for everything

You probably discovered while doing the preceding exercise that schemas have much in common with the notion of stereotype. You may have unconsciously assumed, for example, that the shopkeeper was male. You also may have noticed that schemas aren't normally subject to conscious inspection. We aren't usually conscious of the schemas we are employing, for example, the particular rules we are following in a given social situation. We merely perceive what kind of situation we are in (formal, friendly, intimate, etc.) and act accordingly.

Proper (''expected'') conduct is automatically defined as a part of the particular schema. So if you perceive that you are at the opera, your opera schema causes you to sit quietly in your seat, rather than walking up and down the aisles.

You are probably convinced by now that there are schemas for everything. ''Just as theories can be about the grand or the small,'' writes Rumelhart, ''so schemas can represent knowledge at all levels—from ideologies and cultural truths to knowledge about what constitutes an appropriate sentence in our language to knowledge about the meaning of a particular word to knowledge about what patterns of [sound] are associated with what letters of the alphabet.''[5]

Schemas are connected to one another. A certain schema, such as ''spectator at an opera,'' automatically brings into play a great number of other schemas. For example, you will identify the woman dressed in regal clothing on stage as a singer, rather than some sort of royalty.

Schema activation

So far, we have described schemas in purely psychological terms, but they are presumably embodied in the brain by networks of neurons. Current theory favors the idea that the extent to which a schema is working to organize experience is determined by the degree of activity in its respective neural network.

Freud believed the mind to be divided into three parts: conscious, preconscious, and unconscious. In these terms, the activation of a schema above a critical threshold results in a conscious experience.

Schemas with too little activation to influence any other schemas remain unconscious. Those with sufficient activation to influence the activation of other schemas, but insufficient activation to themselves enter consciousness, are part of the preconscious mind.

An example will clarify these terms. Consider a word representing a schema which is probably not currently activated in your mind: *ocean*. Until you read this word, your schema for ocean was probably lying dormant in your unconscious mind, along with many other schemas that you associate with the ocean. Now, however, you have ocean well activated above your threshold for consciousness. Your ocean schema probably brought several other schemas along with it into consciousness, such as *fish*, *sea gulls*, and *seashore*. You may have thought of the proverb "Only call yours what cannot be lost in a shipwreck."

In addition to raising several schemas to consciousness, the word *ocean* has also activated some schemas to the preconscious level. These are schemas for things that you associate with the ocean, though perhaps not as closely as the things that immediately came to mind. For example, your schema for ship was probably at least slightly activated (though now it is in your conscious mind).

Even if you didn't consciously think of ships, subconscious activation of your ship schema could be demonstrated by showing you Figure 5.1c. Like Steinfeld's subjects who had been told a story about an ocean cruise, you should quickly recognize the figure as a ship. Thus, schemas do not have to be in consciousness to affect your behavior.

A Model of Dreaming

The building of dreams

I suggested that dreams are simulations of the world created by our perceptual systems. The introduction to waking perception that you have just read will help you understand this theory.

Consider, first of all, how sleep modifies the process of perception. During REM sleep, as you learned in chapter 2, sensory input from the outside world and body movement are both suppressed, while the entire brain is highly active. The activity of the brain raises certain schemas above their perceptual thresholds. These schemas enter consciousness, causing the dreamer to see, feel, hear, and *experience* things not present in the external environment.

Ordinarily, if you were to see something that wasn't really there, contradictory sensory input would rapidly correct your mistaken impression. Why doesn't the same thing happen during dreaming? The answer is because there is little or no sensory input available to the brain for correcting such mistakes.

What we are likely to dream about

Our experience in dreams is determined by which schemas are activated above the threshold for consciousness. But what determines which schemas are activated? The same processes that influence waking perception: expectation and motivation.

Expectation shows itself in dreams in many ways. When we construct a dream world we expect that it will resemble past worlds we have experienced. Thus, dream worlds are almost always equipped with gravity, space, time, and air. Likewise, recent experience influences dreaming in the same way it influences waking perception. Freud called this "day residue."

Personal interest, preoccupations, and concerns influence dreaming as well as waking perception. The minister who saw Nebuchadnezzar's fiery furnace in an inkblot might well dream about the mad king of Babylon. Likewise, remember the study which found that police officers were more likely than civilians to expect, and therefore see, crimes that weren't there? Which group do you suppose would be more likely to dream about crime?

Motivation and emotions strongly influence waking perception, and we would expect the same for dreaming. In particular, you are likely to dream about what you desire—wish-fulfillment dreams. Suppose, for example, that you have gone to bed without your supper. Like the hungry schoolchildren who were likely to interpret ambiguous figures as food, you will be likely to dream about food. Freud was so impressed by the prevalence of wish fulfillment in dreams that he made it the cornerstone of his entire theory of dreams. According to Freud, *every dream is the fulfillment of a wish*. However, this appears to be overstating the case; nightmares are an obvious counterexample.

Indeed, just as fear makes you more "jumpy," that is, ready to interpret ambiguous stimuli as danger while awake, it has the same effect in dreams. This is probably why people dream about unpleasant and even horrible situations. The reason is not, as Freud believed, because they are masochistic and unconsciously wish to be frightened. More likely it is because they are afraid of certain events, and therefore in a sense expect that they may happen. You can't be afraid of ghosts if you don't believe in ghosts.

Why dreams seem like stories

By this account, you might expect that dreams would be sequences of disconnected images, ideas, feelings, and sensations, rather than the intricately detailed and dramatic storylike sequences that they often are. However, I believe that schema activation can also account for the complexity and meaningfulness of dreams. To see how, look back at how many more inferences than observations you derived from schemas in the exercise on how schemas take us beyond the information given (page 123). The exercise showed you how a few general-purpose schemas can generate a vast amount of meaningful detail: give a schema a dot, and it will see a fly; give a sleeping brain an activated schema or two, and it will make a dream.

Some dreams have plots as coherent, funny, dramatic, and profound as the best stories, myths, and plays. After awakening from such dreams, it sometimes seems as if the significance of characters or events set up early in the dream became clear only in the denouement. This can give the impression of a complete dream plot worked out in advance.

It is probably this sort of dream that gives people the notion that their unconscious minds have put together a dream film with a message for their conscious minds to watch and interpret. However, I think a simpler explanation is that a *story schema* has been activated throughout the dream.

The notion of a story schema may have taken you by surprise, but remember, there are schemas for everything. The story, or narrative schema, is a basic and universally understood part of human culture. Stories most typically occur as sequences of episodes, which are typically divided into three parts: exposition, complication, and resolution. The exposition introduces the settings and characters, who typically encounter some complication or problem that is finally resolved at the end of the story.

Indeed, Carl Jung described the dream as being like a drama in three acts. Story schemas can specify sequences of events, timing of character introductions, patterns of dramatic tension and release, ''surprise'' endings, and so on. It's not necessary to reify the unconscious mind in the role of ''dream director.''

Why dreams are meaningful

The view of dreams as world models is far from the traditional notion of dreams as messages, whether from the gods or from the unconscious mind. I have presented arguments against the letters-to-yourself view of dreams elsewhere.[6] Be that as it may, interpretation of dreams can be very revealing of personality and can be a rewarding, valuable practice.

The reason for this is straightforward. Think about the inkblot projection test. How is it that what people see in inkblots tells us something about themselves? Their interpretations inform us about their personal interests, concerns, experiences, preoccupations, and personality. Dreams contain much more personal information than inkblots, because the images in them are created by us, from the contents of our minds. Dreams may not be messages, but they are our own most intimately personal cre-

ations. As such, they are unmistakably colored by who
and what we are, and by whom we would become.

The building of dreams: Two examples

The following two examples of hypothetical dreams illustrate several features of dream construction: (1) dreams
are products of an interaction between various parts of
the mind including the conscious, preconscious, and unconscious; (2) schemas, motivations, and expectations
interact in the development of the dream; and (3) there
is no predestination in dreams. Dreams respond as readily
to the lowest as to the highest motivation, to expectations
of disaster or *ad astra*.

DREAM, VERSION 1

I have just entered REM sleep and the activation of my
brain is gradually increasing. Within a minute, some
schema reaches perceptual threshold. Let's say it's a city
street schema that remains activated from my day's experiences. As soon as I see the street, I strongly expect
to see myself on it, and I am there.

Now I notice that it's night and the street is dimly lit.
This activates an associated set of schemas (previously
unconscious or preconscious) relating to the dangers of
being on some streets at night, including the expectation
of someone, perhaps a mugger, who is likely to do me
harm. The same moment that this fearful expectation
emerges, a shadowy figure appears across the street.

Who is he? I can't see him well enough to tell what he
looks like, but the thought crosses my mind that he could
be the mugger I've heard about. And so he now is that
mugger: he looks menacingly in my direction, so I turn
around and start to walk the other way. I am afraid (that
is, I expect) he will follow me, and so he does. I begin
to run, and he runs after me. I try to lose him, going up

and down various streets and alleys, but somehow he always finds me.

Finally, I hide beneath some stairs and feel safe for a moment. Then I think: but maybe he'll find me here too! And he does! I wake in a sweat.

DREAM, VERSION 2

I have just entered REM sleep and the activation of my brain is gradually increasing. Within a minute, some schema reaches perceptual threshold. Let's say it's a city street schema that has some residual activation as a day residue.

As soon as I see the street, I strongly expect to see myself on it, and I am there. Now I notice that it's night and the street is dimly lit.

The experience of being on a street at night activates other schemas related to this experience—the one that comes to the fore is the idea that I must be on my way to a movie. I see a shadowy figure down the street. I can't see him or her well, but the movie schema encourages me to believe that this is a friend I am meeting before seeing the film. When I get closer, I see that it is indeed my friend.

We walk on down the street toward the theater. The street is now clearly one I know well. I seem to have forgotten what film we are to see and I peer at the marquee. Some part of my mind must be aware that I am dreaming—the dream schema is activated, because I see that the marquee reads *The Last Wave* (a film about dreaming). Since I have seen this movie dozens of times, I wonder why I am going to see it again. I look back at the marquee, and it now reads *Dream or Awake*. I cannot miss this unmistakable clue; I now am fully conscious that I am dreaming. My friend has disappeared while I was pondering the dream marquee. I take off into the sky and soar (knowing that the gravity schema is not applicable).

Mental Constraints on Dreaming

Assumptions can be dangerous

As we have seen, schemas are theories, embodying assumptions about the world. If your assumptions are mistaken and, as a result, your schema fails to model the world accurately, what should happen is a process of theory revision and schema modification that the renowned psychologist Jean Piaget called "accommodation." Your accommodated schema will now better fit the facts, and you will have slightly more knowledge than you did before.

If we always accommodate our schemas to new information, our worlds will continuously expand as our schemas become increasingly comprehensive, adaptable, and intelligent. Unfortunately, people don't always accommodate their schemas in the face of new information.

We may not even see the new information, exactly because it doesn't fit the assumptions of our schemas. Instead of noticing the discrepancy, we distort or, in Piaget's terminology, "assimilate" our perception of the real event or object to fit the schema. The difficulty of accurate proofreading illustrates this phenomenon. Or if we do see that something doesn't quite fit, we may regard the discrepant feature or features as irrelevant or defective.

Consider the story in which Nasrudin, the foolish mulla whom the Sufis use to illustrate common human errors, "finds a king's hawk sitting on his windowsill. He has never seen such a strange 'pigeon.' After cutting its aristocratic beak straight and clipping its talons, he sets it free, saying, 'Now you look more like a bird. . . .' "[7]

Just as Nasrudin cut off the hawk's most prominent features because they didn't fit his bird schema, we may suffer from the same self-perpetuating myopia when we attempt to reduce new concepts to fit our current understanding. Incidentally, one of the functions of Nasrudin tales and other Sufi teaching stories is to provide schemas for seeing ourselves in new ways, and to provide a basis for eventual development of higher perceptions.

The general set of schemas guiding our ordinary waking experience also governs our ordinary dream state. We tacitly assume, in both cases, that we are awake, and our perceptions during dreaming are distorted to fit this assumption.

When bizarre dream events occur, we somehow assimilate them into what we consider possible. If we happen to notice or experience them as unusual, we are usually able to rationalize them.

If you want to become a lucid dreamer, however, you must be prepared to accept the possibility that a "strange pigeon" may be a bird of an altogether different feather, and that sometimes the explanation for anomalies is that you are dreaming.

Importance of expectation in the building of dreams

Your expectations and assumptions, whether conscious or preconscious, about what dreams are like determine to a remarkable extent the precise form your dreams take. As I have said, this applies to your waking life as well.

As an example of the effect of assumed limitations on human performance, take the myth of the four-minute mile. For many years it was believed impossible to run that fast—until someone did it, and the impossible became possible. Almost immediately, many others were able to do the same.

Assumptions play a more important role during dreaming than waking perception. After all, in the physical world there are actual limitations built into our bodies, not to mention the constraints of the laws of physics.

Although the barrier of the four-minute mile was not insurmountable, there are absolute limits to human speed.

With the bodies we have today, running a mile in four seconds is presumably impossible. In the dream world, however, the laws of physics are followed merely by convention, if at all.

There may be physiological constraints on a lucid dreamer's actions, deriving from the functional limitations of the human brain. For example, lucid dreamers appear to find reading coherent passages virtually impossible. As the German physician Harald von Moers-Messmer reported in 1938, letters in lucid dreams just won't hold still. When he tried to focus on words, the letters turned into hieroglyphics. (Note that I am not saying we can never read in dreams. I myself have had dreams in which I have done so, but these were not lucid dreams in which the writing was being produced in response to voluntary intention.)

However, possible physiological constraints on dream actions are far fewer in number than those imposed on waking life by physical laws, leaving more room in dreams for psychological influences, such as assumptions, to limit our actions.

If you think you can't, you can't

The Russian philosopher P. D. Ouspensky believed that "man cannot in sleep think about himself unless the thought is itself a dream." Somehow, from this he decided that "a man can never pronounce his own name in sleep." In light of what we now know about the effects of expectation on dream content, you should not be surprised to hear that Ouspensky reported, "as expected," that "if I pronounced my name in sleep, I immediately woke up."[8]

Another lucid dreamer, studied by the English psychologist Celia Green, heard of the philosopher's experiences and theories and tried the experiment for herself. She reported that "I thought of Ouspensky's criterion of repeating one's own name. I achieved a sort of gap-in-consciousness of two words: but it seemed to have some effect; made me 'giddy,' perhaps; at any rate I stopped."[9]

In one more demonstration of the issue, Patricia Garfield described a lucid dream of her own ". . . in 'Carving My Name,' I proceeded to do just that on the door where I was already carving. I read it and realized why Ouspensky believed it is impossible to say one's name in a lucid dream: the whole atmosphere vibrated and thundered and I woke." Garfield, who was also familiar with the experience of Green's subject, concluded that it is "not impossible to say one's own name in a lucid dream, but it *is* disruptive."[10]

I too had read Ouspensky's account, but I accepted neither his conclusion nor his original premise. I was confident that nothing would be easier than saying my name in a lucid dream and soon put my belief to the test. In one of my early lucid dreams I spoke out loud the magic word—"Stephen, I am Stephen."

Beyond hearing my own voice, speaking my own name, nothing unusual happened. Evidently Ouspensky, Green's subject, and Garfield had been strongly conditioned by prior expectations. Of course, the same is true for all of us. In dreams even more than elsewhere in life, if you think you can't, you can't. As Henry Ford said, "Believe you can't, believe you can. Either way you're right."

6

~~~~~~~~

Principles and Practice
of Lucid Dreaming

To Dream or Not to Dream:
How to Stay Asleep
or Wake Up at Will

So far you have learned various techniques for increasing
your dream recall and inducing lucid dreams. Perhaps
you have succeeded in having a few lucid dreams, or
perhaps you know how to induce them more or less at
will. Now that you are learning to realize when you are
dreaming, what can you do with this knowledge? As discussed previously, one of the most fascinating possibilities is the ability to control dreaming. It may be possible
to dream anything you choose, as the Tibetan dream yogis believe. But before you can try it, you need to be able
to remain asleep and retain lucidity.

Novice lucid dreamers often wake up the moment they
become lucid. They can recognize lucidity clues, apply
state tests, and conclude that they are dreaming but are
frustrated because they wake up or fall into nonlucid

sleep soon after achieving lucidity. However, this obstacle is only temporary. With experience, you can develop the capacity to stay in the dream longer. As you will see in a moment, there are also specific techniques that appear to help prevent premature awakening. Continue to apply will and attention to your practice, and you will be able to refine your lucid dreaming skills.

Preventing premature awakening

Informally experimenting in their beds at home, lucid dreamers have discovered various ways of remaining in the dream state when threatened by early awakening. All the techniques involve carrying out some form of dream action as soon as the visual part of the dream begins to fade.

Linda Magallon, editor and publisher of the *Dream Network Bulletin* and an intrepid explorer of lucid dreams, has described how she prevents herself from waking up by concentrating on the senses other than vision, such as hearing and touch. She reports that all of the following activities have successfully prevented awakenings from visually faded dreams: listening to voices, music, or her breathing; beginning or continuing a conversation; rubbing or opening her (dream) eyes; touching her dream hands and face; touching objects such as a pair of glasses, a hairbrush, or the edge of a mirror; being touched; and flying.[1]

These activities all have something in common with the spinning technique described on page 140. They are based on the idea of loading the perceptual system so it cannot change its focus from the dream world to the waking world. As long as you are actively and perceptually engaged with the dream world, you are less likely to make the transition to the waking state.

Magallon may be a dreamer with an unusually active REM system; it may be that she has little trouble staying asleep once she is in REM. However, many others are light sleepers who find it difficult to remain in lucid dreams for long periods of time. These people need more powerful techniques to help them stay in their lucid dreams. Harald von Moers-Messmer was one of the handful of researchers who personally investigated lucid dreaming in the first half of the twentieth century. He was the first to propose the technique of looking at the ground in order to stabilize the dream.[2]

The idea of focusing on something in the dream in order to prevent awakening has independently occurred to several other lucid dreamers. One of these is G. Scott Sparrow, a clinical psychologist and author of the classic personal account *Lucid Dreaming: The Dawning of the Clear Light*.[3] Sparrow discusses Carlos Castaneda's famous technique of looking at his hands while dreaming to induce and stabilize lucid dreams.[4] Sparrow argues that the dreamer's body provides one of the most unchanging elements in the dream, which can help to stabilize the individual's otherwise feeble identity in the face of a rapidly changing dream. However, as he points out, the body isn't the only relatively stable reference point in the dream: another is the ground beneath the dreamer's feet. Sparrow uses this idea in this example of one of his own lucid dreams:

. . . I walk on down the street. It is night; and as I look up at the sky I am astounded by the clarity of the stars. They seem so close. At this point I become lucid. The dream "shakes" momentarily. Immediately I look down at the ground and concentrate on solidifying the image and remaining in the dreamscape. Then I realize that if I turn my attention to the pole star above my head, the dream image will further stabilize itself. I do this; until gradually the clarity of the stars returns in its fullness.[5]

Dream Spinning

Some years ago I had the good fortune to discover a highly effective technique for preventing awakenings and producing new lucid dream scenes. I started by reasoning that since dream actions have corresponding physical effects, relaxing my dream body might inhibit awakening by lowering muscle tension in my physical body. The next time I was dreaming lucidly, I tested the idea. As the dream began to fade, I relaxed completely, dropping to the dream floor. However, contrary to my intention, I seemed to awaken. A few minutes later I discovered I had actually only dreamed of awakening. I repeated the experiment many times and the effect was consistent—I would remain in the dream state by dreaming of waking up. However, my experiences suggested that the essential element was not the attempted relaxation but the sensation of movement. In subsequent lucid dreams, I tested a variety of dream movements and found both falling backward and spinning in the dream to be especially effective in prolonging my lucid dreams. Here is a method for spinning to remain in the dream state.

THE SPINNING TECHNIQUE

1. Notice when the dream begins to fade
When a dream ends, the visual sense fades first. Other senses may persist longer, with touch being among the last to go. The first sign that a lucid dream is about to end is usually a loss of color and realism in your visual imagery. The dream may lose visual detail and begin to take on a cartoonlike or washed-out appearance. You may find the light growing very dim, or your vision becoming progressively weaker.

(exercise continues)

2. Spin as soon as the dream begins to fade

As soon as the visual imagery of your lucid dream begins to fade, quickly, before the feel of your dream body evaporates, stretch out your arms and spin like a top (with your dream body, of course). It doesn't matter whether you pirouette, or spin like a top, dervish, child, or bottle, as long as you vividly feel your dream body in motion. This is not the same as imagining you are spinning; for the technique to work, you must feel the vivid sensation of spinning.

3. While spinning, remind yourself that the next thing you see will probably be a dream

Continue to spin, constantly reminding yourself that the next thing you see, touch, or hear will very probably be a dream.

4. Test your state wherever you seem to arrive

Continue spinning until you find yourself in a stable world. You will either still be dreaming or have awakened. Therefore, carefully and critically test which state you are in (see chapter 3).

Commentary

If I think I have awakened, I always check the time on the digital clock beside my bed. This usually provides a foolproof reality test.

Frequently, the spinning procedure generates a new dream scene, which may represent the bedroom you are sleeping in or some more unusual place. Sometimes the just-faded dream scene is regenerated in all its vivid glory.

By repeatedly reminding yourself that you're dreaming during the spinning transition, you can continue to be lucid in the new dream scene. Without this special effort of attention, you are likely to mistake the new dream for an actual awakening—in spite of many manifest absurdities of dream content.

(exercise continues)

> A typical false awakening would occur if, while spin-
> ning, you felt your hands hit the bed and you
> thought:"Well, I must be awake, since my hand just hit
> the bed. I guess spinning didn't work this time." What
> you should think, of course, is, "Since the spinning hand
> that hit the bed is a *dream hand*, it must have hit a *dream
> bed*. Therefore, I'm still dreaming!" Don't fail to criti-
> cally check your state after using the spinning technique.

Effectiveness of spinning

This method is extremely effective for many dreamers,
including myself. I used this technique in 40 of the 100
lucid dreams in the last six months of the record for my
doctoral dissertation. New dream scenes resulted in 85
percent of these cases. Lucid consciousness persisted in
97 percent of the new dreams. When spinning led to
another dream, the new dream scene almost always
closely resembled my bedroom.

The experiences of other lucid dreamers who have employed this method have been very similar to mine but
suggest that the post-spin lucid dream need not be a bedroom scene. One of these lucid dreamers, for instance,
found herself arriving at a dream scene other than her
bedroom in five out of the eleven times she used the
spinning technique.

These results suggest that spinning could be used to
produce transitions to any dream scene the lucid dreamer
expects. (See spinning a new dream scene exercise,
page 161.) In my own case, it appears that my almost
exclusive production of bedroom dreams may be an accident of the circumstances in which I discovered the
technique. I have tried, with very little success, to produce transitions to other dream scenes with this method.
Although I have definitely *intended* to arrive elsewhere
than my dream bedroom, I cannot say that I fully *ex-*

pected to. I believe I will someday be able to unlearn this
accidental association (if that is what it is). Meanwhile,
I'm impressed by the power of expectation to determine
what happens in my lucid dreams.

How does spinning work?

Why should dream spinning decrease the likelihood of
awakening? Several factors are probably involved. One
of these may be neurophysiological. Information about
head and body movement, monitored by the vestibular
system of the inner ear (which helps you to keep your
balance), is closely integrated with visual information by
the brain to produce an optimally stable picture of the
world. Because of this integration of information, the
world doesn't appear to move whenever you move your
head, even though the image of the world on the retina
of your eye moves.

Since the sensations of movement during dream spinning are as vivid as those during actual physical movements, it is likely that the same brain systems are
activated to a similar degree in both cases. An intriguing
possibility is that the spinning technique, by stimulating
the system of the brain that integrates vestibular activity
detected in the middle ear, facilitates the activity of the
nearby components of the REM sleep system. Neuro-
scientists have obtained indirect evidence of the involvement of the vestibular system in the production of the
rapid eye movement bursts in REM sleep.[6]

Another possible reason why spinning may help post-
pone awakening comes from the fact that when you
imagine perceiving something with one sense, your sensitivity to external stimulation of that sense decreases.
Thus, if the brain is fully engaged in producing the vivid,
internally generated sensory experience of spinning, it
will be more difficult for it to construct a contradictory
sensation based on external sensory input.

What to do if you do awaken prematurely

Even if you find that despite your best efforts to stay asleep you still wake up, all is not lost. *Play dead.* If you remain perfectly motionless upon waking from a lucid (or nonlucid) dream and deeply relax your body, there is a good chance that REM sleep will reassert itself and you will have an opportunity to enter a lucid dream consciously, as described in chapter 4. For some people with a strong tendency to remain in REM sleep, this happens almost every time they awaken from a dream until they decide to move. Alan Worsley is one of the world's most experienced lucid dreamers. He has been conducting personal lucid dream experiments since the age of five. During the 1970s, he was the first person to signal from a lucid dream in pioneering experiments carried out in collaboration with Keith Hearne.[7] Worsley appears to possess this felicitous sort of physiology, and he offers the following advice for dreamers who have just awakened but yearn to return to their lucid dreams: "Lie very still—don't move a muscle! Relax and wait. The dream will return. I've had dozens of lucid dreams in a row with this method."[8]

Preventing Loss of Lucidity: Use Inner Speech to Guide Your Thinking

We have used language to control our thinking and behavior since we first learned to speak. Our parents would tell us what to do and how to do it, and we were guided by their words. When we first did these things under our own direction, we would repeat out loud the parental instructions to remind ourselves of exactly how and what we were trying to do. Now, having fully incorporated the role of parental guide within us, we repeat the instructions silently to ourselves when carrying out complicated new procedures.

We can also use verbal direction of conscious behavior to regulate our behavior in the lucid dream (for instance, to maintain awareness that it is a dream). Until becoming and staying lucid is a well-developed habit, we are all too likely to lose lucidity anytime our attention wanders. The moment we take a bit too much interest in some facet of the dream, lucidity vanishes. If you are a novice lucid dreamer and have problems maintaining your lucidity, a temporary solution is for you to *talk to yourself* in your lucid dreams. Remind yourself that you are dreaming by repeating phrases like "This is a dream! . . . This is a dream! . . . This is a dream!" or "I'm dreaming . . . I'm dreaming . . . I'm dreaming. . . ." This self-reminder can be spoken "out loud" in the dream, if necessary. Otherwise it's better to say it silently to prevent the repetition from becoming the predominant feature of the dream.

Sparrow recommends the same procedure, advising dreamers with shaky lucidity "to concentrate on an affirmation which serves as a continual reminder of the illusory nature of the experience."[9] He considers it essential that the affirmation (for example, "This is all a dream") be learned by heart and cultivated in the waking state in order for it to be an effective aid in the dream state.

After you have acquired some experience, you will learn to recognize the situations in which you tend to lose your lucidity and find that you can maintain your lucidity without conscious effort. Learning to do this can happen fairly rapidly. In my first year of studying lucid dreaming, I lost lucidity in 11 of 62 lucid dreams; in the second year, I lost lucidity in only 1 of 111 dreams; and in the third year, only 1 of 215 dreams.[10] In the following ten years, my rate of lucidity lost has stayed at less than one percent.

Awakening at Will

My first lucid dream arose from my discovery as a child of five that I could wake myself from frightening dreams by trying to shout "Mother!" [11]

I have found a paradoxical-sounding but simple technique for waking at will: "Fall asleep to wake up." Whenever I decide I want to awaken from a lucid dream, I simply lie down on the nearest dream bed, couch, or cloud, shut my dream eyes, and "go to sleep." The usual result is that I immediately wake up, but sometimes I only dream that I wake up, and when I realize I'm still dreaming, I try again to wake up "for real," sometimes succeeding at once, but sometimes only after an amusing sequence of false awakenings. (B.K., Palo Alto, California)

When I was a little girl, about six years old, I came up with a method for awakening myself when dreams got too unpleasant. I don't recall how I came up with the idea, but I would blink my eyes hard three times. This worked well for a while, and got me out of some pretty horrific and surrealistic scenarios, but then something changed, and the method began to produce false awakenings. When I once used this technique to end a mildly distasteful dream, only to find myself awakening in my bedroom just before the arrival of a terrible hurricane, and certain that the experience was real, upon actually awakening I decided to abandon the practice. (L.L., Redwood City, California)

If the secret to preventing premature awakening is to maintain active participation in the dream, the secret to awakening at will is to withdraw your attention and participation from the dream. Think, daydream, or otherwise withdraw your attention from the dream, and you are very likely to awaken.

When five-year-old Alan Worsley called out for his mother in the physical world, he was directing his attention away from the dream as well as possibly activating the muscles of vocalization in his sleeping body, which could awaken him.

But nothing could provide a better illustration of the principle of waking by withdrawing attention from the dream than Beverly Kedzierski's formula "go to sleep to wake up." After all, what does sleep mean but withdrawal of attention from what is around us?

Another way of withdrawing your participation from the dream is to cease making the usual rapid eye movements so crucially characteristic of REM sleep. Paul Tholey has experimented with fixation on a stationary point during lucid dreams. He found that gaze fixation caused the fixation point to blur, followed by dissolution of the entire dream scene and an awakening within four to twelve seconds. He notes that experienced subjects can use the intermediate stage of scene dissolution "to form the dream environment to their own wishes."[12] Artist and dream researcher Fariba Bogzaran describes a very similar technique called "intentional focusing," in which she concentrates on an object in her lucid dream until she regains waking consciousness.[13]

However, the examples here show that using methods to awaken from dreams may lead to false awakenings. Sometimes, the false awakening can be more disturbing than the original dream you were trying to escape. In general, it is probably best not to try to avoid frightening dream images by escaping to the waking state. Chapter 10 explains why and how you can benefit from facing nightmares. An example of a good use for techniques of waking yourself at will from lucid dreams is to awaken yourself while you still have the events and revelations of the dream clearly in mind.

Two Kinds of Dream Control

Before we go on to discuss ways in which you can exercise your will over the images of your dreams, let's consider the uses you can make of your new freedom.

When faced with challenging dream situations, there are two ways you can master them. One way involves magical manipulation of the dream: controlling "them" or "it," while the other way involves self-control. As it happens, the first kind of control doesn't always work—which may actually be a blessing in disguise. If we learned to solve our problems in our lucid dreams by magically changing things we didn't like, we might mistakenly hope to do the same in our waking lives. For example, I once had a lucid dream about a frightening ogre whom I confronted by projecting feelings of love and acceptance, leading to a pleasurable, peaceful, and empowering resolution in my dream. Suppose I had chosen to turn my adversary into a toad, and get rid of him that way. How would that help me if I were to find myself in conflict with my boss or another authority figure whom I might see as an ogre, in spite of my being awake? Turning him into a toad would hardly be practical! However, a change in attitude might indeed resolve the situation.

Generally, a more useful approach to take with unpleasant dream imagery is to control yourself. Self-control means control over habitual reactions. For example, if you are afraid and run away even though you know you should face your fear, you aren't controlling your behavior. Although the events that appear to take place in dreams are illusory, our feelings in response to dream events are real. So, when you're fearful in a dream and realize that it is a dream, your fear may not vanish automatically. You still have to deal with it; this is why lucid dreams are such good practice for our waking lives. We're free to control our responses to the dream, and whatever we learn in so doing will readily apply to our waking lives. In my "ogre dream," I gained a degree of self-mastery and confidence that has served me as well in the waking world as in the dream. As a result of such lucid dream encounters, I now feel confident that I can handle just about any situation. If you'd like to enhance your sense of self-confidence, my advice is that you'd be wise to control yourself, not the dream.

Flying

I read about your work and the techniques you suggested for having lucid dreams. I practiced noticing whether I was dreaming. The first night, after several nonlucid dreams, I suddenly remembered to ask myself if I was dreaming. As soon as I answered "yes," something happened that your article did not mention. Everything in the dream became extremely vivid. The visual aspects were like someone turned up the contrast and the color. I saw everything in great detail. All my dream senses were amplified. I was suddenly intensely aware of temperature, air movement, odors, and sounds. I had a strong sense of being in control. Even though I had not planned to fly, something in the dream made me think about flying, and I simply leaped into the air (Superman style) and flew. The sensation was the most exhilarating and realistic dream experience I have ever had. I flew down a canyon of tall buildings, gradually gaining altitude. The buildings gave way to a park, where I embarked upon some aerial acrobatics. It was my last dream of the night, and the feeling of exhilaration lasted all day. I told everyone who would listen about the experiment and the success I had. (G.R., Westborough, Massachusetts)

One night I was dreaming of standing on a gentle hill, looking out over the tops of maples, alders, and other trees. The leaves of the maples were bright red and rus-

tling in the wind. The grass at my feet was lush and vividly green. All the colors about me were more saturated than I have ever seen.

Perhaps the awareness that the colors were "brighter than they should be" shocked me into realizing that I was in a dream, and that what lay about me was not "real." I remember saying to myself, "If this is a dream, I should be able to fly into the air." I tested my hunch and was enormously pleased that I could effortlessly fly, and fly anywhere I wanted. I skimmed over the tops of the trees and sailed many miles over new territory. I flew upward, far above the landscape, and hovered in the air currents like an eagle.

When I awoke I felt as if the experience of flying had energized me. I felt a sense of well-being that seemed directly related to the experience of being lucid in the dream, of taking control of the flying. (J.B., Everett, Washington)

Flying dreams and lucid dreams are strongly related in several ways. First, if you ever find yourself flying without benefit of an airplane or other reasonable apparatus, you are experiencing a fine dreamsign. Second, if you ever suspect that you are dreaming, trying to fly is often a good way to test your state. And if you want to visit the far corners of the globe or distant galaxies in your lucid dreams, flying is an excellent mode of transportation.

If you think you are dreaming, push off the ground and see if you can float into the air. If you are indoors, after you fly around the room, look for a window. Go out the window and strive for altitude. Curiously, more than a few dreamers (most likely city dwellers) have reported that they sometimes find an obstacle in the form of electrical power lines that seem to prevent their passage. Some of these oneironauts report a surge of energy, often accompanied by a burst of light, when they fly through the "power" lines. Beyond that barrier, oneironauts have flown around the earth, to other planets, distant stars and galaxies, even mythical realms like Camelot or Shangri-la.

Flying is fun and therefore worth doing for the sheer joy of it, even if you aren't determined to reach a specific destination. People seem to be able to fly in just about any manner imaginable, according to the hundreds of reports we have received. Many people fly "Superman style," with their arms extended in front of them. Also common is "swimming" through the air, probably because the closest experience we get to flying in the air is "flying" in the water. Others sprout wings from their backs or their heels, flap their hands, or straddle jet-powered cereal boxes, or flying carpets, or supersonic easy chairs.

One way to challenge yourself and to begin to fly is to jump off tall buildings or cliffs. Uncontrolled falling is a common theme of nightmares, and the following anecdote suggests the potential usefulness of lucid dream flying for overcoming this terror:

My attempts at flying lucidly were the most interesting adventures I've had in lucid dreams. I have a great fear of heights, so falling in dreams, while not nightmarish, is common for me. I always wake up before I land. But attempting the exercise I read in your article, I flew over places which would have terrified me in a dream before— open water, snowy mountains.

One night I was soaring in outer space and coming back to earth. No fear involved. But coming eventually to a small ledge in a mountain, I was afraid to land and almost woke up. Using your techniques (especially spinning), I forced myself to deliberately land on the very edge. I could see the mountains below, feel the cold, even smell the fresh air. It was really a great feeling to know I could not be hurt; because if I started to fall, I could just fly away again. (N.C., Fremont, California)

Extending Your Dream Senses

I gained conscious control in one of my dreams. I took a bicycle ride because I decided I'd like to broaden my sensual experience. As I pedaled, I called out the senses: Hearing! And I heard my own heavy breathing. Smell! And I smelled a whiff of cigarette smoke. I touched a big, rough-barked tree, heard the flapping of sparrow wings, saw much greenery, felt the handles of the bicycle. My senses were so alive, just as good as if I were awake. Yet I knew I was dreaming. This excited me incredibly! I pedaled furiously to get back, to wake up, but I woke up feeling refreshed. (L.G., San Francisco, California)

Most people are astonished to discover that they are dreaming. The astonishment stems from the realization that they have been fooling themselves in a colossal way. It is definitely a surprise, especially the first time, to learn that your normally trustworthy senses are reporting to you an absolutely flawless portrayal of a world that doesn't exist outside the dream. Indeed, one of the most common features of first lucid dreams is a feeling of hyperreality that happens when you take a good look around you in the dream and see the wondrous, elaborate detail your mind can create.

First-time lucid dreamers often note a marked, pleasurable heightening of the senses, particularly the sense of vision. Hearing, smell, touch, taste can intensify instantly, as if you had found the volume control knob for your senses and turned it up a notch. Give it a try. Play with your senses, one at a time, as you explore the dream world. During daily life, we all have very good reasons for tuning out our senses so we can concentrate on getting our jobs done. In your dreams, however, you can learn how to turn them back on again.

Senses are marvelous instruments for providing data about events inside and outside our bodies. Our brains structure this data into the models of the world we experience. We have all learned how to think, perceive, believe, and model the world in a certain way, and the greatest part of this learning took place when we were infants. The world-modeling process was automatic long before we were able to think about it. Therefore, it comes as a surprise when we discover in lucid dreams that the drama we perceive as *real* might only be a kind of stage set, and all the people in it but mental constructions. However, once we get used to the notion, it is natural and empowering to begin to take conscious control of our senses in the dream state.

The dream television

In the early 1980s, continuing his dual role as lucid dream explorer and researcher, Alan Worsley developed an interesting series of "television experiments."[14] In his lucid dreams he finds a television set, turns it on, watches it, and experiments with the controls to change such things as the sound level and the color intensity. Sometimes he pretends that the TV responds to voice control, so that he can ask it questions and request it to display various images.

Worsley reports that "I have experimented with manipulating imagery, as if I were learning to operate by trial an internal computer video system (including 'scrolling,' 'panning,' changing the scene instantly, and 'zooming'). Further, I have experimented with isolating part of the imagery or 'parking' it, by surrounding it with a frame such as a picture frame or proscenium arch and backing away from it ('windowing')."[15]

EXERCISE: THE DREAM TELEVISION

Before bed set your mind to remember this experiment. When you achieve lucidity, find or create a large, ultra-high resolution, total surround sound television set. Make yourself comfortable. Turn it on. Find the volume, brightness, and color saturation controls and slowly experiment with them. Turn the sound up and down. Tweak the color. When the picture is right, imagine the smell of your favorite food wafting right out of the picture tube. If you are hungry, allow it to materialize. Savor a sample. Conjure up velvet pillows and satin pajamas. Give all the senses a workout. Observe what is happening in your mind as you adjust the color or contrast control on your world-modeling television monitor.

Manipulating Lucid Dreams

I dreamed of falling down the side of a building, and as I fell I knew I was still unprepared to face the fall, so I changed the building to a cliff. I grabbed onto foliage and shrubs that grew down the side and began climbing down confidently. In fact, when someone began falling from above me, I caught him and told him to think of footholds and plants to support him because "it's only a dream and you can do what you want in it." And I enjoyed a totally new excitement and headiness of purposely facing danger and risk. It was a deeply gratifying and proud moment in my life. (T.Z., Fresno, California)

In this dream I was at my mother's house and heard voices in another room. Entering the room, I realized without a doubt I was dreaming. My first command was ordering the people in the room to have a more exciting conversation, since this was my dream. At that moment they changed their topic to my favorite hobby. I started commanding things to happen and they did. The more

*things began to happen, the more I would command. It
was a very thrilling experience, one of the most thrilling
lucid dreams I've had, probably because I was more in
control and more sure of my actions.* (R.B., Chicago,
Illinois)

*Two weeks ago I had a dream of being pursued by a
violent tornadic storm. I was on a cliff high above an
open expanse of beach and had been teaching others to
fly, telling them that this was a dream and in a dream all
you have to do to fly is believe you can. We were having
a great time when the storm appeared, coming in from
the ocean. Tornados and I go way back in dreams. They
are some of my pet monsters of the mind.*

*When this one appeared, it was announced by excep-
tionally strong winds and lightning and high waves. A
young boy, a puppy, and I were together for some time
running and seeking shelter, but then we stopped, poised
on the very edge of the last great cliff before the open
sea. Panic was bringing me close to the point of losing
lucidity. But then I thought, "Wait! This is a dream. If
you choose, you can keep on running. Or you can destroy
the tornado or transform it. The storm has no power to
hurt the boy or the puppy. It is you it wants. Anyway, no
more running. See what it is like from within."*

*As I thought this, it was as though some exceptional
force lifted the three of us, almost blurring our forms as
we were pulled toward the tornado. The boy and puppy
simply faded out about midway. Inside the storm there
was a beautiful translucent whiteness and a feeling of
tremendous peace. At the same time it was a living energy that seemed to be waiting to be shaped and at the
same time was capable of being infinitely shaped and
reshaped, formed and transformed over again. It was
something tremendously vital, tremendously alive.* (M.H.,
Newport News, Virginia)

* * *

Taking action in dreams can mean many things—you can command the characters, or manipulate the scenery, as in the examples quoted above, or you can decide to explore part of the dream environment, act out a particular scene, reverse the dream scenario, or change the plot. Although, as explained above, the greatest benefit from lucid dreams may come not from exercising control over the dreams, but from taking control of your own reactions to dream situations, experimenting with different kinds of dream control can extend your powers and appreciation of lucidity. Paul Tholey mentions several techniques for manipulation of lucid dreams: manipulation prior to sleep by means of intention and autosuggestion, by wishing, by inner state, by means of looking, by means of verbal utterances, with certain actions, and with assistance of other dream figures.[16]

Chapter 3 showed how intention and autosuggestion can influence lucid dreams. Manipulation by wishing is amply illustrated by oneironauts who transport themselves and change the dream world simply by wishing it to happen. Manipulation by inner state is particularly interesting. Tholey says this about it, referring to his own research findings: "The environment of a dream is strongly conditioned by the inner state of the dreamer. If the dreamer courageously faced up to a threatening figure, its threatening nature in general gradually diminished and the figure itself often began to shrink. If the dreamer on the other hand allowed himself to be filled with fear, the threatening nature of the dream figure increased and the figure itself began to grow."[17]

Manipulation by means of looking plays an important part in Tholey's model of appropriate lucid dream activities. He cites his own research in support of the hypothesis that dream figures can be deprived of their threatening nature by looking them directly in the eye. Manipulation by means of verbal utterances is explained thus: "One can considerably influence the appearance and behavior of dream figures by addressing them in an appropriate manner. The simple question 'Who are you?' brought about a noticeable change in the dream figures so addressed. Figures of strangers have changed in this manner into familiar individuals. Evidently the inner readiness to learn something about oneself and one's situation by carrying on a conversation with a dream figure enables one to . . . achieve in this fashion the highest level of lucidity in the dream: lucidity as to what the dream symbolizes.''[18]

Spinning, flying, and looking at the ground are examples of manipulation by certain actions: these are actions that stabilize, enhance, or prolong lucidity. Other dream figures may be able to help you manipulate dreams to find answers, resolve difficulties, or just enjoy yourself. Reconciling with threatening dream characters can help you to achieve better balance and self-integration. This application of lucid dreaming is a key topic in chapter 11.

Getting Places in Dreams

On a more basic level, to get the most out of lucidity you need to know how to get around in the dream world. For many lucid dream applications, you may wish or need to find a particular place, person, or situation. One way to achieve this is by willing yourself to dream about your topic of choice. This is often called "dream incubation." It is a timeless procedure used throughout history in cultures that consider dreams valuable sources of wisdom. In ancient Greece people would visit dream temples to sleep and find answers or cures.

Dream temples are probably not necessary for dream incubation—although they certainly would have helped sleepers to focus their minds on their purpose. This is the key: make sure you have your problem or wish firmly in mind before sleeping. To do this, it is helpful to arrive at a simple, single phrase describing the topic of your intended dream. Because, for the purposes of this book, you are trying to induce lucid dreams, you need to add to your focus the intention to become lucid in the dream. Then you put all of your mental energy into conceiving of yourself in a lucid dream about the topic. Your intention should be the last thing you think of before falling asleep. The following exercise leads you through this process.

EXERCISE: LUCID DREAM INCUBATION

1. Formulate your intention

Before bedtime, come up with a single phrase or question encapsulating the topic you wish to dream about: "I want to visit San Francisco." Write down the phrase and perhaps draw a picture illustrating the question. Memorize the phrase and the picture (if you have one). If you have a specific action you wish to carry out in your desired dream ("I want to tell my friend I love her"), be sure to formulate it now. Beneath your target phrase, write another saying, "When I dream of [the phrase], I will remember that I am dreaming."

2. Go to bed

Without doing anything else, go immediately to bed and turn out the light.

3. Focus on your phrase and intention to become lucid

Recall your phrase or the image you drew. Visualize yourself dreaming about the topic and becoming lucid in the dream. If there is something you want to try in the dream, also visualize doing it once you are lucid. Meditate on the phrase and your intention to become lucid in a dream about it until you fall asleep. Don't let any other

(exercise continues)

thoughts come between thinking about your topic and falling asleep. If your thoughts stray, just return to thinking about your phrase and becoming lucid.

4. Pursue your intention in the lucid dream

Carry out your intention while in a lucid dream about your topic. Ask the question you wish to ask, seek ways to express yourself, try your new behavior, or explore your situation. Be sure to notice your feelings and be observant of all details of the dream.

5. When you have achieved your goal, remember to awaken and recall the dream

When you obtain a satisfying answer in the dream, use one of the methods suggested earlier in this chapter to awaken yourself. Immediately write down at least the part of the dream that includes your solution. Even if you don't think the lucid dream has answered your question, once it begins to fade awaken yourself and write down the dream. You may find on reflection that your answer was hidden in the dream and you did not see it at the time.

Creating new settings

Dreams of this degree of lucidity also let me change the shapes of objects or change locations at will. It's lovely to watch the dream images sort of shift and run like colors melting in the sun until all you have all around you is shifting, moving, living color/energy/light—I'm not sure how to describe it—and then the new scene forms around you from this dream stuff, this protoplasmic modeling clay of the mind. (M.H., Newport News, Virginia)

Another way to dream of particular things is to seek them out or conjure them while you are in a lucid dream. In other literature about dreams you may find some objections to the notion of deliberately influencing the content of dreams. Some believe the dream state to be a kind of psychological "wilderness" that ought to be left untamed. However, as discussed in chapter 5, dreams arise out of your own knowledge, biases, and expectations, whether or not you are conscious of them. If you consciously alter the elements in your dream, this is not artificial; it is just the ordinary mechanism of dream production operating at a higher level of mental processing. Dreams can be sources of inspiration and self-knowledge, but you can also use them to consciously seek answers to problems and fulfill your waking desires.

Changing dream scenes at will can also help you to get acquainted with the full illusion-creating power at your disposal. Seeing that the world around you can switch from a Manhattan cocktail party to Martian canals at your command will be much more effective than the words in this book for teaching you that the dream world is a mental model of your own creation.

The increased sense of mastery over the dream gained by knowing that you can manipulate it if you wish will give you the confidence to travel fearlessly wherever the dream should take you. Your power here is precisely as large as you imagine it to be. You can change the color of your socks, request a replay of the sunset, or segue to another planet or the Garden of Eden, simply by wishing. Here are a few exercises you can experiment with in trying to direct your dreams. Not much is known about the best way to achieve scene changes in dreams, so take the following exercises as hints and then work out your own method.

Spinning a new dream scene

In my dream-spinning experiment, I wanted to go to the setting of a book I'm reading. I wanted to solve the mystery in the book. I reached my target. I started at the point the book began, met the characters in proper sequence, and when I went to the point in the book where

*I was with another character in the book who is a wizard,
he took a running start, leaped off a mountain fortress
wall, and turned into a hawk, thereby escaping his enemies. I also jumped off the wall and changed into a hawk.
I dressed and spoke in the manner of the characters and
took an active part in solving the mysteries in the book.*
(S.B., Salt Lake City, Utah)

Spinning during the course of a lucid dream may do more
for you than merely prevent premature awakening. It may
also help you visit any dream scene you like. Here's how
to do it.

EXERCISE:
SPINNING A NEW DREAM SCENE

1. Select a target
Before going to sleep, decide on a person, time, and
place you would like to "visit" in your lucid dream. The
target person and place can be either real or imaginary,
past, present, or future. For example, "Padmasambhava,
Tibet, 850," or "Stephen LaBerge, Stanford, California, the present," or "my granddaughter at home, the
year 2050."

2. Resolve to visit your target
Write down and memorize your target phrase, then vividly visualize yourself visiting your target and firmly resolve to do so in a dream tonight.

3. Spin to your target in your lucid dream
It's possible that just by the intention you might find
yourself in a nonlucid dream at your target. However, a
more reliable way to reach your target is to become lucid
first and then seek your goal. When you are in a lucid
dream at the point where the imagery is beginning

(exercise continues)

to fade and you feel you are about to wake up, then spin, repeating your target phrase until you find yourself in a vivid dream scene—hopefully your target person, time, and place.

EXERCISE:
STRIKE THE SET, CHANGE THE CHANNEL

Think of this as the opposite of the kind of magical transportation involved in spinning and flying. Instead of moving your dream self to a new, exotic locale, simply change the environment of your dream to suit your fancy. Start with a small detail and work up to greater changes. Change the scene slowly then abruptly, subtly then blatantly. Think of everything you see as infinitely malleable ''modeling clay for the mind.'' Some oneironauts have elaborated on Alan Worsley's example of the dream television. When they want to change the scenery, they imagine that the dream is taking place on a huge, three-dimensional television screen and they have the remote control in their hand.

Doing the Impossible

I dreamed that I was at a party recently and having a boring time when I stood back from the dream and knew it was a dream. I then had a great time projecting myself into being whoever was having fun. At first I just tried being women, but then I said, it's a dream, why not be a man and see what that feels like? So I did. (B.S., Albuquerque, New Mexico)

In waking life we are used to restrictions. For almost everything we do, there are rules about how to act, how not to act, and what it is reasonable to try. One of the most commonly quoted delightful features of lucid dreaming is great, unparalleled freedom. When people realize they are dreaming, they suddenly feel *completely unrestricted*, often for the first time in their life. They can do or experience *anything*.

In dreams you can experience sensations or live out fantasies that are not probable in the waking state. You can get intimately acquainted with a fantasy figure. But you could also become that figure. Dreamers are not limited to their accustomed bodies. You can appreciate a beautiful garden. Or you can be a flower. Alan Worsley has experimented with bizarre things like splitting himself in half and putting his hands through his head.[19] Many oneironauts pass through walls, breathe water, fly, and travel in outer space. Forget your normal criteria; seek the kinds of things you can only do or be in dreams.

7

~~~~~

Adventures
and Explorations

Wish Fulfillment

A few years back I was trying to lose weight. I would dream that I was in a grocery store, bakery, or restaurant, and food was everywhere. I was conscious that I was dreaming and therefore could eat whatever I wanted. I proceeded to pig out on the feast before me, even tasting the food. These dreams would satisfy my craving to gorge myself. I would wake feeling satisfied—not full, but satisfied—and if during the day I got the urge to eat something I shouldn't I just thought, "I'll eat it tonight in my dream," and I did! (C.C., Cotati, California)

I always wanted to dance professionally, mostly ballet. My mother, however, always discouraged it because of the hard work and hard life that went along with it. Eventually, I just gave up and never did take it seriously. However, the desire never left and I would have wonderful experiences with it in my dreams and would try new moves or steps that I saw or learned of but could obvi-

ously do nothing with except in my dreams. (B.Z., Salt Lake City, Utah)

The wish-fulfillment aspect of dreams is deeply embedded in our colloquial speech: we speak of "the man of your dreams," or "your dream house," and we say "may your fondest dreams come true." These metaphors show that in our hearts we know that dreams are different from the waking world in at least one important sense—in dreams you can live your wildest fantasies, see your most delightful wishes fulfilled, and experience perfection and joy even when these satisfactions are not possible in your waking life.

In dreams Cinderella can be with her prince and prisoners can conjure sweet freedom; the crippled can walk and the aged can be as young as they like—everyone can feel fulfilled, no matter how impossible their wishes may seem in waking life. The experience of wish fulfillment is not the same as actually living out the same scenarios in waking life, yet the sensations are no less intense and pleasurable when you know it is "only a dream." As the psychologist Havelock Ellis said, "Dreams are real while they last, can we say more of life?"[1]

When you are beginning to shape your dreams, wish fulfillment is a natural thing to pursue. Joyous flights through beautiful countryside, wild lovemaking with your heart's desire, sumptuous feasting, thrilling runs down ski slopes, acts of power and achievement, and any other pleasant experiences that you can imagine are possible in the lucid dream state. One of psychologist Ken Kelzer's lucid dreams provides a vivid illustration of the joys of lucid dreaming:

. . . I have been dreaming for a long time, and now I see myself lying on a brass bed in what looks like an old hotel room . . . Now I stretch out my body full length and begin to fly. My feet stick out through the bars at the foot

of the brass bed, and without any effort or intention on my part, I lift the bed up off the floor. Soon the bed and I are flying together around the room as I seek a way to explore all the rooms in this huge hotel. Suddenly, I realize I am dreaming, and I feel exhilarated as the familiar, light-headed tingling sensations begin . . . I begin to sing, "Beautiful dreamer, wake unto me, Starlight and dewdrops are waiting for thee." I deeply enjoy this song, and I sing it with my heart wide open. As I sing, I hear the gentle tinkling of a music box. The music box plays "Beautiful Dreamer" in perfect accompaniment to my voice, its modulations, its pacing and its rhythms, as I sing the words over and over. I feel how wonderful it is to be lucid again, and I realize that "Beautiful Dreamer" is the perfect theme song for me . . .

Now I see many beautiful colors and lights flashing about me. I see hundreds of rainbow droplets, tiny little spectrums, floating and spiraling circles of white light, and many small, shiny objects of art swirling everywhere. I feel very uplifted as I enjoy this dazzling display of music, light and color. It is a fantastic feast for the senses, a miniature psychedelic light show, though much more delicate, sensuous and uplifting than any that I have ever seen. . . .[2]

Go ahead and indulge yourself in these joys, if you wish. It's good for you. Having fun just for the sake of it is beneficial in several ways. Psychologists and physicians are finding that daily pleasure and enjoyment are good for your health. Educators are also realizing that when tasks are fun, they are easier to learn.

Robert Ornstein and David Sobel recently published a book entitled *Healthy Pleasures*, which discusses myriad ways that pleasure is good for your health.[3] They claim that our innate desire to seek pleasure and persist in activities that feel good helps us to live longer and happier lives. The healthiest people seem to be those who enjoy pleasure, seek it out, and make it for themselves. Some of the benefits attributed to indulging in pleasurable and sensual experiences are lowered blood pressure, decreased risk of heart disease and cancer, improved immune function, and lowered sensitivity to pain. Some people may protest that they do not have time to have fun. But as long as you have time to sleep at night, you have time to enjoy yourself in your dreams. By learning to have lucid dreams, you open for yourself a limitless amusement park full of all the delights you can imagine. Admission is free, and there are no lines!

If you take some time to play and take pleasure in your lucid dreams, you can learn to become more proficient at lucid dreaming. Once you have learned to have lucid dreams whenever you like, you will possess a means of improving your life in many ways. The chapters that follow will discuss how you can use lucid dreaming to help you learn other skills, overcome fears, increase your mental flexibility, and find ultimate fulfillment. But the best way to attain the ability to use lucid dreaming for "serious" tasks may be to start off by using lucid dreams to have a great time. When lucid dreaming is easy and fun for you, then your dreams will be ideal environments for learning and practicing for waking life.

Wish fulfillment may be the ultimate use that many people will make of their lucid dreams, and their lives will be richer for it. But that doesn't have to be the end of the journey. Many of you will want to go deeper, and higher, to gain greater understanding of the dream state, and apply lucidity to problem solving and other practical purposes. However, until you satisfy your urge to pursue the impossible made possible, you are likely to find yourself distracted from more sublime pursuits by your baser impulses. This is one more reason why you should not hesitate to give in to your hedonism and curiosity when you are first learning to have lucid dreams.

Dream sex

My ability to achieve orgasm is highly vulnerable to stress and anxiety. Recently, during a period of several months of nearly constant anxiety, I seemed to have lost the ability to climax. I knew it wasn't related to my feelings about my partner, or anything he was (or wasn't) doing. The frustration ensuing from not being able to achieve sexual release added to the rest of my general stress. But, then, one night, I had the following dream:

I dreamed I was involved in the plot of a horror film. It involved a haunted house, or abandoned abbey, where I supposed awful things were to take place. I walk by what I take to be this haunted building, only it has been transformed into a large, cheerily lit department store. I think this is a neat trick; it will attract people whom it can submit to its horrors. I enter and mill about. Everything looks normal, but I am fearfully looking everywhere for the incipient danger.

But, then, the thought occurs to me that this is a nightmare, and therefore I should face anything fearsome. This thought radically changes my outlook, and with an open and curious attitude I turn to the scenery, now floating along, looking for challenges and anything interesting. I note that some people are operating a video camera at one side of the room and that the video screen is on the other side. I am intrigued by the idea of getting my own image displayed and orient myself in front of the camera, while looking at the screen. The idea becomes sexual and I wish to display myself on the video screen. At first it is a struggle to get the screen to display anything other than my back from the waist up, clothed. But, eventually, I get the right zone on the display and begin to remove my jeans. I begin to experience sexual arousal which intensifies quite rapidly, and within five seconds I have a wonderful orgasm—the first I'd experienced in two months. I awaken immediately afterward, feeling delightful.

The very evening following this dream I easily experienced my first waking orgasm in two months. And in the few weeks following, though the rest of the anxiety-provoking situation remains, I have achieved climax whenever I desired. (A.L., Santa Clara, California)

I am an inmate confined in a federal prison. When I read the article about being conscious while in the dream state I became very interested in it for I was able to do the same thing. I have had such experiences while dreaming and have loved them. They have at times given me a way to escape from being confined.

In one such dream I started realizing that if I wanted to I could control the environment here, for this was created by my subconscious, therefore subject to my conscious will. I thought for a moment of what I would like to do. The first thought that came through my mind was the fact that I had not been with a woman in years and this is what I wanted most, for even though it was only a dream, everything there was just like here, there was no difference.

So as I sat there I looked at these two guys and told them that this was no more than a dream. I then told them that I have been in prison for a while now and that I wanted a woman to have sex with. Neither of them said anything but looked at me in a crazy way. I then repeated my desire and began to think upon it. The guy at the table then told me that I should go into the other room. So I got up, went to the door, and before entering concentrated on my desire.

I was then in the room. There on the bed was lying a woman who had been in the dream earlier. I took my clothes off and got into bed with her. Throughout the entire sexual act I kept concentrating on keeping in a conscious state of mind, because in previous such dreams I would panic or lose myself and fall out of the dream.

There was total awareness of every moment of our sex-

ual act, from beginning to end. After we were finished I rolled over on my side. As my head hit the pillow I felt that drifting feeling coming over me and realized that I was getting ready to pass into the blackness that I always find myself in when I leave these types of dreams and wake up. (D.M., Terre Haute, Indiana)

In this lucid dream, I am in the French countryside riding a beautiful horse along with someone I've always wanted to meet but never have (and have lusted after for many years), the actor Michael York. It is late afternoon, and we have stopped our horses to walk together through fields of exquisitely perfect and very fragrant flowers, which we can both smell distinctly. We then have a "flower fight" and fall together into the softest bed of flowers ever, where we make love, with a cool breeze floating over us. We ride back to a chateau together on one horse; the other follows by my verbal command alone.

When we reach the chateau, Michael takes the horses to the stables and I go upstairs to a huge marble bathroom with a sunken tub trimmed in platinum fixtures and with a stained glass skylight. As I step into the perfectly bubbling and heated bathwater, I think of Michael, naked, walking into the bathroom and joining me, and he appears.

After a long bath, during which we have fallen asleep in each other's arms with the water flowing around us, we adjourn to the bedroom where I once again think of red wine (Margaux '73), biscuits and jam, and it's there. We are wrapped in soft, white, thick sheets made of heavy silk. Just as we bring the wine to the bed, I wake up. (J.B., Long Island City, New York)

As you would expect in a land of complete freedom, sex is a very common theme in many people's lucid dreams. According to the psychologist Patricia Garfield, an experienced lucid dreamer and noted author of books on dreams, "Orgasm is a natural part of lucid dreaming: my own experience convinces me that conscious dreaming *is* orgasmic." She reports that two-thirds of her lucid dreams have sexual content and that about half of these lucid dreams culminate in orgasms that are apparently as good or even better than in waking life. In *Pathway to Ecstasy*, Garfield describes her lucid dream orgasms as being of "profound" intensity; she finds herself "bursting into soul-and-body shaking explosions . . . with a totality of self that is only sometimes felt in the waking state."[4]

There are both psychological and physiological reasons why the lucid dreaming state tends to be a hotbed of sexual activity. In terms of physiology, our research at Stanford has established that lucid dreaming occurs during a highly activated phase of REM sleep, associated, as a result, with increased vaginal blood flow or penile erections. These physiological factors coupled with the fact that lucid dreamers are freed from all social restraint ought to make lucid dream sex a frequent experience.

These findings imply that lucid dreaming could become a new tool for sex therapists, and new hope for those who suffer from some forms of psychosexual dysfunction (some cases of impotence, premature ejaculation, difficulty in achieving orgasm, etc.). Like many new ideas based on the discoveries of lucid dreamers, this one is untested and ripe for research. Nevertheless, it is fairly clear, as shown in the second example given above, that lucid dreaming can provide a sexual outlet for people confined to prisons, working in isolation, or whose activities in waking life are limited by a physical handicap.

The significance of dream sex can vary tremendously. For some, it is just a good time; for others, it means union of opposite parts of the personality. It may even provide the starting point for speculation, as in the case of Samuel Pepys, who recounted a dream in his diary entry for August 15, 1665:

. . . I had my Lady Castlemayne in my armes and was admitted to use all the dalliance I desired with her, and then dreamt that this could not be awake, but that since it was a dream, and that I took so much real pleasure in it, what a happy thing it would be if when we are in our graves . . . we could dream, and dream but such dreams as this, that then we should not need to be so fearful of death, as we are in this plague time.

Exploring and Closely Observing Dream Reality

I am in a garden and feeling lighthearted and joyous about my ability to fly. I spend much time performing all manner of aerial acrobatics, and the sense of freedom I am experiencing is beyond description. I descend then to enjoy the garden at eye level and realize that I am quite alone in this place. At the moment of this realization also comes the awareness that I am in fact asleep in my bed and having a dream. I am fascinated by the seeming so-lidity of my own body within this dream and find great amusement in the act of "pinching myself to see if I am real." I indeed feel as real to myself as anyone feels to themselves while awake! I become then quite serious in pondering this matter and take a seat on a rock at the edge of the garden to think on this. The thought that comes to me is this: "The degree of awareness one is able to achieve while in a dream is in direct proportion to the degree of awareness one experiences in waking life."

I am startled by the ability to have such a complex and concrete thought within a dream and I begin to examine the condition of my waking life from a perspective that seems impossible to do while living in one's waking life. I am further startled at being able to do such a thing within a dream and begin to experience some apprehension over this entire matter. I decide to get up and inspect my surroundings. I notice that the garden is a stage set. All the flowers are painted in luminous color and in great detail on freestanding flats. Being an artist, I am quite taken by the skill inherent in the painting of them. I then wander "backstage" through a hallway that is papered in red flocked wallpaper. Still aware that this is a dream I am in, I am taken by the amount of detail I am able to observe here and touch the wallpaper to feel the flocking. At the end of the hallway is a bookcase and I am fascinated by the ability to read the titles of the books, the feel of their leather bindings, the details of the drawings on them. (D.G., Woodland Hills, California)

I was traveling down my local, mountainless, two-lane highway in broad daylight when it became pitch dark in a split second. I almost smashed into the rear end of a slow-moving tractor-trailer in front of me. I followed it awhile up a steeper and steeper mountain. Then, as I glanced to my right there was the dark outline of another tractor-trailer pulled off on the right shoulder of the road. As I crept farther down the road, I saw imbedded lengthwise in the side of the mountain another tractor-trailer. As I took my eyes off the tractor and glanced at the road ahead, my car bolted forward down the road alone, and I shot out into the universe at a breathtaking, totally exhilarating velocity. I knew I was dreaming as I could hear my sleeping husband breathing beside me and knew my body was on the bed. I was a speck of light traveling at a tremendous force through space and I was elated. I shouted, "Yes! Yes!" and I could see 360° around me. Ahead and to the right I saw our planet bathed in light; to my left and higher still was another bright spinning globe. Around the middle of the globe, unfolding like a ribbon, were the most beautiful, bright stained-glass colors pulsating energy, and I became one with them. Next, from the unfolding ribbon came musical notes which I could see but not hear. Then came letters of the alphabet in no particular order. Then numbers, again in no particular order. Finally came symbols: the circle and the triangle and a few others. Then many I had never seen before. "This is all the wisdom of the universe," was the message I received telepathically. As I started to go around the curve—in back of the globe—I thought I must be dying, having a heart attack or stroke (although I felt no pain), and I came back to my body.

While I was out there I had no feeling of being a wife, mother, grandmother, retired legal secretary, etc. (which I am). Out there I was alone, but not alone, like part of a whole. It was warm, still, bright, and seemed to me to be a whisper of something. I was infinitely more alive there than I've ever felt here, and I've always been a very active woman. I wish I hadn't been afraid to "round that curve." (A.F., Melrose, New York)

Exploring lucid dreaming offers many delights and rewards. The worlds of lucid dreams are fascinating, and constantly changing, with many vistas of breathtaking and unearthly beauty in which the impossible and unexpected regularly happens. They are at least as interesting and rewarding to explore as anyplace a waking world traveler might want to visit. In fact, the lucid dream world offers several advantages: it doesn't cost anything but a little effort to get there, and unlike Paris, China, or Tahiti, you will never see all the sights. Moreover, you won't get seasick, stuck in airports, or have your bags stolen.

Lucid dream travel is guaranteed to be safe and for most people, almost always pleasant. We aren't saying that lucid dreamers don't sometimes face demanding, anxiety-provoking situations, but that while they are undergoing fully realistic harrowing experiences (for example, being chased by demons, axe murderers, or other monsters from the id) they are actually safely asleep in bed. Whatever they do in their lucid dreams, they will soon find themselves safely returned to the physical world. If, for example, you unsuccessfully attempt to avoid a dreamed danger, you may awaken in a sweat but physically unscathed. Even better, if you use your lucidity to help you face and overcome fears, you will awaken triumphant and inspired.

"Travel broadens the mind" because it brings people into new and challenging situations outside their normal limited and habitual world. Lucid dreaming presents many opportunities for broadening the mind. Intrepidly exploring your dreams with an open mind is bound to enhance your knowledge of both yourself and others. As Goethe put it, "If you want to know yourself, observe the behavior of others. If you want to understand others, look in your own heart."[5] There is much to be learned through lucid dreaming. If you are sensitive and attentive in your observations, you may discover great treasure in the course of exploring your dream world—you may even find yourself.

Another benefit of observant exploration and examination of dream reality is that it helps you become better acquainted with your dreams. As a result, you will more easily recognize dreamsigns, which will help you to become lucid more frequently. Experience will teach you how to avoid misconceptions about the difference between waking and dreaming. Novice lucid dreamers often fail to recognize that they are dreaming, because they are tricked into accepting the "reality" of dream scenes. They appear quite like ordinary reality to casual observation. The following dream shows how this tendency caused one of us to fail to become lucid in a dream with an ironic dreamsign:

Finding myself driving with my father to JFK airport, I begin to wonder what will happen to the car after we park it and fly off to San Francisco. Then I realized that I had no memory of transporting that car to New York in the first place. Something was very wrong! I looked at my father, and he gave me a quizzical grin. Yes, he seemed to be indicating, something is wrong, but you don't get it yet. So I looked at the cars around us on the freeway. They were absolutely lifelike, filled with strangers on their way to unknown destinations. They all had dents and license plates. The upholstery in my car was exactly the same as it should be. The moment I awakened, I realized that my father has been dead for ten years and felt foolish to have failed to become lucid in the presence of such an obvious dreamsign, simply because the dream had seemed so realistic. I firmly resolved to avoid this mistake in the future. The next night, seeing a dead friend in a dream, I ignored the absolutely realistic look of the place I met him and realized I must be dreaming. (H.R. Mill Valley, California)

By observing while lucid how real the dream world can appear, you will be less likely to make the mistake of accepting that "seeing is believing," and that vividness has anything to do with the reality of an experience. You will learn instead to distinguish the two worlds by becoming familiar with the characteristics that make them different—in dreams, all things are much more transitory than in waking life, physical laws are frequently broken, dead or imaginary characters appear among the living, wishes become horses, and beggars do ride.

Adventure: From Walter Mitty to the Hero's Journey

The first controlled dream I can clearly recall was when I was five or six. I used to dream that I was flying around the Earth in a rocket I had made from a garbage can. The bottom was glass and I had a lovely aerial view of the world as I flew wherever I wanted. When it was time to land (my rocket was not equipped for landing), during the descent I would tell myself, "Time to wake up," and I'd wake myself up. Though sometimes I would get perilously close to the ground, I was never afraid of the inevitable crash because I knew I was dreaming and could wake myself up at any time. I had a lot of enjoyment from this dream for about six months. (K.M., Rathdrum, Idaho)

What a wonderful discovery it was when I read an article about your research on lucid dreaming today! All my life I have flown throughout many nights and taken wondrous adventures upon the wings of my imagination while dreaming. I have talked to bears, dogs, raccoons, and owls; I have swum with dolphins and whales, breathing underwater as if I had gills. (L.G., Chico, California)

I'm an astronomer, and I pride myself on my powers of detailed observation; I would like to add to our knowledge of the sleep state. I have saved the Earth from nuclear war, the Galaxy from its core exploding, the Universe from final heat Death. I have inhabited a score of other bodies and personalities, from the distant past to the technological future. One of my more interesting lucid dreams lasted for over five years in the dream time frame, during which I lived in the far distant future, in a body very different from my present one. I would actually fall asleep in this "nest" life. Interestingly, I did not

*have lucid dreams in this alter life, but each time I awak-
ened from the "nested" sleep I would become instantly
aware that I was having a lucid dream, and each time I
chose to stay in the dream. This was far in the future,
when the moon had broken up to form lovely multicolored
rings, which I would watch with my wife and little girl
in the cool evening twilight.* (S.C., El Paso, Texas)

From fairy tales to fiction, from fantasies to daydreams
(and nightdreams!), the human imagination is a limitless
source of adventure. Great storytellers are rare, but we
all seem to have a deep capacity for appreciating stories
and inventing personal ones to fulfill our need for excitement. James Thurber's classic tale "The Secret Life of
Walter Mitty" has provided the American archetype of
the armchair adventurer.

Walter Mitty was meek and undistinguished in the external world, but in his fantasies he was a hero. Whether
or not we are meek in waking life, we all can be heroes
in our dreams. Many people have written to us about
their lucid dream experiences, noting that they began to
become conscious of their dreams as children and used
the opportunity to live out high adventures as knights on
horseback, princesses, or space explorers. In this sense,
lucid dreaming can be used as a kind of wish-fulfillment
tool for the adventurous at heart—or for those who would
like just a taste of adventure.

Some of our correspondents have written that they have
enjoyed regular nighttime adventures for decades—just as
some people can spend a lifetime enjoying travel stories
or science fiction novels or westerns. The ability to vicariously enjoy the experiences of fictional characters
gives us raw material from which to construct our own
adventures. You can start out as Ivanhoe or Mata Hari
and experience for yourself the scenes you have read
about or seen on a movie screen. Unlike a book or a
movie, however, your lucid dream adventure can con-

tinue indefinitely, with a new episode each night or each
REM period.

EXERCISE:
HOW TO SCRIPT YOUR OWN ADVENTURE

*I have always looked at my dreams as being an ongoing
story in which I have cast myself in the leading role.
Things that happen in everyday life or on television or
in a movie are molded into scenes for my "story." Sometimes it can be a man that I have met. For the most part,
my dreams are made up of situations that I would really
like to happen in real life.* (D.W., Brooklyn, New York)

Not uncommonly, oneironauts have reported that they
have consciously scripted, directed, and starred in their
own lucid dream productions. One woman wrote that she
even rolled credits at the end and woke up laughing at
her own joke. In writing your own script for adventure,
you can start out with a simple plot. Feel free to borrow
from Shakespeare, fairy tales, or comic books (Superman is a frequent persona adopted in lucid dreams). Be
open to variations. When something new happens, something that wasn't in the original script, then follow it and
see where it goes. If and when you grow tired of experiencing known scenarios, sketch out a simple one of
your own while you are awake, concentrate on it before
you go to sleep, and see if you can "produce" it like a
film when you become lucid.

Here are a few suggested titles for the kind of adven-
tures you might try when you start. Choose one that ap-
peals to you:
  • Frontier explorer
  • Seeker of the Holy Grail
  • Vision quest
  • Astronaut
  • Time traveler

The Hero's Dream

Fantasies and adventures can operate on many levels of the mind. At the lowest level, they satisfy our needs for excitement and wish fulfillment. However, they can also help us focus our goals, create futures for ourselves and the world, and, on the highest level, model the search for truth and meaning in life. For those of you with an interest in the psychological and mythological aspects of storytelling who want to put your lucid dream scenarios to work on a deeper level of adventure, we recommend reading the late mythologist Joseph Campbell's book, *The Hero With a Thousand Faces*.[6]

Early in the book, Campbell points out that the heroic adventures of all mythologies, regardless of their origins, seem to follow a standard pattern. His theories suggest that mythologies reflect symbols that are not dependent on a particular culture but are deeply embedded in the human psyche. By acting out the classic myths, lucid dreamers can explore the paths of initiation and human development represented by myths in the microcosm of their own minds. Campbell's monomyth pattern can help you in scripting your dream adventures:

The standard path of the mythological adventure of the hero is a magnification of the formula represented in the rites of passage: *separation—initiation—return*: which might be named the nuclear unit of the monomyth. "A hero ventures forth from the world of common day into a region of supernatural wonder: fabulous forces are there encountered and a decisive victory is won: the hero comes back from this mysterious adventure with the power to bestow boons on his fellow man."[7]

You find the same story everywhere you go, Campbell claimed, although the characters and settings may change names. George Lucas acknowledges that the *Star Wars* trilogy was strongly influenced by Campbell's book. Let us examine the way the adventures of Luke Skywalker adhere to the formula quoted above, so you will have a better idea of how to devise your own personal variation.

At the beginning of the trilogy, Luke is just an ordinary boy, unaware that vast forces are about to focus on him. He does not realize that the appearance of Obi-Wan Kenobe (the wise old man character) signals a turning point in his life—the "departure" phase that Campbell calls "the call to adventure." Luke, cut off from his familiar world by the murder of his aunt and uncle, sets off on a journey. Along the way he experiences a victory over himself—making contact with the "Force" within him, which allows him to save a world from the evil plans of Darth Vader (a dark-cloaked and masked "shadow figure" right out of the pages of Jung).

You may choose to begin your own dream hero's journey from familiar territory. Perhaps you will reject the temptation to indulge in one of your typical lucid dream pastimes, and instead set off in search of new experience. Your mission might involve the defense of freedom, the discovery of a legendary land, such as Shambhala or Oz, or the recovery of a magical object, such as a ring of power.

In Campbell's schema, the departure phase proceeds through the stages of "refusal of the call" (fear of leaving known territory), "supernatural aid" (your wise old man or fairy godmother), "the crossing of the first threshold" (a step away from the familiar), and "the belly of the whale" (no turning back). By this time, ordinary life has been left far behind. The initiation phase begins with "the road of trials," wherein dragons and villains, disasters and sinister forces, fear and monstrous perils, are confronted and defeated. The final stage of initiation is "the ultimate boon"—the attainment of the goal. The maiden is liberated. The Ring of Power is recovered. The Tin Woodsman finds a heart. But in myth, as in lucid dreaming, the arrival at the goal is not the end of the story. The final and most heroic phase is when the hero returns to the ordinary (waking?) world, bringing something to enrich not only the hero's life, but that of the community. He may marry the princess and become the beneficent ruler of the land.

EXERCISE:
YOU ARE THE HERO

Think of a hero's story that appeals to you. You can use the structure of a classical myth or story, or you may invent your own, based on the pattern described above. If you want a little vicarious practice before taking your own journey, immerse yourself in *Star Wars*, or *The Arabian Nights*, or Wagner's *Ring of the Nibelüngen*. Examine the characters and the action as they progress through the stages of the monomyth cycle. You don't have to invent elaborate plots or construct dialogue. Simply note possible scenes in the journey of your chosen hero-identity that fit with this model. Write them down in simple sentences. Read the script before you go to sleep. The next time you attain lucidity, remember your script: turn your back on the familiar, be open to guidance, and begin your quest.

Commentary

On the deepest level, Campbell suggests that anyone who seeks the ultimate meaning of life must make this journey on a psychological and spiritual level, and that the journey's structure is often manifested spontaneously in dreams. Thus, you may find that your dream story takes on powerful significance for you. In chapter 12 we will return to the idea of using lucid dreams in the quest for your true self.

8

~~~~~~

Rehearsal for Living

Lucid Dreaming and Peak Performance

It was the night before my first 10 km road run and I was apprehensive. It was my first such race, the course was hilly, and I had never run on a hill in my life; all my training had been on an indoor track. That night I dreamed of running on hills using techniques I'd only read about. I remember knowing I was dreaming during the dream and remarking to myself that this would give me a chance to learn how to run hills. It worked. During the actual run the techniques I'd practiced in my dreams felt exactly the same and worked just as well in reality. (B.E., Alexandria, Virginia)

When I was about twelve years old, my mother made my sister and me take tennis lessons one summer. Toward the end of the four weeks of lessons I found out there would be a tournament and a trophy for the winner. That night in my dream I realized I was dreaming and I decided to master the game of tennis. I took what I had seen on TV, on other people's tennis games and tried to remember the way they hit and served, etc. By the end of the dream I was doing pretty good on swinging and incredibly on serving, because with serving the ball, once you have the technique down it's really very basic and repetitious.

When it came to the tournament I beat everyone and walked away with the trophy. The teacher couldn't believe how well I played, and neither could I. (B.Z., Salt Lake City, Utah)

Authors Charles Garfield and Hal Bennett popularized the term "peak performance," referring to those extraordinary moments when body and mind seem to operate together at the very top of their capacity. Research on how to cultivate peak performance suggests that lucid dreaming may prove to be an ideal training ground, not only for athletics, but also for any area in which skill can be developed.

Garfield, president of the Peak Performance Center, interviewed hundreds of successful athletes about those moments when they performed extraordinarily well. He identified mental conditions that seemed to characterize personal peaks for the majority of athletes. Peak performers, he found, were relaxed, confident, optimistic, focused on the present, highly energized, extremely aware of the environment, in control, and completely in touch with their powers and skills.[1] The athletes were mentally, as well as physically, prepared to perform.

Interest in peak performance has spread from sports psychology to business. Businesses have discovered that mental practice can boost performance levels on the job as well as on the playing field. Yoga, breathing, and meditation have been successfully employed for both material and spiritual achievement. Even greater improvements in performance have resulted from the use of controlled mental imagery and mental rehearsal.[2]

Lucid dreaming is a very powerful type of mental imagery. Waking mental images are weak sensory impressions that resemble actual experience but are generally not as vivid. For example, imagine an apple in front of you. If you are like most people, you can sort of "see" the apple, its shape, color, and position on the table. You can imagine what it would smell like if you could pick it up and sniff it, and what it would taste like if you could bite into it. However, you are not likely to mistake it for a real apple—if you visualize an imaginary apple next to a real apple, you will know which one you can really eat. Dreams, however, are mental images of completely convincing vividness. While in a dream, you may pick up and eat a dream apple and be absolutely certain that you are really eating an apple. If you become lucid, you have the power to realize that dream apples, despite their apparent reality, are not really real—they do not fill your stomach. However, this realization does not diminish the vividness of the experience.

Dreams are the most vivid type of mental imagery most people are likely to experience. The more the mental rehearsal of a skill feels like the real thing, the greater the effect it is likely to have on waking performance. Because of this, lucid dreaming, in which we can make conscious use of dream imagery, is likely to be even more useful than waking mental imagery as a tool for learning and practicing skills.

Mental Practice

In the dream I was in a rink with a number of other people. We were playing hockey and I was skating in the manner I always had, competent yet hesitant. At that moment I realized I was dreaming, so I told myself to allow my higher knowledge to take over my consciousness. I surrendered to the quality of complete skating.

Instantly there was no more fear, no more holding back and I was skating like a pro, feeling as free as a bird.

The next time I went skating I decided to experiment and try this surrender technique. I brought back the quality of that dream experience into my wakened state. I remembered how I was feeling during the dream and so in the manner of an actor in a role, I "became" the complete skater once again. I hit the ice . . . and my feet followed my heart. I was free on the ice. That occurred about two and a half years ago. I have skated with that freedom ever since, and this phenomenon has manifested itself in my roller skating and skiing as well. (T.R., Arlington, Virginia)

While the idea of mental rehearsal as a way of refining motor skills was once a radical hypothesis, research in this area has now burgeoned into a rich, interdisciplinary field. Studies have shown that new skills can be learned to some extent merely by thinking about performing them.[3] Learning improves when mental and physical practice are combined.

How can merely imagining doing something help you to actually do it better? First of all, remember the laboratory work at Stanford showing that when people dream of performing an action, such as singing or engaging in sexual activity, their bodies and brains respond as if they were actually doing it, except that their muscles remain paralyzed by the REM process. Apparently, the neural impulses from the brain to the body are still active and quite similar, if not identical, to those that would accompany the same acts in waking.

Likewise, researchers of mental imagery have found that "vivid, imagined events produce innervation in our muscles that is similar to that produced by the actual physical execution of the event."[4] For example, Richard Suinn monitored the electrical activity in the legs of a downhill skier as he mentally relived a race.[5] He found

that the skier's muscles exhibited activity in a sequence
that corresponded to the layout of the run, showing more
activity at times when the skier was imagining navigating
turns and rough sections. Imagery rehearsal may work to
improve motor skills by strengthening the neural pathways used to elicit the patterns of movement that are
required by the skill.

There is, however, an important difference between
dreamed action and imagined action. When we are
awake, the neural impulses to the muscles created by
imagining an action must be somehow attenuated to keep
us from acting out what we imagine. If they were not,
think what would happen each time you fantasized doing
something—say, on a hot day, while sitting at your desk,
you think how nice it would be to dive into a lake. If the
neural messages caused by your fantasized action were
as great as those evoked when you really intended to
dive, you would be likely to break your neck in your
resultant attempt to dive off the desk. While we dream,
our muscles are actively inhibited from moving by the
REM process through a different neural pathway than the
one that transmits directions to act. The neural messages
to our muscles in dreams can be as strong as they are
when we are awake. The evidence for the presence of
intact, full-strength messages from the brain to the muscles in REM sleep comes from studies with cats. French
researcher Michel Jouvet blocked the process that causes
muscular paralysis during REM in cats. He found that
the cats then moved around in REM, as if they were
acting out their dreams.[6]

Thus, lucid dreaming may be more powerful than waking mental imagery for motor skill enhancement not only
because of the vividness of the imagery, but also because
the physiological nature of REM sleep is ideal for estab-
lishing neural patterns without actual movement. Through
imagery, or lucid dreaming, athletes could even practice
performing movements for which their bodies are not yet

physically prepared, setting up neural and mental models for skills; this way the movement models will be ready when the muscles are.

Another basis for the usefulness of mental practice is the idea of "cognitive coding." More complicated skills require the construction of a conscious map of the skill in addition to the establishment of the neural pathways that facilitate a movement. This is called *symbolic learning*.[7] Symbolic learning theory proposes that imagery rehearsal can help you to codify the sequence of movements involved in your skill. For example, a swimmer might codify the correct sequence for optimally performing the breaststroke by thinking "pull, breathe, kick, pull, breathe, kick . . ." Using imagery, you can set up symbols in your mind before going through the actual motions—when so much of your energy may be required to perform the action correctly that you may not be able to simultaneously analyze its structure. Lucid dreams could easily be used for this purpose, again because of the vividness of dreamed experience.

Improving Physical Skills in Lucid Dreams

At the age of ten I became the proud owner of a real Shetland pony for about a year. One little chore that simply defeated me was trying to cinch up the girthstrap on a saddle. (It is equivalent to learning how to tie a man's necktie.) One night I realized I was dreaming and dreamed that I was trying to learn this art, and in the dream I studied the configurations involved and "saw" how to do it. The next day, I walked out to the barn and went straight to the saddle and cinched it exactly as I had learned the night before. Perfectly. (K.A., Portland, Oregon)

* * *

As we mentioned earlier, researcher Paul Tholey, a sports psychologist, has done pioneering work investigating the use of lucid dreaming for skill training in sports.[8] Tholey provides several suggestions on how lucid dreamers can use their dreams to work on motor skills.

He asserts that "sensory-motor skills which have already been mastered in their rough outlines can be optimized by using lucid dreams." If you more or less know how to swing a bat, jump over a hurdle, or juggle three balls, then lucid dream practice can help you learn to do it better.

Furthermore, Tholey proposes that new sensorimotor skills can be learned using lucid dreaming. He cites the experience of a skier as an example:

Jetting, with its strong shift of the center of gravity backwards, had always made me so afraid that I constantly fell and came home to the cabin covered with bruises. When I learned lucid dreaming that following summer I began to dream about skiing over moguls. I often used the hump to initiate a flying experience, but at some point I also began to lean back shortly before the hump, thereby taking my weight off the skis in order to change direction with my heels. That was a lot of fun and after a few weeks it became clear to me during lucid dreaming that my movements corresponded to jetting. When I went on a skiing vacation again the following winter and took a course, I mastered jetting in one week. I am absolutely convinced that it was connected to my summer-night exercises.[9]

In another example, Tholey quotes a martial arts practitioner who found it difficult to retrain himself in the soft style of aikido after years of hard-style karate:

* * *

On this particular evening, after still not succeeding in wearing down the attacker and taking him to the mat, I went to bed somewhat disheartened. While falling asleep the situation ran through my mind time and again. While defending myself, the correct balancing movement collided with my inner-impulse to execute a hard defensive block so that I repeatedly ended up unprotected and standing there like a question mark . . . a ridiculous and unworthy situation for the wearer of a black belt. During a dream that night, I fell down hard one time instead of rolling away. That day I had made up my mind to ask myself the critical question in this situation: "Am I awake or am I dreaming?" I was immediately lucid. . . . I went to my Dojo, where I began an unsupervised training session on defense techniques with my dream partner. Time and time again I went through the exercise in a loose and effortless way. It went better every time.

The next evening I went to bed full of expectations. I again reached a state of lucid dreaming and practiced further. That's the way it went the whole week until the formal training period started up again. Even though I was totally relaxed, I amazed my instructor with an almost perfect defense. And even though we speeded up the tempo I didn't make any serious mistakes. From then on I learned quickly and had received my own training license after one year.[10]

According to Tholey, once a technique or skill has been learned, lucid dreaming can be used to perfect routines before performance. In addition, he suggests that athletes, especially those involved in risk-taking sports, should go a step beyond practicing optimal actions in lucid dreams and work on acquiring flexibility of action in the face of unusual or stressful situations. We will discuss the idea of the benefits of mental flexibility in more detail in chapter 11.

Tholey further hypothesizes that lucid dreaming can affect performance by improving the psychological state of the athlete: "By changing the personality structure, lucid dreaming can lead to improved performance and a higher level of creativity in sport."[11] The key change, in Tholey's opinion, is from an "ego-centered personal outlook," which he feels leads to a distortion of perception, to a more flexible, responsive, "situation-oriented personal outlook." The skier who is thinking about beating an opponent is more likely to lose his balance when he hits an unseen bump than the skier who has learned to relax, pay attention to the terrain, and react fluidly to the unexpected. Tholey remarks that this shift from ego-centered to situation-centered outlook is applicable to the life beyond sports.

EXERCISE: LUCID DREAM WORKOUT

1. Set your intention before going to bed

During the day and in the evening before bedtime, think about the skill you would like to practice in your lucid dreams. Or actually practice it during the day, and notice the problems you need to work on. Think about what it would feel like to do it exactly right. If you can, study the performances of experts or masters in your skill. While practicing, thinking, or studying, remind yourself that you want to practice in a lucid dream tonight.

2. Induce a lucid dream

Use your favorite lucid dream induction technique (see chapters 3 and 4) to stimulate a lucid dream. While practicing the technique, visualize yourself becoming lucid, and see yourself practicing your sport or skill. You can also use the lucid dream incubation technique (page 158) to induce a lucid dream about working out.

3. Set up your practice environment

When you are in a lucid dream, first make sure you are set up to practice. If you need to change your environ-

(exercise continues)

---

ment, do so—travel to the gym or field, or create one around you. However, remember that you may not need to go to a special place just because you ordinarily do while awake. You can dance on a rooftop as well as in a studio.

4. Practice, aiming for the best

Practice! Each moment you execute your skill, concentrate on achieving perfection. Recall how it looks when a master does your skill, and try to duplicate what that would feel like as you do it. Lucid dream practice is ideal for working on the feel of the skill, how it all fits together, and performing it smoothly.

5. Push the boundaries of your potential

In a lucid dream you can go beyond what you know you can do. When you have felt what it is like to perform the skills you know perfectly, try out more advanced skills, even things you have never tried before. Remember that you cannot hurt yourself by straining muscles, getting overtired, or making an error of judgment, because your muscles aren't actually moving. You may be able to get the feeling of a new skill in your dream, and this will prepare you to learn it faster when you are awake.

Rehearsal for Living

I have called a meeting in a conference room. Present are big shots and team colleagues of mine. I am moderating this meeting, and at the same time I am an observer. The scene is undisturbed by my omnipresence. As an observer I can watch each person's expressions, detect interpersonal nuances, read each person's thoughts. I make sure I never interfere with their free will, I want to know what their reactions are to what the moderator (me again) has to say. As an observer I can freeze the proceedings and zoom in on an individual and read his thoughts. As an observer I can wipe out from everyone's memory one presentation or words from the moderator and start over with a new opinion.

This can go on indefinitely. Usually it serves me as a rehearsal for a meeting I'll have the next day or in a few days. It also gives me an indication of what someone may ask (so I can do research in advance) or where loose logic needs to be strengthened. (M.C., West Chazy, New York)

As a teen I would make myself dream how I would act the next day in school or any social activities. I won my first tennis tournament the night before in my dream. I also dreamed myself through several college interviews before actually going through one. After nursing school, I dreamed how I would manage a cardiac arrest and most any stressful new thing in my career. I can make myself dream just about anything that I need to "practice" before doing it. (C.A., Jacksonville, Florida)

Before I went to sleep, I was mulling over ways in which I could present my internship experience to my classmates. While dreaming, and knowing I was dreaming, I wheeled a cart of stuff into the classroom, set it up, and did a wonderful presentation. I saw overheads outlining my talk, slides, posters—everything I would need. When I woke up it was very clear how I should organize and present the material, so I did, and it went beautifully. (M.K., Wildwood Crest, New Jersey)

These examples show that lucid dreaming can be used to rehearse for anything in life. Just as with sports, we can set up patterns of action and behavior in advance that allow us to perform more smoothly when the time comes for the actual event. We can rehearse specific anticipated performances, such as an oral exam, a dance routine, a meeting with an influential business associate, a surgical procedure, or a difficult discussion with a loved one.

The next section presents another application of lucid dream practice to your ability to perform.

Reducing Performance Anxiety

This dream helped me overcome an irrational fear. My dream began with me walking up a driveway toward a large white house. There were dozens of people with candles going in. I did not have a candle and I felt afraid I would be unable to enter. When I came up to the door I had to squeeze my way in. Inside the main room were hundreds of people. While standing in line I noticed a guitar. Although I could play, I was afraid nobody would like my music. In the back of my mind I realized I was dreaming and that it was okay to do what I wanted.

Since I had always wanted to play at a party, I went ahead and picked up the guitar. I was really amazed at how well I could play the music I wanted and I really enjoyed putting on my impromptu performance. Many of the people around me said to me how much they too enjoyed my songs. I felt as if a burden had been lifted. I then went through the crowd making friends. (J.W., Sacramento, California)

Learning a skill is sometimes not enough. Often, you must learn to perform in front of an audience. Most people are at least a little nervous about being in front of a group. Many are nearly paralyzed by the prospect of making a presentation at work or a speech at a testimonial dinner, or of appearing in a public athletic or artistic performance. We have received quite a few letters demonstrating that people can conquer this obstacle by rehearsing performances in dreams, where it is possible for them to let go of anxiety about the audience because they know it is not composed of real people. The next exercise will help you do this.

EXERCISE:
PLAYING TO THE DREAM AUDIENCE

1. Set your intention before going to bed

During the day, think about what you want to do in your lucid dream. If you can, practice your performance, your concerto, dance, batting, whatever. As you do so, remind yourself that you want to perform in front of an audience in your lucid dream tonight. If you can't practice, imagine your performance and see yourself performing in a lucid dream tonight.

2. Induce a lucid dream and go to your performance arena

Use your favorite lucid dream induction technique (see chapters 3 and 4) to produce a lucid dream. When you become lucid, go to the recital hall or athletic field or meeting room where your feared performance is to take place. Or use the lucid dream incubation technique (page 158) to create a dream about your performance. If you can't get yourself there in the dream, try to set yourself up to perform right where you are.

3. Accustom yourself to the audience

Look around at the people in the audience. If they look unfriendly, remember this is the result of expectations of disaster caused by your performance anxiety. Smile at the audience and welcome them. If you do this sincerely, they will almost certainly become friendly and appreciative. In any case, you don't need to fear their criticism or what they will think of you in the morning—after all, they won't be there. But in your lucid dream, they can help you perform to your utmost capacity.

4. Perform

Do your act, give your speech, play your piece, or whatever. Enjoy it!

(exercise continues)

Commentary:
If you do the above and still have difficulty with the idea of an audience, try this variation: Be alone in the performance arena. Concentrate on feeling relaxed and unpressured. Then think of the ideal nonthreatening person sitting in the back row—a trusted friend, or maybe yourself. Fill the back row with other nonthreatening persons. When the house is filled with an appreciative-looking audience personally created by you, pick up your cello or your tennis racket and play to your heart's content.

Increasing Self-Confidence in Dreams and Waking Life

I am working with my psychiatrist to become more assertive. In my lucid dreams I am always with a group of people in a room where everyone seems to be doing or saying exactly what they feel. I am usually sitting back, not saying much of anything, and feeling very badly inside. Suddenly, I realize that I am dreaming and I decide to change my behavior in the dream and say exactly what is on my mind. It's a little scary doing this because it is new for me, but at the same time it feels good and makes me feel clearer. I wake up from these dreams feeling especially good about myself. It shows me how it feels to act aggressively rather than passively. You can see how these dreams are allowing me to make progress in my therapy. (K.G., Charlotte, North Carolina)

The epiphany was a dream that confronted my insecurities and lack of confidence. Right after a friend of mine died, I had dropped out of a doctoral program and was convinced there wasn't anything I could do that was useful. In the dream, my friend (the one who had died) and

I went to another world to learn about flying. Everyone in this world was flying—animals, men, women. The landscape was very beautiful, serene, peaceful. My friend told me I should fly as well and I said that I couldn't, that this was "his world" and I couldn't fly because I wasn't dead. So he said, "No problem, you just have to create the solution." And then he took off and I turned to find a booth renting wings for 25 cents. I put the wings on and leaped off a cliff and was happily flying until I suddenly realized that it was ridiculous that a pair of cheap rented wings could sustain me. With that thought, I started plummeting to the ground, screaming. In that moment of panic I groped for some salvation and thought to myself, "But I was flying just a moment ago with these wings," and was easily aloft again.

This conflict between belief and disbelief, falling and flying, repeated two more times, until I realized this was a dream and that it was my belief that I could fly that enabled me to fly—not any artificial devices or other means of external support. And at that moment I also realized that this was true in my waking life as well. The dream experience instantly transposed itself into a gut feeling that if I believed in myself I could do anything.

The next week, I interviewed for a job. During the interview, I could see that the person thought I was wrong for the job, and I was about to give up when I thought about my lesson in self-confidence. I found myself saying positive things about my resourcefulness and commitment to hard work. I was hired and became a consultant, ironically, in a field I knew nothing about. My employer later told me she hired me because I seemed so positive and confident that she knew I could pick up the technical skills quickly. (A.T., San Francisco, California)

We tend to try only what we think we can do, which is generally less than we are capable of. Lucid dreaming provides us with one way of expanding our belief in our own potentials: we can safely test new behaviors while dreaming, and the increased self-confidence will make it easier to carry out the same behaviors in waking life.

Albert Bandura, an eminent psychologist at Stanford University, has proposed what he calls *social cognitive theory* to explain higher human functions in terms of reciprocal relationships between our behavior, our experience, and what goes on inside our heads.[12] Several aspects of Bandura's model can be useful to lucid dreamers, because they offer a clear explanation of why actions in dreams can have real effects on the dreamer's personality. According to Bandura, people learn to behave by observing the results of their own actions, and vicariously by observing the behaviors of others. Observed actions are then modeled in the mind, and the models are called up when they seem to apply to a new situation.

As we have seen, the observations we make of how things work in the waking world are projected onto dreams. However, in lucid dreams, since we know that we are not in the waking world, we are free to consciously create new models. We can test the results of new kinds of actions, both by ourselves and by other dream characters. And if we find that the new behaviors work well, we will add them to our repertoire of possible ways to respond.

For example, if you are usually a timid and shy person, in lucid dreams you can practice being open and assertive with dream characters. If you like the results, you will find it easier to do the same while awake. Even if the results of your dream experiments are not wholly positive, the practice will probably decrease the effort it takes to apply the new approach in waking life. You will learn that, even though an experience may not feel good at the time, you can handle it, and the end result may be an improvement in your overall situation in life.

Creating Positive Futures

As a further hint on how lucid dreams can help us plan our waking lives, consider this statement from Bandura: "Images of desirable future events tend to foster the behavior most likely to bring about their realization."[13] When we conceive of what we would like the future to bring, what we would like our lives to become, we are preparing ourselves to attain that future. The act of creating a concrete mental image in which we see ourselves as happy, or successful, reinforces our intentions to behave in ways that help us achieve the image in our heads. This is the basis of the innumerable self-help books and tapes on the market that instruct you to "see yourself as rich," or "visualize yourself being thin."

Lucid dreams, as extremely vivid mental images, are the perfect place to set up images of your future success. If you wish to lose weight, you can dream you are as thin and fit as you like, experience how it feels to be that way, and increase your motivation to achieve that state in waking life. Perhaps you want to stop smoking. In a lucid dream you could dream yourself as eighty years old and healthy, cheerily hiking up a mountainside without huffing and puffing. This future is not likely to come to pass if you continue to smoke, so if you enjoy the hike in the dream, you will be encouraged to break your addiction to cigarettes.

The happy futures you conjure in your lucid dreams can extend beyond your own success and pleasure. Perhaps the more people there are in the world who create potent images of peace and joy for all the inhabitants of Earth, the more likely we will be to survive the current crises of this planet and grow on to achieve the greatest potential of the human race.

Idries Shah refers to a closely related idea in the preface to his *Caravan of Dreams*:

In one of the best tales of the Arabian Nights, Maruf the Cobbler found himself daydreaming his own fabulous caravan of riches.

Destitute and almost friendless in an alien land, Maruf at first mentally conceived—and then described—an unbelievably valuable cargo on its way to him.

Instead of leading to exposure and disgrace, this idea was the foundation of his eventual success. The imagined caravan took shape, became real for a time—and arrived.

May your caravan of dreams, too, find its way to you.[14]

9

~~~~~~~~

Creative Problem
Solving

Creative Dreams

*I'm a department store manager in a home furnishings
store at a mall. In the housewares department we do a
lot of floor moves—moving fixtures, relocating mass dis-
plays of goods, etc. When the idea comes up between the
store manager, the display manager, and myself that the
floor needs some revamping, I go home, go to sleep, and
I will dream of being in the store by myself. I try doing
a floor move. I move fixtures around (always quickly in
the dream, just by a flick of my finger). I know that I'm
in the dream and I want to find the troublesome mer-
chandise that's always difficult to display and find a place
for it in my dream. I always remember these dreams.
Actually, it is a joke at work because it has happened
often. (J.Z., Lodi, New Jersey)*

*If I'm working on my car and try to repair something
complicated and finally at midnight find myself unable to
proceed, I give up and go to bed. I purposely dream about*

the problem and, knowing it to be a dream, try different approaches to solving the problem. Always before morning I find a way to do the job, and when I try it the next day, it works! It seems to me that concentrating on a problem holds me to "tunnel vision," while the dream state has unlimited dimensions. (J.R., Seattle, Washington)

In the fall of 1986, while I was taking chemistry, I began to solve problems while sleeping. The majority of these problems were molecular equations involving two compounds and 4–6 elements. I would realize that I was dreaming and proceed to work out the problem, breaking it down to an ionic equation. If you have done this type of problem, you can understand the difficulty involved. Every time I would be almost done with the problem, the scene would begin to fade and I would have to reinduce lucidity. I did this by shaking my head or spinning. After strengthening the lucid dream, I would have to rewrite the problem and do it again, only faster. Upon awakening, I would simply write it down and check it. My dream answers were correct 95 percent of the time. What was great about solving problems this way was that I usually woke up with a better understanding of the processes involved. I had about five dreams of this type a week. (K.D., Lauderhill, Florida)

Throughout recorded history, dreams have been regarded as a wellspring of inspiration in nearly every field of endeavor—literature, science, engineering, painting, music, and sports.

Well-known examples of dream-inspired figures from literature include Robert Louis Stevenson, who attributed many of his writings to dreams, including *The Strange Case of Dr. Jekyll and Mr. Hyde*; and Samuel Taylor Coleridge and his opium-dream poem, "Kubla Khan." In science there is Friedrich Kekulé's dream discovery of the structure of the benzene molecule, and Otto Loewi's dream-inspired experiment demonstrating the chemical mediation of nerve impulses. In the field of engineering, there are several instances of inventions revealed in dreams, including Elias Howe's sewing machine. Painters such as William Blake and Paul Klee have also attributed some of their works to dreams. Composers, including Mozart, Beethoven, Wagner, Tartini, and Saint-Saëns, have credited dreams as a source of inspiration. In sports, one of the most familiar cases is master golfer Jack Nicklaus, who claimed to have made a discovery in a dream that improved his game by ten strokes—overnight! These examples and those quoted at the beginning of this chapter should make clear the remarkable creative potential of dreams.[1]

Given that dreams are such fertile fields for inspiration, why is there not yet a school of dreaming in the Western world? The answer may lie in the fact that dreams are unpredictable. Though a great breakthrough may appear in a dream, rarely can an artist or thinker decide, "Tonight I will find the solution to my problem." Dream incubation techniques are one step toward deliberately accessing the creativity of dreams. Since the age of Egyptian civilization, people have used dream incubation to try to induce dreams about the problem they are trying to solve. A more efficient method, however, may be to seek answers to problems in *lucid* dreams. One can try to incubate a lucid dream on the problem, or once in a lucid dream intentionally turn one's will toward the question in mind. Instead of waiting for the muse to visit, the artist can call on her.

The examples above suggest a very wide range of potential applications, from car repairs to painting to mathematics. We believe you can learn from the experiences of others how to use the creative potential of your lucid dreams to solve problems and invoke inspiration. Once researchers have investigated creativity in dreams more thoroughly they should be able to give you more precise guidance in how to use your sleeping time to solve problems and be creative. Meanwhile here are some ideas.

The Creative Process

I discovered in high school that I was a lucid dreamer when I learned that I could study complicated mathematical and geometry problems before going to bed and discovered that I was able to solve the problems when I awakened.

This phenomenon followed me through college and medical school. When I was in medical school, I began to apply my sleep-solving abilities to medical problems, quickly running through the questions of the day and usually finding useful solutions or useful additional questions in the process (even today I will occasionally wake up at 3:00 in the morning and call the hospital to order a special laboratory test on a problem patient, the possible solution of which had occurred to me in a lucid dream).

At this point, the greatest use to which I have been able to put this facility is in the practice of surgery. Each night before retiring I review my list of surgical cases and I actually practice these cases in my sleep. I have gained a reputation for being a rapid and skilled surgeon with almost no major complications. This surgical "practice" has allowed me from the very beginning to constantly review the anatomy and to refine and polish technique by eliminating unnecessary motions. I am presently able to perform most major complex procedures in 35 percent to 40 percent of the time taken by most of my peers. (R.V., Aiken, South Carolina)

With both my husband and myself finishing college in May, we can now think about starting a family. Lately, I have been concerned with names for babies. During this latest lucid dream I talked with Robert, my husband, about names I liked. (Of course, he agreed with me on my favorite names because I wanted it that way.) I even dreamed that I borrowed a baby to try out the names. I took the baby to both sets of parents and reran the same scene over and over. "Mom and Dad, this is Chris." "Mom and Dad, this is Justin," etc. This went on and I watched for my parents' reaction to the names. Finally, I settled on a boy's and a girl's name. When I awakened, after having another dream, I couldn't remember the two names I had felt so good about during the earlier dream. I thought about it all day long, but couldn't remember them. That night I started another lucid dream and stopped it in the middle. I remembered that in the "name dream" I had told a girlfriend the two names, so I called her in the dream and asked her. She told me. I woke myself up immediately and said the names over and over out loud. Now I remember the names. (L.H., Hays, Kansas)

Creativity means different things to different people. Some people may find the word threatening, because we are often taught that creativity is a rare talent that only artists really know how to use. However, all creativity means is the use of the imagination to produce some new thing, from a work of art to a homework paper. We can't help being creative. The essence of creativity is the combination of old ideas or concepts into a new shape. Each sentence we speak, if it is not a direct quotation, is creative. How creative a thing or act is depends on the uniqueness of the use of the elements involved. What makes high creativity so elusive is that, in general, we do not know how to evoke the state of mind in which we can easily make new, unique, and useful associations between ideas. The key issue in creativity research is to discover a means of readily accessing such states of mind at will. Dreams can be a fabulous source of creativity. An introduction to what is currently known about the creative process will help you understand why.

There are degrees of creativity, just as there are of lucidity. Like the ability to solve problems, creativity is a universal human capacity. As explained earlier, this ability is not restricted to the fine arts or to any formal discipline; it can be applied to anything that can be done innovatively, imaginatively, flexibly, spontaneously.

Everybody is creative at one time or another, and some people are creative a lot of the time. As the psychotherapist Carl Rogers put it: "The action of the child inventing a new game with his playmates; Einstein formulating a theory of relativity; the housewife devising a new sauce for the meat; a young author writing his first novel; all of these are, in terms of our definition, creative. . . ."[2]

Creativity researchers agree that creative expression is a process. Inspirations often seem to appear suddenly, out of nowhere, in a flash of illumination. However, there is evidence that the "sudden" realization is only the part of the process that emerges above the threshold of awareness. While analyzing his own discoveries, the great nineteenth-century German scientist Hermann Helmholtz first described the stages of the creative process: saturation, incubation, and illumination.

In the saturation stage, problem solvers gather information and try different approaches without complete success. These preparations might consist of reading, talking to experts, observing, recording, photographing, or measuring. The problem solvers then think about the problem—concentrate, meditate, model it in their minds, review the research. This is the point at which the mechanic stares at an engine, the painter at a blank canvas, the writer at an empty page (or computer screen). At the end of this stage, the problem solver says to himself or herself, "Okay, I've studied the problem. I've thought about it. I've looked at it. Now, what's the answer?"

The next stage is to do nothing. Incubation begins when a problem solver gives up actively trying to solve the problem, handing it over to the realm of the unconscious. Many creative dreamers in the historical literature have decided at this point to take a nap. Other problem solvers have incubated their solutions while taking a drive or a long walk. If they have studied enough, analyzing the right aspects of the problem, and if they have fostered the right psychological conditions for the emergence of a creative solution, the incubation phase will then give birth to illumination: "Eureka!"—the sudden arrival of the solution. This is the time of the switching on of the proverbial light bulb.

A good example of illumination in a dream, born out by verification while awake, comes from Nobel Prize winner Otto Loewi. As the physiologist recounted the story, he had a hunch early in his career about the nature of the nerve impulse but forgot about the idea for seventeen years, because he couldn't think of an experiment to test his hypothesis. Nearly two decades later, he had a dream which presented him with the method of successfully testing his theory. According to Loewi's account:

> I awoke, turned on the light, and jotted down a few notes on a tiny slip of thin paper. Then I fell asleep again. It occurred to me at six o'clock in the morning that during the night I had written down something important, but I was unable to decipher the scrawl. The next night, at three o'clock, the idea returned. It was the design of an experiment to determine whether or not the hypothesis of chemical transmission that I had uttered seventeen years ago was correct. I got up immediately, went to the laboratory, and performed a simple experiment on a frog's heart according to the nocturnal design.[3]

Loewi eventually won the Nobel Prize for proving that chemicals assist in the transmission of information through neurons.

States of Mind and Creativity

The above discussion of the creative process, while noting that the illumination would come if the thinker had fostered the right psychological conditions for creativity, left open the question of what those conditions might be. A few researchers have made a start on this question by exploring the notion that different kinds of knowledge seem to be accessible from different states of consciousness.

Elmer and Alyce Green, biofeedback researchers at the Menninger Foundation, examined physiological aspects of the relationship between creativity and conscious states. By measuring the bodily processes of people involved in the different stages of creative problem solving, the Greens were able to make strong correlations between the illumination phase and at least one physiologically distinguishable state of consciousness.

They wrote:

> The entrance, or key, to all these inner processes [is] a particular state of consciousness in which the gap between conscious and unconscious processes is voluntarily narrowed, and temporarily eliminated when useful. When that self-regulated reverie is established, the body can apparently be programmed at will, and the instructions given will be carried out, emotional states can be dispassionately examined, accepted or rejected, or totally supplanted by others deemed more useful, and problems insoluble in the normal state of consciousness can be elegantly resolved.[4]

The state of consciousness the Greens refer to is not lucid dreaming but the hypnagogic or reverie state. Nevertheless, their conclusions would seem to apply even more precisely to the lucid dreaming state, in which the conscious and unconscious minds meet face to face.

Carl Rogers also looked at the relationship between creativity and psychological states. In *On Becoming a Person*, he proposed that three psychological traits are especially conducive to creativity.[5] The first trait, openness to experience, is the opposite of psychological defensiveness, or rigidity about concepts, beliefs, perceptions, and hypotheses. It implies tolerance of ambiguity and the ability to process conflicting information without finding it necessary to either believe or disbelieve it. As you have seen, the very act of becoming lucid in a dream requires the ability to process the conflicting, ambiguous, and often improbable information presented by the dream flexibly enough to come to the unusual conclusion that your experience in the dream is illusory. So, once you have succeeded in become lucid, the trait of openness to experience is already prepared for you.

The second trait is possessing an internal source of evaluation. This means that the value of the creative person's product is established not by the praise or criticism of others, but by the individual. This could be nowhere more true than in the lucid dream, where the dreamer is responsible for creating and evaluating the entire experience.

The final trait postulated to be conducive to creativity by Rogers is the ability to toy with elements and concepts, to play spontaneously with ideas, colors, words, relationships—to juggle elements into impossible juxtapositions, propose wild theories, explore the illogical. Because lucid dreamers have the potential to do anything in their dreams, lucid dreams could be the ideal experimental workshop. Furthermore, as we will discuss in the next section, the tools available in that workshop may be far more versatile than those we are familiar with in the waking world.

Tacit Knowledge

The most important idea behind our belief that lucid dreaming can help boost the illumination phase of the creative process is the concept of "tacit" knowledge. The things you know that you know and can spell out explicitly, such as your street address or how to tie your shoe, are called "explicit" knowledge. Tacit knowledge, on the other hand, includes what you know but can't explain (how to walk or talk), and what you know but don't think you do (say, the color of your first-grade teacher's eyes). This latter form of knowing is demonstrated by recognition tests in which individuals think they are only guessing but in fact do better than chance would allow.

Of the two kinds of knowledge, the tacit variety is by far the more extensive: we know more than we realize. In dreams we have greater contact with our tacit knowledge than we do while awake. If you remember your dreams, you can surely recall having had one in which the likeness of a person whom you have met only once was reproduced with amazing detail in comparison to any description you could have made of him or her while awake. The explanation for this phenomenon is our access to tacit knowledge in dreams. In dreams we have conscious access to the contents of our unconscious minds. Therefore, in our dreams we are not limited, as we are while awake, to working with only that tiny portion of our accumulated experience to which we normally have conscious access.

Without lucidity, it seems we have no way to determine when, or even if, a creative dream might occur. However, through lucid dreaming we may be able to bring the extraordinary creativity of the dream state under conscious control. Consider this next example, in which an oneironaut managed to find a specific piece of tacit knowledge in the form of a book. In this instance, the dreamer did not find the specific solution in the dreamed book, but upon awakening he did find it in the real book. The knowledge discovered in this case was that this book contained a clue to the problem—a good example of something you can know without knowing you do:

I recently pulled second place in a math competition. When I received a copy of the problems (five in all), I spent most of the day mulling over various approaches. When I went to sleep that night, I dreamed lucidly of looking through a particular math reference book I own. I don't think I dreamed of reading anything in particular in the book, just the act of flipping through it. Subjectively, the dream was only a couple of seconds long. When I woke, I didn't have an opportunity to look through the book until that evening. When I did, I discovered the trick I needed to solve one of the problems. (T.D., Clarksville, Tennessee)

Mental Modeling

If our hypotheses about creativity in dreams are true— that lucid dreams permit deliberate access to a wide store of knowledge, and that dreams themselves are conducive to creativity—then how can a lucid dreamer make use of this potential? For a hint, take another look at the examples of lucid dreams quoted at the beginning of this chapter. The floor manager dreamed of a dream model of the store, filled with the items to be displayed. The person who solved automobile repair problems did so by bringing the elements of the problem into his dream and manipulating them until a solution emerged. The chemistry student simply continued working on problems as he would while awake.

The following letter is an example of another kind of mental model building, in which the lucid dreamer was able to model a highly abstract concept (note that the dreamer had already been through the preparation and incubation phases):

A little over a year ago, I was in a linear algebra class that introduced me to vector spaces. I was having a lot of trouble understanding the topic on more than a superficial level. After about a week of serious studying, I had a lucid dream about an abstract vector space. I perceived directly a four-dimensional space. The dream did not have a visual component, but such abstract dreams are not uncommon for me. The best I can describe that dream is to say that I perceived four coordinate axes that were mutually perpendicular. Since that night, both math and dreaming have been more fun for me, and I've had relatively little trouble understanding vector space calculus. (T.D., Clarksville, Tennessee)

A computer programmer uses her mind's logical processes to model the function of her programs while lucid:

I have had programs to write for a class and before I write them on the computer, I test my way of solving the program during a lucid dream. I have found that many of my ideas wouldn't work, or needed something additional. This has saved me many hours of programming outside of class. I actually "run" my programs in my mind before I ever sit down at the computer. (L.H., Hays, Kansas)

The use of lucid dreams to create mental models of problem situations is the basis of the exercises that follow. Mental modeling methods can also be useful to artists.

Fariba Bogzaran, artist and dream researcher, uses her lucid dreams to discover the subject of her forthcoming works. She becomes lucid anytime she enters an art gallery in her dreams. In her dream gallery she finds an art piece that she wishes to bring into the waking world. She carefully observes the medium, texture, and color of the piece. To ensure that she remembers her lucid dream and can later reproduce the artwork, she fixes her gaze on the art object until she awakens (as described in chapter 5). In 1987 she had a lucid dream that inspired her to learn paper marbling:

I am in an art studio teaching a class. One of the students calls me over to look at his work. As I approach, I become aware that I am dreaming. I stand still and look around the room. The art medium looks very unfamiliar to me. I see two water trays with different colors floating on top of the water. Next to the tray I see many small jars with a variety of colors in them. I take a closer look at the art work—close enough to touch the paper. At this point I realize that this must be the marbling technique. . . .

I recorded the dream right away and made a sketch of the marbled paper which the student created in the dream. My curiosity about this medium led me on a search for a teacher who could instruct me in this beautiful art technique. . . . Thereafter, marbling became the medium for my self-expression. [6]

One of the most frequent problems we face in everyday life is decision making. Lucid dreaming can help us arrive at informed decisions, as in the following example:

I have been wrestling with the decision to buy a new, double-wide mobile home and then whether or not I should keep my old one and rent it out. That was what I had decided to do, after months of worry and thought.

Then, Sunday night I went to bed. I was asleep but I was awake (that sounded demented until I read your article). I was at a big table, kind of like a desk, there were papers before me and though I saw no one, someone answered my questions from over my shoulder . . . in my dream the problem was all laid out neatly and orderly, the pros and cons of my decisions were examined. I asked questions, I got answers. I woke up an hour after going to bed and knew what I was going to do about the entire problem. Not only was I sure of what I was going to do (buy a new home, and sell the old), but I was so comfortable with the decision! It was like I had talked to someone with great authority, someone who knew my needs, my insecurities and capabilities. (K.A., London, Arkansas)

Producing Creative Lucid Dreams

This discussion has mentioned two primary approaches to deliberately utilizing the creativity of dreams. One is to seek the answer to your problem once you are in a lucid dream. The other is to incubate a dream about the problem and include in your incubation a reminder to become lucid in the dream.

Lucidity, though not absolutely necessary for creative dreaming, offers important advantages. Once you learn how to have lucid dreams frequently, you can have a creative dream whenever you wish, just by acting on your desire to seek an answer or create in your next lucid dream. Of course, the age-old method of dream incubation may help you find answers in nonlucid dreams, but even here lucidity can help.

If you use incubation to stimulate a lucid dream about a particular topic, then your lucidity will give you the power to act freely and consciously, knowing you are dreaming. You could incubate a dream of visiting an expert on your difficulty or of a place you are thinking of moving to. Or with another kind of problem you could incubate a dream in which you try a new way of dealing with someone in your life. Being lucid in the dream allows you to reflect on exactly why you are there: to ask Einstein a question about physics, to explore San Francisco and see if you would like to live there, to look in libraries for stories to write, or to try being warm and supportive to your child instead of overcritical. Without lucidity, you might forget your purpose.

Another way lucidity can add to the usefulness of creative dreams is by ensuring that you are aware that you are dreaming and that you must be careful to do all you can to recall the dream upon awakening. In nonlucid dreams, even ones of great potential value, there is always a risk that you may forget. Fariba Bogzaran is able to use her intentional focusing technique, which brings her to full awakening with her art image clearly in mind, because she is aware that she is dreaming. The following exercises include an instruction to help you remember to awaken from your creative lucid dreams while your answer or inspiration is still vivid.

LUCID DREAM PROBLEM SOLVING

1. Phrase your question
Before going to bed, choose a problem you'd like to solve or a creative breakthrough you would like to make. Frame your problem in the form of a single question. For example, "Which investments should I make?" or "What will be the theme of my short story?" or "How can I meet interesting people?" Once you've selected a problem question, write it down and memorize it.

(exercise continues)

2. Incubate a dream about your problem

Use the lucid dream incubation technique (page 158) to try to evoke a dream about your question.

3. Use your lucid dream to generate solutions

Once in a lucid dream, ask the question and seek the solution to your problem. Even if you became lucid in a dream that doesn't exactly address your problem, you can still seek the answer. You can look for or conjure up the person or place you need, or seek your solution where you are. It may help to question other dream characters, especially if they represent people who you think might know the answer. For example, if you were trying to solve a physics problem, Albert Einstein might be a good person to ask in your dream. To visit an expert advisor, try using the spinning a new dream scene exercise (page 161). Or simply explore your dream world with your question in mind, while remaining openly receptive to any clues that may suggest an answer. Remember that you unconsciously know many more things than you imagine; the solution to your problem may be among them.

4. Remember to awaken and recall the dream once you have an answer

When you obtain a satisfying answer in the dream, use one of the methods suggested in chapter 5 (or your own) to awaken yourself. Immediately write down at least the part of the dream that includes your solution. Even if you don't think the lucid dream has answered your question, once it begins to fade awaken yourself and write down the dream. You may find on reflection that your answer was hidden in the dream and you did not see it at the time.

Building a Lucid Dream Workshop

I do this frequently. I have a certain computer program to design. At night I will dream that I am sitting in a parlor (an old-fashioned one that Sherlock Holmes might use). I'm sitting with Einstein, white bushy hair—in the flesh. He and I are good friends. We talk about the program, start to do some flowcharts on a blackboard. Once we think we've come up with a good one, we laugh. Einstein says, "Well, the rest is history." Einstein excuses himself to go to bed. I sit in his recliner and doodle some code in a notepad. Then the code is all done. I look at it and say to myself, "I want to remember this flowchart when I wake up." I concentrate very hard on the blackboard and the notepad. Then I wake up. It is usually around 3:30 A.M. I get my flashlight (which is under my pillow), get my pencil and notepad (next to my bed), and start writing as fast as I can. I take this to work and usually it is 99 percent accurate. (M.C., West Chazy, New York)

It might be possible to build a mental model not of a specific problem, but of a workshop for solving all manner of problems or stimulating creative breakthroughs. We've already seen evidence for the potential of this approach in the lucid dream garage implied by the mechanic, in the parlor equipped with Albert Einstein and blackboard used by the computer programmer, and in other creative dreams in which the lucid dreamer created tools and situations applicable to the problem.

Remember the fairy tale about the cobbler and the elves who did his work while he was sleeping? At least one well-known man of letters, the writer Robert Louis Stevenson, created his own dream workshop replete with assistants—his "brownies," as he called them, who helped him produce many of his most famous works. Stevenson remarks on his dream helpers:

The more I think of it, the more I am moved to press upon the world my question: Who are the Little People? They are near connections of the dreamer's beyond doubt; they share in his financial worries and have an eye to the bankbook . . . they have plainly learned like him to build the scheme of a considerable story and to arrange emotion in progressive order; only I think they have more talent; and one thing is beyond doubt, they can tell him a story piece by piece, like a serial, and keep him all the while in ignorance of where they aim. Who are they then? And who is the dreamer?[7]

Stevenson was not explicit about whether his brownies were characters of lucid dreams. It appears from his reports that they were mental images that appeared during lucid hypnagogic reverie. The technique the writer used was to lie in bed with his forearm perpendicular to the mattress. He found that he could drift easily into his familiar fantasy workshop, and if he fell into a deeper sleep, his forearm would fall to the mattress and awaken him. Stevenson credited his brownies with coming up with the plot for his famous story, *The Strange Case of Dr. Jekyll and Mr. Hyde*.

EXERCISE:
BUILDING A LUCID DREAM WORKSHOP

Here are some ideas for building a lucid dream workshop of your own. You will need an inspiring environment, gifted helpers, powerful tools. The first step is to create the environment. If you feel you need magnificent surroundings, you can create them. If the atmosphere you seek is that of a starving artist in a garret, so be it. If you are a computer programmer, you can seat yourself at your ultimate "dream computer." You can create a "fortress of solitude" on an uninhabited planet or surround yourself with companions. Give your rooms doors and windows into other dimensions where help might be found. After initially creating your workspace in a lucid dream, each time you visit it you can add finishing touches: put treasure chests, reference libraries, or workbenches into your structure—whatever you might possibly need to inspire and empower your creative work.

When you are satisfied with your environment, enlist helpers—experts, teachers, assistants, wizards, consultants, muses, galactic councils. If you want to learn to paint, summon Rembrandt. Go fishing with Hemingway or Hesse and talk about that novel you've always wanted to write. Ask your helpers to get you started on your specific problem or creative challenge. Build or conjure tools—an idea machine, or a magical paintbrush.

If this exercise works for you, don't forget to return to your workshop every once in a while. Your mental model will grow increasingly capable of empowering your creativity. The more problems you solve there, the more inspirations you find there, the more power the workshop will have for you.

10

Overcoming Nightmares

What are Nightmares?

I began to try to recognize my dreams as products of my mind, even as I dreamed them. The breakthrough came one night soon after a nightmare. I decided I could not live fully while I let my fears roam about on their own power, so to speak. I entered the dream state determined not to yield. I had read somewhere that a fear could only be dissipated by friendliness and trust. Anger, threats, aggressiveness were out. These reactions were actually fearful reactions. So I made up my mind to be friendly.

The dream evolved, and I barely had time to remind myself to smile before the nightmare began. This time it was an almost childish nightmare, in which my collective fears took the shape of a large, nebulous but very scary monster. I quailed and almost turned tail, but by sheer will (I was really scared) I stayed and let it approach. I said to myself "it's my dream, and if I forget this, I'll have to go through it again," and I smiled as sincerely as I could. What's more, I spoke as calmly as I could, a big step since waking or sleeping terror leaves me speech-less. I said something like "I'm not afraid. I want to be friends. You're welcome to my dream!" and almost as soon as I said it, the monster became friendly, delight-edly so. I was ecstatic. Needless to say, I awoke quickly, still saying "I did it!" (T.Z., Fresno, California)

I know that I can change a frightening situation in a lucid dream, so I don't let myself get scared or panic. I never run away from things or persons in my dreams anymore. And the strange thing is that in waking life I don't run away either, anymore. I face things head on and don't drag situations out forever. My lucid dreams have changed the way I look at life. People think I've changed through the years, but the fact is that this is the real me coming out. (V.F., Greensboro, North Carolina)

Nightmares are terrifying dreams in which our worst fears are brought to life in fully convincing detail. Whatever horrors you personally believe to be the worst things that could happen, these are the most likely subjects of your nightmares. All people, in every age and culture, have suffered from these terrors of the night. People's under-standing of the origins of nightmares has varied as much as their understanding of dreams. In some cultures, nightmares have been the true experiences of the soul wandering another world as the body slept. To others, they have been the result of the visitation of demons. Indeed, the word *nightmare* comes from the Anglo-Saxon *mare*, for goblin or incubus. (An incubus is a demon who comes in the night to steal the sexual favor of ladies; its female counterpart is the succubus.)

In Western culture today, most people are content to say of nightmares that they are "only dreams," meaning they are imaginary and of no consequence. Thus, when a business executive awakens with his heart pounding from a dream of being pursued by zombies through the jungle, he is grateful to be able to recite the comforting refrain, "Thank God, it was only a dream," get a glass of water, and return to bed. However, when just a few minutes before the stinking corpses with eyes like pits to hell were breathing down his neck, the executive had no doubts about their reality. The zombies may have been imaginary, but the terror was real. So, to lightly dismiss the real terror of horrific dreams as illusory is an error that leaves us with no choice but to submit ourselves again and again to the greatest fear we are likely to ever experience.

What gives nightmares their special terror? In dreams, anything is possible. This limitlessness can be wonderful, since it allows us to experience delights of fantasy and pleasure unachievable in waking life. However, turn over the stone, and anything you can imagine that you would *not* like to experience, however unlikely in waking, can happen as well.

In nightmares we are alone. The terrifying worlds we create in our minds are populated with our personal fears. We may dream that we are accompanied by friends, but if we doubt them they can just as easily turn into fiends. If we run from an ax-wielding maniac, he can find us no matter where we hide. If we stab a devil with a knife, he may not even notice, or the knife may turn to rubber. Our thoughts betray us; if we think, I only hope he doesn't have a gun—lo! he has a gun. It is no wonder we are grateful to return from nightmares to the relative sanity and peace of the waking world.

Thus, it is understandable that people who realize they must be dreaming in the midst of nightmares frequently choose to wake up. However, if you become fully lucid in a nightmare, you will realize that the nightmare can't really hurt you, and you don't need to "escape" it by awakening. You will remember that you are already safe in bed. It is better, as discussed below, to face and overcome the terror while remaining in the dream.

Nightmare Causes and Cures

Studies show that one-third to one-half of all adults experience occasional nightmares. A survey of college students found that almost three-quarters of a group of 300 had nightmares at least once a month. In another study, 5 percent of college freshmen reported having nightmares at least once a week.[1] If this rate applies to the general population, then we might find that more than ten million Americans are plagued by wholly realistic horrifying experiences every week!

Some factors that seem to contribute to nightmare frequency are illness (especially fever), stress (caused by such situations as the difficulties of adolescence, moving, and hard times at school or work), troubled relationships, and traumatic events, such as being mugged or experiencing a serious earthquake. Traumatic events can trigger a long-lasting series of recurrent nightmares.

Some drugs and medications can cause an increase in nightmares. The reason for this is that many drugs suppress REM sleep, producing a later effect of REM-rebound. If you go to sleep drunk, you may sleep quite soundly but dream little, until five or six hours into sleep. Then, the alcohol's effect has mostly worn off and your brain is prepared to make up for the lost REM time. As a result, you will dream more intensely than usual for the last few hours of your sleep time. The intensity is reflected in the emotionality of the dream, which often will be unpleasant.

There are a few drugs that seem to increase nightmares by increasing the activity of some part of the REM system. Among these are L-dopa, used in the treatment of Parkinson's disease, and beta blockers, used by people with some heart conditions. Since research has shown that lucid dreams tend to occur during periods of intense REM activity, I believe that drugs that cause nightmares may also facilitate lucid dreaming.[2] This is a topic I plan to research in years to come. I think that whether an intense REM period leads to dreams that are pleasantly exciting or terrifying depends on the attitude of the dreamer.

Thus, it is to the dreamer's attitude that I think we should look in seeking a treatment for nightmares. For example, people rarely experience nightmares in the sleep laboratory, because they have a feeling of being observed and cared for. Likewise, children who awaken from nightmares and crawl into bed with their parents feel safe from harm and thus are less likely to have more bad dreams.

I believe the best place to deal with unpleasant dreams is in their own context, in the dream world. We create our nightmares out of the raw material of our own fears. Fears are expectations—why would we fear something we thought would never happen? Expectations affect our waking lives, but even more so, they determine our dream lives. When in your waking life you walk down a dark street, you may fear that someone will threaten you. However, for some dark figure to actually leap out at you with a knife depends on there really being some knife-bearing thug hiding in an alley nearby waiting for a victim. On the contrary, if you *dream* of walking down a dark street, fearing attack, it is almost inevitable that you will be attacked, because you can readily imagine the desperate criminal waiting for you. But if you had not thought that the situation was dangerous, there would be no thug, and no attack. Your only real enemy in dreams is your own fear.

Most of us harbor some useless fears. Fear of speaking in public is a common example. In most cases, no harm will result from giving a speech, but this fact does not prevent many people from being as frightened of public speaking as they would be of a life-threatening situation. Likewise, to be afraid in a dream, while understandable, is unnecessary. Even when fear is useless, it is still quite unpleasant and can be debilitating. An obvious way to improve our lives is to rid ourselves of unnecessary fear. How is this done?

Research on behavior modification treatment for phobias shows that it is not enough for a person to know intellectually that the object of their fear is harmless. Snake phobics may ''know'' perfectly well that garter snakes are harmless, but they will still be afraid to handle one. The way to learn to overcome fear is to face it—to approach the fearsome object or situation little by little. Each time you encounter the feared thing without harm you learn by experience that it cannot hurt you. This is the kind of approach we propose for overcoming nightmares. Many anecdotes demonstrate that the approach is effective and can even be used by children.

None of our proposed treatments for nightmares require that you interpret the symbolism of the unpleasant images. Much fruitful work can be accomplished in dreams by working directly with the images. Waking analysis (or interpretation while in the dream) may help you understand the source of your anxieties but will not necessarily help you outgrow them. For instance, consider again the fear of snakes. The classical interpretation of snake phobia is that it is a disguised anxiety about sex, especially regarding the male member, and in fact most snake phobics are women. A much more plausible biological explanation is that humans come into the world prepared to learn to fear snakes, because avoiding venomous snakes has obvious survival value. However, providing this information doesn't cure the phobia. What does help, as mentioned above, is for the phobic to become accustomed to dealing with snakes. Likewise, dealing directly with dream fears, learning they cannot harm us, can help us to overcome them.

The Uses of Anxiety

According to Freud, nightmares were the result of masochistic wish fulfillment. The basis of this curious notion was Freud's unshakable conviction that every dream represented the fulfillment of a wish. "I do not know why the dream should not be as varied as thought during the waking state," wrote Freud, tongue-in-cheek. For his own part, he continued, "I should have nothing against it. . . . There is only a trifling obstacle in the way of this more convenient conception of the dream; it does not happen to reflect reality."[3] If for Freud, every dream was nothing but the fulfillment of a wish, the same thing must be true for nightmares: the victims of nightmares must secretly wish to be humiliated, tortured, or persecuted.

I do not see every dream as necessarily the expression of a wish; nor do I view nightmares as masochistic wish fulfillment but rather as the result of maladaptive reactions. The anxiety experienced in nightmares can be seen as an indication of the failure of the dreamer to respond effectively to the dream situation.

Anxiety arises when we encounter a fear-provoking situation against which our habitual patterns of behavior are useless. People who experience anxiety dreams need a new approach for coping with the situations represented in their dreams. This may not be easy to find if the dream results from unresolved conflicts which the dreamer does not want to face in waking life. In severe cases, it may be difficult to treat the nightmare without treating the personality that gave rise to it. But I believe that this qualification applies mainly to chronically maladjusted personalities.[4] For relatively normal people whose nightmares are not the result of serious personality problems, lucid dreams can be extremely helpful. However, if you are to benefit from our method of overcoming nightmares, you must be willing to take responsibility for your experiences in general and, in particular, for your dreams.

To illustrate how lucidity can help you work through anxiety-provoking situations, consider the following analogy. The nonlucid dreamer is like a small child who is terrified of the dark; the child really believes there are monsters there. The lucid dreamer would perhaps be like an older child—still afraid of the dark, yet no longer believing that there are really monsters out there. This child might be afraid, but he or she would know that there was nothing to be afraid of and could master the fear.

Anxiety results from the simultaneous occurrence of two conditions: one is fear in regard to some (possibly ill-defined) situation we find threatening; the other is an uncertainty about how to avoid an unfavorable outcome. In other words, we experience anxiety when we are afraid of something and have nothing in our behavioral repertoire to help us overcome or evade it. Anxiety may serve a biological function: it prompts us to scan our situations more carefully and reevaluate possible courses of action in search of an overlooked solution to the situation—in short, to become more conscious.[5]

When we experience anxiety in our dreams, the most adaptive response would be to become lucid and face the situation in a creative manner. In fact, anxiety seems to result spontaneously in lucidity fairly frequently (for example, in a quarter of the sixty-two lucid dreams I had in the first year of my records).[6] It may even be the case that anxiety in dreams would always lead to lucidity for people who are aware of this possibility. With practice, dream anxiety can become a reliable dreamsign, no more dangerous than a scarecrow, pointing to where you need to do some repair work. There is no cause for fear in dreams.

Facing the Nightmare

In the midst of a lucid dream I saw a series of gray-black pipes. Out of the largest pipe emerged a black widow [spider] about the size of a cat. As I watched this black widow, it grew larger and larger. However, as it was growing I was not the least bit afraid and I thought to myself "I am not afraid" and I made the black widow vanish. I was very proud of my achievement since I had always been terrified of black widows. The earliest nightmare I can remember was about a large black widow which I couldn't escape. For me, black widows were a very strong symbol of fear itself. (J.W., Sacramento, California)

About twenty-six years ago I realized that the monster in my nightmares couldn't really hurt me. I told it I wasn't afraid anymore and it changed into a toothless, whimpering witch and went away. Yesterday I read the article about your work in Parade *magazine, and last night the monster returned. This time, knowing I was dreaming, I enjoyed the intricacy of detail, changing from one revolting, menacing shape to another, second by second. I remember the black kitten you had described from one of your dreams and I told it to smile. I was stunned as I watched the bulging eyes recede, the snarling mouth try to relax into a smile. It didn't know how. The shark teeth changed into horse teeth and it beamed. It was the silliest damn thing I ever saw, and I woke up laughing my head off. I feel like a sixty-seven-year-old kid with a new toy.* (L.R., Jacksonville Beach, Florida)

"There is no cause for fear," wrote the Sufi teacher Jalaludin Rumi seven centuries ago. "It is imagination, blocking you as a wooden bolt holds the door. Burn that bar. . . ."[7] Fear of the unknown is worse than fear of the known, and this seems nowhere more true than in dreams. Thus, one of the most adaptive responses to an unpleasant dream situation is to face it, as can be seen in the following account of a series of nightmares experienced by the nineteenth-century lucid dream pioneer the Marquis d'Hervey de Saint-Denys:

I wasn't aware I was dreaming, and I thought I was being pursued by frightful monsters. I was fleeing through an endless series of interconnecting rooms, always experiencing difficulty in opening the dividing doors and closing them behind me, only to hear them opened again by my hideous pursuers, who uttered terrible cries as they came after me. I felt they were gaining on me. I awoke with a start, bathed in sweat.

. . . I was all the more affected on waking because, when this particular dream came upon me, I always lacked, through some curious twist of fate, that consciousness of my state that I so often had during my dreams. One night, however, when the dream returned for the fourth time, at the moment my persecutors were about to renew their pursuit, a feeling of the truth of the situation was suddenly awakened in my mind; and the desire to combat these illusions gave me the strength to overcome my instinctive terror. Instead of fleeing, and by what must indeed under the circumstances have been an effort of will, I leaned against the wall and resolved to contemplate with the closest attention the phantoms that I had so far only glimpsed rather than seen. The initial shock was, I confess, strong enough; such is the difficulty that the mind has in defending itself against an illusion that it fears. I fixed my eyes on my principal attacker, who somewhat resembled the grinning, bristling demons which are sculpted in cathedral porticos, and as the desire to observe gained the upper hand over my emotions, I saw the following: the fantastic monster had arrived within several feet of me, whistling and cavorting in a manner which, once it had

ceased to frighten me, appeared comic. I noted the claws on one of its paws, of which there were seven, very clearly outlined. The hairs of its eyebrows, a wound it appeared to have on its shoulder and innumerable other details combined in a picture of the greatest precision—one of the clearest visions I have had. Was it the memory of some Gothic bas-relief? In any case, my imagination added both movement and colour. The attention I had concentrated on this figure had caused its companions to disappear as if by magic. The figure itself seemed to slow down in its movements, lose its clarity and take on a wooly appearance, until it changed into a kind of floating bundle of rags, similar to the faded costumes that serve as a sign to shops selling disguises at carnival time. Several insignificant images appeared in succession, and then I awoke.[8]

That seemed to be the end of the marquis's nightmares. Paul Tholey also has reported that when the dream ego looks courageously and openly at hostile dream figures, the appearance of the figures often becomes less threatening.[9] On the other hand, when one attempts to force a dream figure to disappear, it may become more threatening, as in the following case of Scott Sparrow's:

I am standing in the hallway outside my room. It is night and hence dark where I stand. Dad comes in the front door. I tell him that I am there so as not to frighten him or provoke an attack. I am afraid for no apparent reason.

I look outside through the door and see a dark figure which appears to be a large animal. I point at it in fear. The animal, which is a huge black panther, comes through the doorway. I reach out to it with both hands, extremely afraid. Placing my hands on its head, I say, ''You're only a dream.'' But I am half pleading in my statement and cannot dispel my fear.

I pray for Jesus' presence and protection. But the fear is still with me as I awaken.[10]

Here the dreamer uses his lucidity to try to make his frightful image disappear. There is little difference between this and running from dream monsters. If, upon reflection, Sparrow had recognized that a dream panther could not hurt him, the thought alone should have dissipated his anxiety. Fear is your worst enemy in dreams; if you allow it to persist it will grow stronger and your self-confidence will diminish.

However, many novice lucid dreamers may at first tend to use their new powers to find more clever ways to escape their fears. This is because of our natural tendency to continue in our current frame of mind. If, in a dream in which you are fleeing from harm, you realize you are dreaming, you will still tend to continue escaping, even though you should now know that there is nothing to flee from. During the first six months of my personal record of lucid dreaming, I occasionally suffered from this sort of mental inertia until the following dream inspired a permanent change in my lucid dreaming behavior:

I was escaping down the side of a skyscraper, climbing like a lizard. It occurred to me that I could better escape by flying away, and as I did so, I realized that I was dreaming. By the time I reached the ground, the dream and my lucidity faded. The next thing I knew I was sitting in the audience of a lecture hall, privileged to be hearing Idries Shah (an eminent Sufi teacher) comment on my dream. "It was good that Stephen realized he was dreaming and could fly," Shah observed with a bemused tone, "but unfortunate that he didn't see that since it was a dream, there was no need to escape."

I would have had to be deaf not to get the message. After this dream lecture, I resolved to never use my lucidity to avoid unpleasant situations. But I wasn't going to be content to passively avoid conflicts by doing nothing. I made a firm resolution regarding my lucid dreaming behavior: anytime I realized I was dreaming, I was required to ask myself the following two questions: (1) Am I now or have I been running away from anything in the dream? (2) Is there now or has there been any conflict in the dream? If the answer was yes to either, then I was honor-bound to do everything I could to face whatever I was avoiding and to resolve any conflict. I have easily remembered this principle in almost every subsequent lucid dream and have attempted to resolve conflicts and face my fears whenever it was called for.

"Escaping" from a nightmare by awakening only removes you from the direct experience of the anxiety-provoking imagery. You may feel a certain relief, but like the prisoner who digs through his prison wall and finds himself in the cell next door, you haven't really escaped. Moreover, aware of it or not, you are left with an unresolved conflict that will doubtless come back to haunt you some other night. In addition, you may have an unpleasant and unhealthy emotional state with which to start your day.

If, on the other hand, you choose to stay in the nightmare rather than waking from it, you can resolve the conflict in a way that brings you increased self-confidence and improved mental health. Then when you wake up you will feel that you have freed some extra energy with which to begin your day with new confidence.

Lucid dreaming gives us the power to banish the terror of nightmares and at the same time to strengthen our courage—if we master our fear sufficiently to recognize our most disturbing images as our own creations and face them.

Sleep Paralysis

My first experience of this terror of being awake but not in control of my body was when I was young, sick with a fever, and in my mother's bedroom. I saw a black shadow pass the window, enter the room and try to take the covers off of me. Inside I was screaming and frantic, outside I knew that nothing was happening. I was dreadfully scared of people coming in through that window, and this somehow helped me realize that it was a black shadowy figure, not a person. I fought it off and woke up. In the past year I have had a repeat of that dream complete with the feeling of flesh on my shoulder—I was terrified. Also recently, in another such dream, something awful was trying to kill me. I remembered something my husband had told me he'd done in the same situation when he was dreaming, so I turned and faced the "thing," and essentially challenged it to go ahead and kill me, asserting that I was not afraid. I felt strongly that it could not hurt me if I put out my strength and began summoning up an image of goodness and purity (God) and praying. The "thing" was defeated and I woke up feeling very good. (K.S., Etobicoke, Ontario)

The experience of sleep paralysis can be terrifying, as in the example above. In a typical case, a person awakens, but then finds he cannot move. It may feel like a great weight is holding him down and making it difficult to breath. Hallucinations may appear, often loud buzzing noises, vibrations in the body, or people and threatening figures nearby. The dreamer may feel things touch his body, body distortions, or "electricity" running inside him. As the experience progresses, the surroundings may begin to change, or the person may feel he is leaving his body, either by floating up or by sinking through the bed. Quite often, the dreamer knows the experience is a dream but finds it very difficult to awaken.

The probable cause of sleep paralysis is that the mind awakens, but the body remains in the paralysis state of REM sleep. At first, the dreamer actually perceives the environment around him, but as the REM process takes over again, strange things begin to occur. Anxiety seems to be a natural concomitant of this physiological condition, and it is worsened by the dreamer's feeling that he is awake, his belief that these peculiar things are really happening, and the sensation of being unable to move. If the dreamer goes more completely into REM sleep, he loses the awareness of his body, which causes him to feel paralyzed. At this point, he may experience the sensation of "leaving his body," as his mental body image is freed from the constraints of perceptual input from his actual body.[11]

Sleep paralysis experiences are likely to be the cause of some of the strangest night phenomena, such as visitations by demons, incubi, and succubi, and out-of-body experiences. They don't need to be terrifying, however, if you reflect as they are happening that they are dreams and that none of the bizarre events are dangerous. People in these states commonly try to cry out for others to awaken them, or to force themselves to move in order to awaken. This usually only makes matters worse, however, since it increases their feelings of anxiety. Anxiety itself may help to perpetuate the condition. A better approach is to (1) remember it is a dream and therefore harmless, and (2) relax, and go with the experience. Adopt an attitude of intrepid curiosity. Dreams that proceed from paralysis experiences are often quite intense and wonderful.

Practicum for Overcoming Nightmares

I was on top of a mountain at the edge of a cliff. I seemed to be a prisoner of two guys who had a dog and a lion with them. I felt they were going to throw me off the cliff, so I rushed them and knocked the two guys off the cliff along with the lion, but I went over too, into the water. I was all right and now my hands were free. I swam to the side and started to climb up the mountain but the lion was in front of me and he was angry because I pushed him into the water. He would not let me up, so I tried to scare him by throwing water and rocks at him. He just got angrier. He started to get closer to me and I moved back into the water. He started to roar and jumped in after me, but I jumped to the rocks. Now I was on my back and knew I couldn't get away, so I faced him, and as he attacked I said, "Come on." I put my hands out and suddenly I realized I was dreaming. In mid-attack his expression changed from rage to friendly and playful. When he landed on me I hugged him, and we play wrestled and rolled. I kissed him and he licked me. I felt really great that I was lucid and playing with a lion. Then he rolled over and turned into a naked black woman. She was beautiful with large nipples on her breasts. I started to play with her, and was getting excited, but I had this feeling that getting back to the top of the cliff was more important, so I said, let's go back. As we started I woke up. (D.T., Lindenwold, New Jersey)

I had a fear of death but cured it through a lucid dream. I was walking through a Hell-like environment and realized that this could not be, as I was asleep in my bed. At that instant, I was stabbed in the back. "Feeling" the pain, I decided to see what "dying" would be like. I felt myself in a catatonic state. I willed my dream "soul" to depart from my dream "body." It was a strange feeling to see my dream "body" beneath me. I also had a sense of all-pervading peace and calm. I said to myself that if this is what dying is like, it isn't so bad. From that day forward, I have had no fear of dying. I even remain calm in life-threatening situations. (K.D., Lauderhill, Florida)

* * *

Anyone who ever suffers from nightmares can benefit from using lucidity as a response to severe anxiety in dreams. Readers who have nightmares frequently will be able to put the advice we provide here to use right away. But others would do well to study these materials and have them ready in mind for the next time they find themselves in a frightening dream.

Several approaches to dealing with unpleasant dream experiences appear in dream literature. They can all be assisted by lucidity, because when lucid we are sure of our context (dreaming) and know that waking world rules don't apply. One of the first proposed systems for overcoming nightmares was that attributed to the Senoi people of Malaysia by Kilton Stewart in his paper "Dream Theory in Malaya."[12] Patricia Garfield brought Stewart's ideas to the public in her inspiring book *Creative Dreaming*.[13] The basic principle of the Senoi system is to confront and conquer danger. This means that if you encounter an attacker or an uncooperative dream figure, you should aggressively attack and subdue it. If necessary, you are advised to destroy the figure, and thereby release a positive force. Once you have subdued the dream figure, you must force it to give you a valuable gift—something you can use in your waking life. Another suggestion is that you enlist friendly and cooperative dream characters to help you overcome the threatening character.

People have reported positive, empowering results with the "confront and conquer" approach. However, as Paul Tholey has found, attacking unfriendly characters may not be the most productive way to handle them. The reason for this will be discussed in detail in chapter 11, but in brief, the idea is that hostile dream figures may represent aspects of our own personalities that we wish to disown. If we try to crush the symbolic appearances of these characteristics in dreams, we may be symbolically rejecting and attempting to destroy parts of ourselves.

Another idea associated with the Senoi is valuable to keep in mind regarding nightmares. Falling is a very common theme in anxiety dreams. The Senoi system proposes that when you dream of falling, you shouldn't wake yourself up but go with it, relax, and land gently. Think that you will land in a pleasant and interesting place, especially one that offers you a useful insight or experience. As a next step, it is suggested that in future dreams when you are falling, you should try to fly, and travel to somewhere intriguing and worthwhile. In this way, you can turn a frightening, negative experience into one that is fun and useful.

Tholey, who has researched the efficacy of various attitudes toward hostile dream characters, concludes that a conciliatory approach is most likely to result in a positive experience for the dreamer.[14] His conciliatory method is based on the practice of engaging in dialogues with dream characters (see the following exercise). He found that when dreamers tried to reconcile with hostile figures, the figures often transformed from "lower order into higher order creatures," meaning from beasts or mythological beings into humans, and that these transformations "often allowed the subjects to immediately understand the meaning of the dream." Furthermore, conciliatory behavior toward threatening figures would generally cause them to look and act in a more friendly manner. For example, Tholey himself dreamed:

I became lucid, while being chased by a tiger, and wanted to flee. I then pulled myself back together, stood my ground, and asked, "Who are you?" The tiger was taken aback but transformed into my father and answered, "I am your father and will now tell you what you are to do!" In contrast to my earlier dreams, I did not attempt to beat him but tried to get involved in a dialogue with him. I told him that he could not order me around. I rejected his threats and insults. On the other hand, I had to admit that some of my father's criticism was justified, and I decided to change my behavior accordingly. At that moment my father became friendly, and we shook hands. I asked him if he could help me, and he encouraged me to go my own way alone. My father then seemed to slip into my own body, and I remained alone in the dream.[15]

To have a good dream dialogue, you should treat the dream figure as being your equal, as in the example. The following questions may open up fruitful lines of dialogue with dream figures:

"Who are you?"
"Who am I?"
"Why are you here?"
"Why are you acting the way you are?"
"What do you have to tell me?"
"Why is such-and-such happening in this dream?"
"What do you think or feel about such and such?"
"What do you want from me? What do you want me to do?"
"What questions would you ask of me?"
"What do I most need to know?"
"Can you help me?"
"Can I help you?"

EXERCISE:
CONVERSING WITH DREAM CHARACTERS

1. Practice imaginary dialogues in the waking state
Choose a recent dream in which you had an unpleasant encounter with a dream figure. Visualize the character

(exercise continues)

before you and imagine yourself talking to the dream character. Begin a dialogue by asking questions. You may choose a question from the list above or substitute any personally relevant question. Write down your questions and the responses you get from the character. Try not to let critical thoughts interrupt the flow, such as "This is silly," or "I'm just making this up," or "That's not true." Listen, and interact. You can evaluate later. Terminate the dialogue when it runs out of energy or when you achieve a useful resolution. Then evaluate the conversation and ask yourself what you did right and what you would do differently next time. Once you are successful with this, try the same exercise on another dream.

2. Set your intention
Set a goal for yourself that the next time you have a disturbing encounter with a dream character you will become lucid and engage the character in dialogue.

3. Converse with problem dream figures
When you encounter anyone with whom you feel conflict, ask yourself whether or not you are dreaming. If you find that you *are* dreaming, continue as follows: Stay and face the character, and begin a dialogue with one of the opening questions from the list above. Listen to the character's responses, and try to address his, her, or its problems as well as your own. See if you can come to an agreement or make friends. Continue the dialogue until you reach a comfortable resolution. Then be sure to awaken while you still remember the conversation clearly, and write it down.

4. Evaluate the dialogue
Ask yourself if you achieved the best result you could. If you feel you did not, think about how you could improve your results next time. You can use Step 1 to relive the dialogue to attain a more satisfying result.

(Adapted from Kaplan-Williams[16] and Tholey.[17])

In contrast to the positive results of conciliatory dialogue, Tholey found that when dreamers attacked dream characters either verbally or physically, the dream figures often regressed in form, for instance, from a mother, to a witch, then to a beast. We might assume that the other characters in our dream worlds are more helpful as friendly humans than as subdued animals, so the aggressive approach may not be the best choice most of the time.

I say most of the time, because in some instances it may not be advisable to open yourself to a dream attacker. The circumstances that might make this true are in cases of dreams that replay real life events in which one was abused by someone—say, a rapist or child molester. In such cases, a more satisfying resolution may result from the Senoi approach of overcoming, destroying, and transforming the dream attacker. However, in many instances, Tholey's research has shown that aggressive attacks on dream characters can result in feelings of anxiety or guilt, and the subsequent emergence of dream "avengers." So, I would advise avoiding such behavior unless it truly seems to be the best option.

I have a few suggestions to add to these ideas for how to resolve nightmare situations. One is an extension of the "confront and conquer" approach. Though I cannot wholly recommend conquering dream characters, the intention to confront all danger in dreams is fully in accordance with my conception of a constructive dream life. Remember that nothing can hurt you in dreams, and consider if there is any reason why you should not allow yourself to experience the things you are trying to avoid in the dream. An excellent example of enduring the dreamed danger is provided by Patricia Garfield:

I was in a subway like the London tube system. I came to an escalator. The first three or four steps weren't going. I figured I had to walk up. After I got up the first few steps, I found that it was working. I looked up toward the top and saw all this yellow machinery above the escalator. I realized that if I kept on going, I would be smashed by the machinery. I became frightened, and started to wake up. Then I said to myself, "No, I have to keep on going. I have to face it. Patty says I can't wake up." My heart began pounding and my palms sweating as I was carried nearer and nearer. I said, "This is bad for my heart," but I kept on going. Nothing happened. Somehow I passed it and everything was all right.[18]

In another case, a woman dreamed that she was having difficulty avoiding being struck by cars as she crossed a busy street. As she had an unusually intense fear of traffic in waking life, upon becoming lucid she decided to directly confront her fear and leaped into the path of an oncoming pickup truck. She described that she felt the truck pass through her and then she, in an ethereal form, rose heavenwards, feeling elevated and amused.

This "let it happen to you" approach may not be best when dealing with dream characters, however. In Tholey's research, "Defenseless behavior almost always led to unpleasant experiences of fear or discouragement."[19] Hostile dream figures would tend to grow in size and strength relative to the dreamer. The reason for this may be that dream characters often are projections of aspects of our own personalities, and by giving in to their attacks, we may be allowing untransformed negative energies within us to overpower our better aspects.

Chapter 11 discusses this idea in greater depth and proposes another method for placating hostile dream figures: opening your heart and accepting them as part of yourself. This may not require any words at all and can have an astonishingly positive effect.

Prescriptions for Nightmares

The following is a list of some of the more common nightmare themes, with suggested methods of transforming the dream to achieve a positive outcome. Make yourself a goal that whenever you next find yourself in a nightmare, you will become lucid and overcome your fear. If the nightmare features one of the following themes, try the suggested responses.

THEME 1: BEING PURSUED
Response: Stop running. Turn to face the pursuer. This in itself may cause the pursuer to disappear or become harmless. If not, try starting a conciliatory dialogue with the character or animal.

THEME 2: BEING ATTACKED
Response: Don't give in meekly to the attack or flee. Show your readiness to defend yourself, then try to engage the attacker in a conciliatory dialogue. Alternatively, find acceptance and love in yourself and extend this toward the threatening figure (see chapter 11).

THEME 3: FALLING
Response: Relax and allow yourself to land. The old wives' tale is false—you will not really die if you hit the ground. Alternatively, you can transform falling into flying.

THEME 4: PARALYSIS
Response: When you feel trapped, stuck, or paralyzed, relax. Don't allow anxiety to overcome your rationality. Tell yourself you are dreaming and the dream will soon end. Let yourself go along with any images that appear or things that happen to your body. None of it will hurt you. Adopt an attitude of interest and curiosity about what happens.

THEME 5: BEING UNPREPARED FOR AN EXAMINATION OR SPEECH

Response: First of all, you don't need to continue with this theme at all. You can leave the exam or lecture room. However, you might enhance your self-confidence in such situations by creatively answering the test questions or giving a spontaneous talk on whatever topic suits you. Be sure to enjoy yourself. When you wake up, you may want to ask yourself whether you should actually prepare for a similar situation.

THEME 6: BEING NAKED IN PUBLIC

Response: Who cares in a dream? Have fun with the idea. Some find being naked in a lucid dream erotically exciting. If you wish, have everyone else in the dream remove their clothes. Remember, modesty is a public convention, and dreams are private experiences.

Recurrent Nightmares

After waking up from the nightmare, I would go back to sleep while thinking of a point in the dream before it went bad. I would go back to that point and redream the dream, changing it, re-creating it so that it would turn out well and end up as a good dream. (J.G., Kirkland, Washington)

From a friend I received the advice that to just "stand there" in a dream could change its course. At that time I was having frequent terrifying dreams. I would wake up screaming for help—thus ending the dream. And, of course, the overtones of helpless fear carried over into the day. So before I went to sleep I began to say to myself that whatever happened in my dreams, I was simply going to stand there and meet the danger and just see what the dream would do about that.

An example of what happened is the elevator dream. I was stuck in an elevator. It wouldn't go up or down and I couldn't get out. Finally, I climbed out the top and while I was on the roof of the elevator, it began to go up very quickly and I would have been crushed against the top of the elevator shaft. Instead of screaming for help, I simply responded as an observer and recognizing that this was a dream, I said to the dream that I was going to sit there on the elevator. "Now, how will you handle that?" The elevator stopped short of the top. No harm was done. Not only that, the dream was no longer out of control. Until that time the elevator dream had been recurring. It never returned. (V.W., Lincoln, Nebraska)

Since I was three years old, twice a month, I have had nightmares about tidal waves engulfing me; the details varied but the feeling was always the same: terror and helplessness. Until . . . in a half-awake state I determined to have a lucid dream about diving into a big wave. I did it! With my heart beating wildly, I ran toward the stormy sea, chanting that it's just a dream. I dove in headfirst. For a fearful moment I felt water in my lungs, but then began to enjoy the sensation of bobbing about in the powerful currents and waves . . . after several (very pleasant) minutes of this, I washed up on shore.

I had one other lucid dream about facing the wave and enjoying being underwater. Since then, I have had no more nightmares of tidal waves. (L.G., San Francisco, California)

When thinking about a nightmare becomes so painful that we avoid it, it is not surprising that it recurs. However, even the most terrible images become less frightening when we examine them. I believe Saint-Denys sheds light on the mechanism of recurrent nightmares in the following comment on his living gargoyle dream, quoted earlier in this chapter:

* * *

I don't know the origin of the dream. Probably some pathological cause brought it on the first time; but afterwards, when it was repeated on several occasions in the space of six weeks, it was clearly brought back solely by the impressions it had made on me and by my instinctive fear of seeing it again. If I happened, when dreaming, to find myself in a closed room, the memory of this horrible dream was immediately revived; I would glance towards the door, the thought of what I was afraid of seeing was enough to produce the sudden appearance of the same terrors, in the same form as before. [20]

I believe nightmares become recurrent by the following process: in the first place, the dreamer awakens from a nightmare in a state of intense anxiety and fear; naturally, he or she hopes that it will never happen again. The wish to avoid at all costs the events of the nightmare ensures that they will be remembered. Later, something in the person's waking life associated with the original dream causes the person to dream about a situation similar to the original nightmare. The dreamer recognizes, perhaps unconsciously, the similarity and expects the same thing to happen. Thus, expectation causes the dream to follow the first plot, and the more the dream recurs, the more likely it is to recur in the same form. Looking at recurrent nightmares in this way suggests a simple treatment: the dreamer can imagine a new conclusion for the dream to weaken the expectation that it has only one possible outcome.

Veteran dreamworker Strephon Kaplan-Williams describes a technique for redreaming the end of a nightmare; he calls it "dream reentry." The technique can be practiced with any dream that you feel unsatisfied with the outcome of, but it seems especially apt for recurrent nightmares, in which you are stuck time after time with the same set of disturbing events.

Dream reentry is practiced in the waking state. People begin by selecting dreams to relive, then come up with alternative ways of acting in the dreams to influence the progression of the events toward more favorable or useful outcomes. They relive the dream in imagination, incorporating the new action, and continue to visualize being in the dream until they see the result of their alternative behavior. Kaplan-Williams offers an example of dream reentry from his own experience. He had dreamed: "I am in this house and there is something scary to confront. I don't want to do it and am all alone. I'm quite afraid. I wake up." He resolves to reenter the dream and face the fear. In this case, he actually fell asleep as he was practicing the reentry process, which added to the intensity of his experience:

This time I make myself enter the bathroom where the source of my fears seems to be. I am afraid, so afraid that the flow of images stops. But through sheer will I make myself enter the bathroom ready for anything. I think of taking my machete and thrashing around with it if I am attacked. But I decide against this because I want to confront my fear by willing myself to stay with the situation no matter what. . . . I am ready to face that which could overwhelm me and exist with it rather than try to defeat it.

. . . When I do [enter the bathroom], there seems to be a hulking luminescent figure there. It does not attack me but changes into a dwarf-like figure, long arms, roundish head, like Yoda. We face each other. I have stayed with the situation. No attack comes. My fear goes away when I experience what is there behind the door, and has been there so many years going back to childhood. What has been there behind every door and scary place is fear itself and my inability to fully deal with it.[21]

* * *

Several years ago, I used a similar approach with someone suffering from recurrent nightmares. A man telephoned me asking for help. He feared going to sleep, because he might have "that terrible dream" again. In his dream, he told me, he would find himself in a room in which the walls were closing in, threatening to crush him. He would desperately try to open the door, which would always be locked.

I asked him to imagine he was back in the dream, knowing it was a dream. What else could he do? At first he was unable to think of anything else that could possibly happen, so I modeled what I was asking him to do. I imagined I was in the same dream and I visualized the walls closing in. However, the moment I found the door locked, it occurred to me to reach into my pocket where I found the key, with which I unlocked the door and walked out. I recounted my imaginal solution and asked him to try again. He imagined the dream again—this time he looked around the room and noticed that there was no ceiling and climbed out.

I suggested to him that if this dream should ever recur, he could recognize it as a dream and remember his solution. I asked him to call me if the dream came back, but he never did. Unfortunately, we cannot be sure about what happened. But I think that having found some way to cope with that particular (dream) situation, he had no need to dream about it again because he no longer feared it. As I have hypothesized elsewhere, we dream about what we expect to happen, both what we fear and what we hope for. I believe that the approach I have outlined can provide the basis for an effective treatment for recurrent nightmares and look forward to it being tested clinically.

Some evidence has appeared in psychotherapy literature indicating that rehearsal (redreaming) can help people overcome recurrent nightmares. Geer and Silverman successfully treated an otherwise normal patient who suffered for fifteen years from a recurrent nightmare with five sessions of relaxation followed by seven sessions of mentally reexperiencing the nightmare (rehearsal).[22] The frequency of nightmares began to decrease after the third rehearsal session, when the patient was instructed to say to himself "It's just a dream." After the sixth rehearsal session, several weeks later, the nightmare disappeared. Marks described a case in which a recurrent nightmare of fourteen years' duration disappeared after the patient relived the dream three times while awake, then wrote three accounts of the nightmare with triumphant endings.[23] Bishay treated seven cases of nightmares with simple rehearsal of the nightmare and/or rehearsal with an altered ending.[24] A one-year follow-up of five patients in the latter study showed complete relief from nightmares in the four patients who successfully imagined masterful endings, and marked improvement in a patient who was only able to imagine a neutral outcome.

Rehearsal redreaming is done while awake. However, a similar technique can be practiced *during* the recurrent nightmare, if the dreamer is lucid. Instead of imagining how the dream might turn out if the dreamer tried something new, while lucid the dreamer can try the alternative action right there in the nightmare. The resultant resolution should be all the more empowering, because of the enhanced reality of the dream experience. Practicing altering the course of recurrent nightmares both in waking and dreaming may be even more effective. Sometimes, the waking redreaming exercise is enough to resolve the problem created in the dream so that it never recurs again. However, if the dream does occur again, then the dreamer should be prepared to become lucid and consciously face the problem. The following exercise incorporates both reentry techniques.

EXERCISE:
REDREAMING RECURRENT NIGHTMARES

1. Recall and record the recurrent nightmare

If you have had a particular nightmare more than once, recall it in as much detail as you can and write it down. Examine it for points where you could influence the turn of events by doing something differently.

2. Choose a reentry point and new action

Choose a specific part of the dream to change, and a specific new action that you would like to try at that point to alter the course of the dream. Also select the most relevant point before the trouble spot at which to reenter the dream. (If it is a long dream, you may wish to begin at the part that immediately precedes the unpleasant events.)

3. Relax completely

Find a time and place where you can be alone and uninterrupted for between ten and twenty minutes. In a comfortable position, close your eyes and practice the progressive relaxation exercise (page 53).

4. Redream the nightmare, seeking resolution

Beginning at the entry point you chose in Step 2, imagine you are back in the dream. Visualize the dream happening as it did before until you reach the part at which you have chosen to try a new behavior. See yourself doing the new action, then continue imagining the dream until you discover what effect your alteration has on its outcome.

5. Evaluate your redreamed resolution

When the imagined dream has ended, open your eyes. Write down what happened as if it were a normal dream report. Note how you feel about the new dream resolution. If you are not satisfied, and still feel uncomfortable

(exercise continues)

about the dream, try the exercise again with a new alternative action. Achieving a comfortable resolution with the waking exercise may be enough to stop the recurrence of the nightmare.

6. If the dream recurs, follow your redreamed plan of action
If the dream occurs again, do in the dream what you visualized during waking reentry. Remember that the dream cannot harm you and be firmly resolved to carry through with your new behavior.

Children's Nightmares

I learned as a child of five or six to control nightmares. For example, a dinosaur was chasing me, so I inserted a can of spinach into the plot, and upon eating it gained Popeye's strength and "vanquished" my foe. (V.B., Roanoke, Virginia)

I had this lucid dream when I was ten years old. Feeling like a frightened victim, I am high in a stone tower with my younger sister Diane. A witch has tied us up and is about to stuff us into gunnysacks and throw us out the window to drown in the water far below. My sister is crying and near hysteria. Suddenly my panic turns to lightness and wonder. I laugh. "Diane! This is only a dream! My dream! Let her throw us out the window because I can make us do anything we want!" The witch is now background material, no longer the imposing "control." We laugh as we fall through the air, gunnysacks melting away. The warm, friendly water gently supports us to the shore where we run, giggling, in the grass. For days after that dream I felt an inner strength, a sense that fear is now what I'd let it be up to that point. (B.H., Sebastapol, California)

* * *

As a child I participated in and controlled many of my own dreams. My own lucid dreaming started when I was about nine or ten years old. One night I had a dream in which I was being chased by an evil giant. In the dream I suddenly remembered my parents telling me there are no such things as monsters. It was then that I realized I must be dreaming. In the dream I stopped running, turned around, and let the giant pick me up. The outcome of the dream was good, and I awoke with a pleasant and confident feeling. Over the next two years I developed more skill at lucid dreaming, so much so that bedtime became exciting because of this new world I had discovered where anything was possible and I was the Boss. (R.M., Toronto, Canada)

Many people have reported discovering lucid dreaming as a means of coping with childhood nightmares, as in the cases above. Children tend to have more nightmares than adults, but fortunately, they appear to have little difficulty putting into practice the idea of facing their fears with lucid dreaming.

In her book *Studies in Dreams* published in 1921, Mary Arnold-Forster mentioned having helped children overcome nightmares with lucidity.[25] I can relate a similar experience myself. Once, when I was making long-distance small talk with my niece, I asked her about her dreams. Madeleina, then seven years old, burst out with the description of a fearful nightmare. She had dreamed that she had gone swimming, as she often did, in the local reservoir. But this time, she had been threatened and terrified by a shark. I sympathized with her fear and added, matter-of-factly, "But of course you know there aren't really any sharks in Colorado." She replied, "Of course not!" So, I continued: "Well, since you know there aren't really any sharks where you swim, if you ever see one there again, it would be because you were dreaming. And, of course, a dream shark can't really do you any harm. It is only frightening if you don't know that it's a dream. But once you know you're dreaming, you can do whatever you like—you could even make friends with the dream shark, if you wanted to! Why not give it a try?'' Madeleina seemed intrigued. A week later, she telephoned to proudly announce, ''Do you know what I did? I rode on the back of the shark!''

Whether or not this approach to children's nightmares always produces such impressive results we do not yet know, but it is certainly worth exploring. If you are a parent with children suffering from nightmares, you should first make sure that they know what a dream is and then tell them about lucid dreaming. For more information on children's nightmares and how to treat them, see Patricia Garfield's excellent book *Your Child's Dreams*.[26]

That lucid dreaming promises to banish one of the terrors of childhood seems reason enough for all enlightened parents to teach the method to their children. In addition, an important bonus of the lucid dreaming approach to children's nightmares is that it results in an increased sense of mastery and self-confidence as can be seen in all of the examples above. Think of the value of discovering that fear has no more power than you let it have, and that *you* are the master.

11

$\sim\!\sim\!\sim\!\sim$

The Healing Dream

Wholeness and Health

Health can be defined as a condition of adaptive responsiveness to the challenges of life. This definition applies in both physiology and psychology. For responses to be adaptive they must resolve challenging situations in ways that do not disrupt the integrity, or wholeness, of the individual. Taking medication that helps you sleep but prevents you from functioning the next day is not very adaptive. However, getting more exercise can make you sleepier at night *and* increase your general health and vigor. This is a truly adaptive response to a difficulty. Optimal responses result in a creative adaptation that leaves the person at a higher level of functioning than before the challenge. In a psychological frame, avoiding situations that make you nervous may prevent you from feeling anxiety, but it also may limit your enjoyment of life. Learning to face those situations will increase the options available to you.

In this sense, being healthy involves more than the

mere absence of disease. If our familiar behaviors are inadequate to cope with a novel situation, a truly healthy response requires learning new, more adaptive behaviors. Learning new behaviors is part of psychological growth, which leads to increased wholeness, a concept close to the ideal of health. It is no accident that the words *whole*, *healthy*, and *holy* come from the same root.

Self-Integration: Accepting the Shadow

Psychologist Ernest Rossi has proposed that an important function of dreaming is *integration*: the synthesis of separate psychological structures into a more comprehensive personality.[1] Human beings are complex, multileveled biopsychosocial systems. Our psyches have many different aspects; these different parts may or may not be in harmony. When one part of a personality is in conflict with another part, or denies the existence of other parts, unhappiness or antisocial behavior can result. Achieving wholeness requires reconciling all aspects of one's personality. Integration, however, need not be only a matter of repairing malfunctional relationships between the different parts of the personality. It can also be a natural developmental process.

Psychotherapeutic theory, once based on the idea that the goal of therapy was to help people overcome developmental flaws, or neuroses, has been broadened by theories encompassing the idea that even healthy people can integrate disparate parts of their personality to enrich their experience of life—to grow. According to Rossi, integration is the means by which personality growth takes place:

> In dreams we witness something more than mere wishes; we experience dramas reflecting our psychological state and the process of change taking

place in it. Dreams are a laboratory for experimenting with changes in our psychic life. . . . This constructive or synthetic approach to dreams can be clearly stated: Dreaming is an endogenous process of psychological growth, change, and transformation.[2]

Lucidity can greatly facilitate this process. Lucid dreamers can deliberately identify with and accept, and thereby symbolically integrate, parts of their personalities they had previously rejected, or disowned. The stones once rejected by the builder of the ego can then form the new foundation of wholeness.

In the same vein, the poet Rainer Maria Rilke advised:

If only we arrange our life according to that principle which counsels us that we must always hold to the difficult, then that which now seems to us the most alien will become what we most trust and find the most faithful. How should we be able to forget those ancient myths that are at the beginning of all peoples, the myths about dragons that at the last moment turn into princesses; perhaps all the dragons of our lives are princesses only waiting to see us once beautiful and brave. Perhaps everything terrible is in its deepest being something helpless that wants help from us.[3]

Carl Jung observed that disowned features of the personality are frequently projected onto others and symbolized in dreams, taking the form of monsters, dragons, devils, and so on. Jung referred to these symbolic figures as ''The Shadow.'' The presence of shadow figures in dreams indicates that the ego model of the self is incomplete. When the ego intentionally accepts the shadow, it moves toward wholeness and healthy psychological functioning.

The importance of being willing to take responsibility for the shadow elements in one's dreams is illustrated by the difficulties that plagued the dream life of lucid dreaming pioneer Frederik van Eeden: "In a perfect instance of the lucid dream," he wrote, "I float through immensely wide landscapes, with a clear blue, sunny sky, and a feeling of deep bliss and gratitude, which I feel impelled to express by eloquent words of thankfulness and piety."[4] Van Eeden found that these pious lucid dreams were unfortunately very frequently followed by what he called "demon-dreams," in which he was typically mocked, harassed, and attacked by horned devils to whom he attributed independent existence as "intelligent beings of a very low moral order."[5]

Jung would have probably considered van Eeden's demon-dreams as an example of compensation, an attempt to correct the mental imbalance produced by his ego's sense of self-righteousness and inflated piety. In Nietzsche's words, "If a tree grows up to heaven, its roots reach down to hell." In any case, van Eeden could not bring himself to believe that it was his own mind that was responsible for "all the horrors and errors of dream-life."[6] Because he could not understand this, he was never able to free himself from his "demon-dreams." Rather than denying responsibility for his own demons, he should have accepted them as a part of himself.

So, how does one go about accepting shadow figures in dreams? There are many approaches, all of which involve entering into a more harmonious relationship with the darker aspects of yourself. One approach mentioned in chapter 10 is to engage shadow figures in friendly dialogues.[7] This will make a difference with most people you encounter in dreams (or waking life) and might have surprising effects when you try it on threatening figures. Don't slay your dream dragons; make friends with them.

Paul Tholey's dialogue approach is illustrated by a case reported by Scott Sparrow. Sparrow explains that the following dream of a young woman was "one of a long series of nightmares in which she continually fled from an aggressive, somewhat mentally unbalanced man. This dream was the first in which she became lucid; and, as we might suspect, it was one of the last dreams in this series":

I'm in a dark, poor section of a city. A young man starts chasing me down an alley. I'm running for what seems like a long time in the dream. Then I become aware that I am dreaming and that much of my dream life is spent running from male pursuers. I say to myself, "Is there anything I can do to help you?" He becomes very gentle and open to me and replies, "Yes. My friend and I need help." I go to the apartment they share and talk with them both about their problem, feeling compassionate for them both.[8]

Remember that evil, like beauty, may be in the eye of the beholder. As the Afghan Sufi master Hakim Sanai observed eight hundred years ago:

> If you want the mirror to reflect the face,
> hold it straight and keep it polished bright;
> although the sun does not begrudge its light,
> when seen in a mist it only looks like glass;
> and creatures comelier than angels even
> seem in a dagger to have devil's faces.[9]

To the extent that your thinking is distorted by fear, greed, anger, pride, prejudice, and faulty assumptions, you cannot tell what is really reflected in your consciousness. If your mind resembles a fun-house mirror, don't be surprised if in your dream an angel seems a demon. Therefore, you would do well to assume the best. When you meet a monster in your lucid dream, sincerely greet him like a long-lost friend, and that is what he will be.

One of Gary Larsen's *Far Side* cartoons illustrates the proper approach: Two old ladies behind their locked front door are peering out the window at a "monster from the Id" standing on their doorstep. The wiser of the two ladies says, "Calm down, Edna . . . Yes, it's some giant hideous insect . . . but it could be some giant hideous insect in need of help."[10]

You don't need to talk to shadow figures to make peace with them. If you can find it in your heart to genuinely love your dream enemies, they become your friends. Embracing the rejected with loving acceptance symbolically integrates the shadow into your model of your self, as illustrated by one of my own dreams: I was in the middle of a riot in a classroom. A violent mob of thirty or forty was taking the place apart, throwing chairs and people through windows, grappling convulsively with each other, and letting fly random shrieks, war cries, and insults; in short, the sort of thing that is likely to happen in certain grade schools when the teacher steps out of the classroom for a moment. The leader, a huge, repulsive barbarian with a pockmarked face, had locked me in an iron-clad grip and I was desperately struggling to get away. Then, I realized that I was dreaming, and in a flash, I remembered the lessons of past experience.

I stopped struggling, for I knew that the conflict was with myself. I reasoned that the barbarian was a dream personification of something I was struggling with in myself. Or perhaps it represented someone, or some quality in another, that I disliked. In any case, this barbarian was a shadow figure if I had ever seen one! Experience had shown me that in the dream world, if nowhere else, the best way to bring hate and conflict to an end was to love my enemies as myself. What I needed to do, I realized, was to completely accept with open arms the shadow I had been attempting to disown.

So, I tried to feel loving as I stood face to face with the shadow barbarian. I failed at first, feeling only repulsion and disgust. My gut reaction was that he was simply too ugly and barbarous to love. Determined to overcome the initial shock of the image, I sought love within my heart. Finding it, I looked the barbarian in the eyes, trusting my intuition to supply the right things to say. Beautiful words of acceptance flowed out of me, and as they did, my shadow melted into me. The riot had vanished without a trace, the dream faded, and I awoke, feeling wonderfully calm.

Seeking Opportunities for Growth

I became lucid when I realized the absurdity of what was happening: I was at a swim meet where we were about to begin a race, swimming across the carpeted floor of a locker room. Delighted to be lucid, I was about to fly out of the room to find an outdoor vista. But then I reflected on my goal of approaching and resolving problems in dreams. Looking about the room I asked myself if anything there was a problem to me. My eyes settled on a woman whom I had a great distaste for in waking life. I recognized that such strong dislike was unwarranted and probably stemmed from my wishing to disown some aspect of myself represented by her. So, I walked over to her, took her hands in mine, and looked into her eyes. I looked for tenderness inside of myself and projected it toward her. Her aspect transformed to that of a young, helpless, and shy girl. I felt compassion for her. At this I woke up, and realized that I now understood why she behaved in the way that annoyed me. I also understood that the same kind of fearfulness that motivated her behavior was also a part of myself. (C.L., Palo Alto, California)

In reality I have a great fear of water, and swimming was one of the possible choices for me to try in a lucid dream.

In the dream I'm in my backyard and am immediately aware that I'm dreaming. I decide that it would be great fun to swim. Instantly there is water all around me. I swim several hundred feet and make many adjustments to my swimming form. I start to stand up in what is chest-deep water and start to feel fearful. I remind myself that in a dream there is no reason for fear. I immediately feel comfortable and start to walk back around the house, when I observe that the water has disappeared. (L.B., Willow Street, Pennsylvania)

I am in high school, in a hall. I don't know why I'm there and think I'm supposed to go downstairs to the basement and find the gym. I get in the elevator, but the door slams shut on me. Then the buttons don't work. I notice there's a button for a lower level and a basement. I'm afraid of the lower level and manage to get the elevator to stop in the basement. I find the pool there, but it's in a big, dark room. Then, somehow, I know I'm dreaming. I ponder what to do. I think of Tholey's article and that I should seek the darkest and lowest. I find I am quite afraid of doing this. I realize, however, that I like the idea of self-integration. So, I decide to go to the lower level. I go to the stairs, sit, and look down. It's dim and scary. I wonder what I fear to find. I go down, peering about nervously. There's no one and no living thing. It looks like a hall of lab rooms. I fly down the hall making sounds that in the echoey hall sound like eerie ghost wails. I think I'm seeing how it feels to be a ghost. I see two mirrors on top of the lockers and fly up to look at my naked body, and focus on developing a positive appreciation of myself. I'm interrupted by a dark-haired woman with a gun. I float on my back as she points it at me. She is pointing it at my crotch and I think it's funny. Clearly, she thinks I ought to be afraid. I say things like, "Put it to me, baby!" Momentarily, I'm afraid of what sensation might be produced if she did shoot. But then she kisses

*me. I encourage her. She is still angry, but she does it
again, until I think I've convinced her to do that instead
of threaten me. Then she says, "Go to sleep," and I
close my eyes and wake up.* (A.L., Redwood City, California)

*I had this dream when I was in third grade. . . . On the
other side of the street instead of seeing the usual line of
houses, there are all kinds of huge, beautiful flowers, like
a scene out of Alice in Wonderland. They're really nice
and I just stand there admiring them until all of the sudden I get this incredible realization that this is all my
dream. It's my dream, I control what goes on, and no
matter what happens I am always in control: nothing can
harm me! Anything I want to have happen will happen if
I will it. So I look at these fine pretty flowers and decide
to try my skill. "All you pretty flowers there," I think to
myself, "You all think you're so great. Well, you can just
all turn into horrible, ugly, man-eating plants!" There is
a moment's pause, then suddenly the whole scene went
from color to black and white and the flowers had indeed
turned into horrible, ugly man-eating plants. I find myself
faced with a jungle of grotesque, slobbering, terrifying
creatures, all gnashing their teeth at me. I was quite
taken aback that it had really worked, and was even
afraid. Then I remembered that it was my dream and
nothing can hurt—not even these hideous things before
me. I decide to take the challenge; still a little apprehensive, I walk right into the jaws of the menacing man-eaters. As I do, they all disappear, and I wake up.*

*And ever since then I've always been able to control
my dreams if they get too scary or too intense.* (B.G.,
Marin, California)

"If you have no difficulties, buy a goat," advises an
Eastern proverb.[11] Beyond the obvious admonition that
goats are troublesome, this aphorism holds a deeper

meaning. We grow in wisdom and inner strength by learning to cope with difficulties. Challenging experiences force us to consider who we really are and what is of real importance. As long as we are content and never face any conflicts or dilemmas, *we have no need to think*. The great Sufi master Jalaludin Rumi put it thus:

> Exalted Truth imposes on us
> Heat and cold, grief and pain,
> Terror and weakness of wealth and body
> Together, so that the coin of our innermost
>   being
> Becomes evident.[12]

As hard as it may be to believe at first, our worst experiences can be our best friends. As Rilke suggests in the passage quoted earlier, if we hold to the difficult, and do not run from our troubles, the whole world can become our ally.

Thus, we propose that in your lucid dreams you can benefit from *seeking out* difficulties, facing and overcoming them. At the least, when faced with a terror you cannot escape—a pursuer or attacking monster, for instance—you should stay with the dream and resolve the conflict, using the methods suggested in this book. As a next step, if anything appears in your dream world that causes you discomfort, you can take its presence as an opportunity to investigate that problem and see if you can resolve or accept whatever it is that repels you.

Those who are even more adventurous or serious about their desire to find personal wholeness can deliberately "look for trouble" in their lucid dreams. This means to search the dream world for things that you find frightening or distasteful. Psychologist Paul Tholey recommended this idea to subjects in a study of the use of lucid dreaming for promoting self-healing. He quotes the German psychologist Kuenkel as stating that "the true way to healing" is to seek out the "barking dogs of the unconscious" and reconcile with them. Emotional balance, according to Kuenkel, can only be obtained through this process.[13]

Tholey gave his subjects several hints on how to find the hidden "barking dogs" of the psyche in dreams. These were to move from areas of light to areas of darkness, from higher places to lower ones, and from the present to the past. This makes sense, if you consider that we tend to associate deep, dark places with fear and evil, and that childhood generally holds more terrors than adulthood.

The participants in Tholey's self-healing study clearly benefited by coming to terms with threatening figures and situations in lucid dreams. Sixty-six percent of the sixty-two subjects resolved some problem or conflict in their life with their lucid dreams. The program also improved the general quality of their waking lives. Many felt less anxious and more emotionally balanced, open-minded, and creative. However, negative consequences in the form of increased anxiety or discouragement occasionally appeared if the participant forgot the instructions and fled from a threatening figure.

Tholey analyzed his findings further, and concluded that facing fearful situations in dreams contributes to people's self-reliance and ability to respond flexibly to challenging situations. In the terms used in this book, Tholey's subjects became better adjusted both within themselves and in regard to the world, because of their learning to cope with difficult circumstances in dreams.

The following exercise is to guide your efforts to reconcile yourself with your personal anxieties and difficulties. If you wish to try this exercise, it is important that you firmly set your intention to do so while awake. Otherwise, you may find that in the emotional heat of the dream, you will lack the willpower to face your fear.

EXERCISE: SEEKING OPPORTUNITIES FOR INTEGRATION

1. Set your intention

Resolve now, while you are awake, that the next time you are lucid you will deliberately seek out a problem: something that frightens, disgusts, or disturbs you. Assert that you will courageously and openly face the difficulty until you can accept it or no longer fear it. Encapsulate your intention in a pithy phrase, such as "Tonight I will openly face a fear in my dreams." Repeat the phrase to yourself until your intention is set.

2. Induce lucidity

Using your preferred technique (see chapters 3 and 4), induce a lucid dream.

3. Look for problems in the dream

Repeat your intention phrase when you realize you are dreaming. Look around for anything that is a problem to you. Is there any thing or character that you wish to avoid? If not, seek out a place where you might find a difficulty. For example, go into a basement, a cave, or a dark forest, or find some scary place from your childhood. In frightening or disturbing places, you are likely to find problems.

4. Face the difficulty

Deliberately approach the problem person, thing, or situation you have selected. Be open and ask yourself why this thing bothers you. If it is a character, involve it in a dialogue. (See the exercise on conversing with dream characters, page 238.) Try to reconcile with the character, or accept the fearful or distasteful thing. Assert to yourself that *you can handle it*. Do not turn from it until you are comfortable in its presence. It may help to talk to yourself, because this helps you to focus your will. For example, say, "This is okay. I can deal with this. See, it does not harm me. I wonder if it can be of use to me, or if I can help it?"

(exercise continues)

---

5. Reward yourself with pleasure
When you have resolved the problem, or when it disappears, indulge in any pleasure you like in the lucid dream. Doing this will reward you for courageously facing difficulties, making it more likely that you will want to do it again. If you awaken before you reach this step, reward yourself while awake with something you especially enjoy.

Letting Go: Finishing Unfinished Business

When my grandmother died several years ago, I was terribly unhappy for many months. She had been my artistic inspiration and mentor. I had been extremely close to her, how close I did not realize until after her death. Nothing I did seemed to help me feel all right about it.

My husband reminded me of my ability to have lucid dreams. I had been dreaming about her and he suggested that I could use seeing her as a lucidity cue. I decided to do so, for once lucid I could ask her how she was and where she was, and to tell her once again how I loved her and how much she had given me as an artistic legacy.

The next time she appeared in my dream, I was too sad; I didn't remember my intention to recognize I was dreaming, so I couldn't carry out my plan.

A few nights later I dreamed of her again. I had prepared myself in advance by telling myself during the days, "If I dream of Grams, I will remember that it is a dream." This time, I did become lucid. I knew clearly it was a dream, and yet she was so vivid and real; it was just as if she were alive. When I asked her how she was, she answered with some despair, "Oh darling, I don't know. . . . I don't seem to know where I am. . . ." This dream left me feeling both elated that I had made contact with her, and distraught that she was disturbed. Of course, many questions tumbled out from my troubled mind: Is she really "someplace"? Is this only my imagination? I was unsure what to think. So I was eager to talk with her again.

Two weeks later I dreamed of her again and immediately became aware that I was dreaming. I asked her how she was, and where she was. She said, "I am not feeling so unsettled, Laurie," and said something I could not quite understand, about existing fairly happily "somewhere." I hugged her a long time and told her, trying not to cry more than a little, how I loved her and always would, and how she had inspired my dancing, and that she would always be with me. In the dream, she looked exactly like she had in life, with her beautiful, noble face, and I awoke reassured.

Perhaps I truly contacted her spirit; perhaps I simply spoke with my inner self. I do not know. I just know that after those two dreams, something settled in me; I felt in touch with some part of my grandmother and had said what I had so much wanted to say to her. I was able very soon after these dreams to let my sadness slip away from me. (L.C., Portola Valley, California)

When I was thirty I broke up with a boyfriend that I had dated for nearly nine years. It was very difficult and especially hard on me when he married only one year later. Through a series of nonlucid dreams I started to accept the situation that he had married someone else—I came to meet his wife, his in-laws, and experienced seeing them together. One of the last dreams regarding them and my acceptance was a lucid dream. It went like this:

I dreamed I met K. and his wife, only this time he invited me to his house for dinner, along with his folks and sister. I remember noticing that K. and his wife appeared to get along quite well, and that they seemed everything he and I weren't. A twinge of melancholy went through me, but in general I felt that everything seemed alright. They were both very nice to me and liked my company. As I left the house at the end of the evening I suddenly wanted to thank them again for the wonderful evening. It occurred to me to wait and call later on the phone, but then I realized I wouldn't be able to reach them in the morning because I'd be awake in the "waking reality," unable to reach these dream characters. I decided to walk back and leave a note. Just then they walked out of the house and saw me. I explained that I wanted to thank them again, especially his wife, who was so pleasant toward me. I explained that in fact they were dream characters in my dream, but to me they seemed very real. I hoped that a part of me was really meeting with a part of them at some level, although I realized they would never recall this meeting in the waking world. They smiled and said they understood and felt that in spite of what the "outside" world remembers, they felt that a side of them had interacted with me. I woke up shortly after that and felt quite happy and assured that our parting was for the best. (B.O., Arlington, Massachusetts)

Recently, I had a wonderfully comforting dream in which my father, who died only a year ago, came to me early in the morning to tell me it was almost time to get up— just like he used to do when I was a little girl. He never spoke to me in the dream but we were communicating. He came into my room to tell me to get up soon. Then he walked from room to room in my house. He conveyed to me that everything looked good—there were some things that needed to be done, but nothing I could not handle. He also conveyed to me the thought that while he was not there with me physically, his presence would always be with me. Then he came and sat on the side of the bed and held my hand. I kept saying, "thank you" to him and woke up feeling that he really had been there with me. I knew I was dreaming while I was dreaming, but I would not have interfered with that dream in any way. (J.A., Knoxville, Tennessee)

My father died of cancer this summer, and I had a long series of dreams in which I was aware that I was dreaming, and insisted that I didn't want to wake up because I was talking to my father, telling him once more that I loved him, but he'd insist that I wake up and accept that he was fine and had to go off on his long journey. In a dream I finally saw him off at the station and was relieved that he'd made the train: he'd delayed so long in saying goodbye that he'd almost missed his connections to go off to his wonderful vacation. That last dream was the last in the series. (C.M., Framingham, Massachusetts)

When I was twenty-three, my family moved from Florida to Washington, leaving some family, including one special grandfather who was very ill. We had been settled in our new home only a week when he died. I was very close to him; he raised me from the age of six. I flew home, feeling very bad that I had left in the first place. I returned to my new home two weeks later. About a month after that, I had a fantastic dream. I dreamed that I had stayed in Florida and had taken my granddad home with us when he was ready to die. I took care of him as if he were only asleep. At this point I realized this was a dream and awoke to discover I was crying. My pillow was soaked. However, I wanted it to continue. When I went back to sleep, I found myself in his room, aware that I was continuing the dream. Very calmly, he started to tell me that he loved me, that he was fine and that I could leave him now to live my own life with my family. At that point he returned to his sleep state. When I awoke, I realized that I had begun to accept his death. (L.L., Yacolt, Washington)

* * *

Seeking and resolving difficulties in lucid dreams can help you achieve greater emotional balance and ability to cope with life's troubles. It may help you solve problems that you were not conscious of but that, nonetheless, were limiting your happiness. Lucid dreaming can also be used intentionally to address specific difficulties that people are very much aware of. Personal relationships can be the source of some of the most trying problems people have to deal with. In many cases, we cannot work out the difficulty with the person involved and have to deal with it on our own. Such problems fall into the category of internal maladjustment, since they cannot be resolved by changing one's interactions with the world. As demonstrated by the examples above, lucid dreaming can help people settle unfinished emotional business with family members and intimate friends.

When an important relationship ends, people often find that they are left with unresolved issues that cause anxiety and possibly even strain later relationships. In waking life, it is impossible to say those things you never said to your father before he died. And, in waking life, it is often impractical to track down a former mate and talk about unresolved issues.

In lucid dreams, however, it is possible to achieve resolution. Of course, the absent partner is not really there, but the missing person's representation in your own mind is present. This is enough, since it is your own inner conflicts that you need to settle. Dreams do not raise the dead. But, as the examples above testify, lucid dream encounters with the dead are real enough to allow us to feel we are with them once more, and that they live on in our hearts. As Jalaludin Rumi's epitaph reminds us: "When we are dead, seek not our tomb in the earth, but find it in the hearts of men."[14]

Tholey has studied the use of lucid dreaming as a means of achieving resolution of such unfinished relationships.[15] He concludes that it is possible to achieve resolution with inner representations of important people in one's life by engaging in conciliatory dialogues during lucid dreams.

Mindfulness and Mental Flexibility

I was sliding along a snow-covered country road on my belly, but without a sled. On both sides of the road were dense forest and huge rocks. The road was very hilly and curvy and I was going at a good rate of speed, fearing I was going to slide at any moment into a tree or rock. While I was moving along I said to myself: "This is a dream, so I can't get hurt, even if I do crash, so why not go faster?" I willed myself to go at a breakneck speed over this dangerous road only to find myself having the time of my life. I actually controlled the whole dream, knowing it was a dream and no danger was involved! (K.H., Chicopee, Massachusetts)

Lucidity greatly enhances your mental flexibility, making it easier to master whatever challenges your dream world presents. Experiencing how it feels to be flexible, knowing what it's like to trust your ability to come up with imaginative solutions to unforeseen problems, can become a resource in your waking life. Flexibility can help you choose the best actions to get what you want and live in harmony with the rest of the world. Indeed, responding creatively may be the only course of action available. You can't always get other people to act the way you want them to. But you can always creatively reframe your situation, flexibly control your behavior, mindfully create multiple perspectives, and optimize your outlook.

The Harvard psychologist Ellen Langer has studied two contrasting modes of mental function: mindfulness and mindlessness.[16] Mindfulness is a state of attentive awareness in which environmental information is consciously controlled and manipulated while people are engaged in the process of making new distinctions and constructing new categories.

Mindlessness, in contrast, is a state of reduced awareness, in which people process information from their environments in an automatic manner. They rely on habitual categories and distinctions without reference to possible novel aspects of the information, resulting in behavior that is rule-governed and rigid. According to Langer's research, "much of the behavior we assume to be performed mindfully instead is enacted rather mindlessly; . . . unless there is a well-learned script to follow or effortful response to make, people may process only a minimal amount of information to get them through their day."[17] As an example, in one study, people about to use a Xerox machine were asked in one of several ways to let another person use it first. We will compare only the two most interesting conditions. One of two requests were made: (A) "Excuse me, I have five pages. May I use the Xerox machine?" or (B) "Excuse me, I have five pages. May I use the Xerox machine because I have to make some copies?" Sixty percent of the people given Request A agreed, but 93 percent given Request B agreed.[18] In the case of Request B, the people seemed to respond to the fact that they were given a reason to relinquish their place in line. Even though the "reason" was empty of content, they responded without thinking.

Our mental functioning in ordinary dreams frequently exhibits remarkable mindlessness; this is how we can fail to notice and correctly interpret the most absurd anomalies. Mental functioning during lucid dreams, in contrast, is characterized by mindfulness.

People have generalized expectancies about the degree to which they can influence the world. They locate the control of their experience either within themselves (internals) or in the outside world (externals). Internals are people who believe their own behavior has a substantial impact on events. They are flexible in their approach to the world, because they believe that they can affect the course of their lives by changing their own behavior. Externals don't believe their behavior has much influence on the course of events; they think that most of what happens in their lives is the result of luck, chance, fate, or other external influences and powers beyond their personal control. If you think this way, please reflect upon the following:

> Two men looked out from prison bars;
> One saw mud, the other stars.[19]

Properly practiced, lucid dreaming can enhance your ability to see the "stars" in any situation, to mindfully look for a better way of doing things, to become an active shaper of your destiny, to move your control expectations from external toward internal. Very little of the external world can be controlled by any of us, but our "inner worlds" can in principle be reprogrammed to reflect any reality we choose. By adopting a flexible attitude we can enhance our ability to act in a way that will help us find in the myriad of potential realities the most useful and rewarding actuality.

Ellen Langer's research suggests "that mindfulness, a creatively integrative mastery of life experience, leads to improved health and longevity either directly or by increasing awareness of adaptive responses."[20] If this is so, given the connection between mindfulness and lucid dreaming, this may be one of many ways that lucid dreaming can lead to improved health. The next section illustrates how lucid dreaming may even be effective for promoting physical healing.

Healing the Mind, Healing the Body

In 1979 I cracked my foot. I am a dancer and there was no way I could afford to be out of work, nor did I have any desire to stay off my foot for three months. The doctor said I had better not think of dancing for at least six months. So every night I tried to dream about that day at dance rehearsal when the accident happened, until I could change in my dream the dance move that made me land on my foot in the wrong way. It took several tries, but eventually in my dream the fall didn't happen and I tried to set that in my mind. After three weeks of this, I started to dance on my bad foot. I went back to the doctor after three months and didn't tell him I'd been dancing. He said my foot was mending very well and to continue to stay off it. (D.M., Studio City, California)*

In 1970 I was hit by a car when I was a passenger on a motorcycle. I received a broken leg and some injuries to my gallbladder. I underwent emergency surgery to remove my gallbladder. A few days after the surgery when I was recovering in the hospital, I had a dream in which I was whole and floating about the hospital room. I saw my body lying in bed with the casted leg suspended slightly above my body and various tubes in every orifice, it seemed. I hovered over my own body, sometimes feeling the pain of my injuries and sometimes feeling the wholeness and ability of my dream body to fly about the room. I decided in the dream state to give the gift of this wholeness to my physical body. I told my physical body that I loved it and that it would recover. When I awoke that day I was able to stop taking medication for pain and had all tubes removed. On the next day I was able to convince the staff that I was ready to start hopping around on crutches. (R.B., Spokane, Washington)*

* * *

These experiences suggest that lucid dreaming might be useful for physical as well as mental healing. Although this is one of the most speculative ideas for the application of lucid dreaming, anecdotal and theoretical evidence supports the possibility. The use of dreams for healing was widespread in the ancient world. The sick would sleep in temples of healing, seeking dreams that would cure or at least diagnose their illnesses and suggest a remedy. Of course, we have no means of evaluating the validity of claims of such antiquity.

Most people assume that a major function of sleeping and dreaming is rest and recuperation. This popular conception has been upheld by research. Thus, for humans, physical exercise leads to more sleep, especially delta sleep. Growth hormone, which triggers growth in children and the repair of stressed tissues, is released in delta sleep. On the other hand, mental exercise or emotional stress appears to result in increases in REM sleep and dreaming.

Health is usually defined as a state of optimal functioning with freedom from disease and abnormality. This chapter begins with a definition of health framed in broader terms, as a condition of adaptive responsiveness to the challenges of life. "Adaptive" means, at minimum, that the responses must resolve challenging situations in ways that do not disrupt the integrity, or wholeness, of the individual.

Being healthy is something more vigorous than the mere absence of disease. For example, if we cannot cope with a novel situation, it would be healthy to learn more adaptive behaviors. This sort of psychological growth helps us to become increasingly better equipped to deal with the challenges of life.

Human beings are extremely complex, multileveled living systems. As I wrote in *Lucid Dreaming*:

It is useful, although an oversimplification, to distinguish three main levels of organization that make up what we are: biological, psychological, and social. These reflect our partial identities as bodies, minds, and members of society. Each of these levels affects every other level, to a lesser or greater extent. For example, your blood sugar level (biology) affects how good that plate of cookies looks to you (psychology) and perhaps even whether you are hungry enough to steal (sociology). On the other hand, the degree to which you have accepted society's rules and norms affect how guilty you feel if you do so. So how the cookies appear (psychology) depends on how hungry you are (biology) as well as on who else is around (sociology). Because of this three-leveled organization, we can view humans as "biopsychosocial systems."[21]

When we sleep, we are relatively withdrawn from environmental challenges. In this state we are able to devote energy to recovering optimal health—that is, the ability to respond adaptively. The healing processes of sleep are holistic, taking place on all levels of the biopsychosocial system. The healing processes of the higher psychological levels probably are normally accomplished during the dreams of REM sleep. However, due to maladaptive mental attitudes and habits, dreams do not always properly fulfill this function, as we have seen in the case of nightmares.

Lucid dreaming, as a form of mental imagery, is related to daydreaming, hypnagogic reverie, psychedelic drug states, and hypnotic hallucinations. Dr. Dennis Jaffe and Dr. David Bresler have written that "mental imagery mobilizes the latent, inner powers of the person which have immense potential to aid in the healing process and in the promotion of health."[22] Imagery is used in a great variety of therapeutic approaches ranging from psychoanalysis to behavior modification, and to help physical healing.

For purposes of illustration, let us examine one well-studied form of potent imagery—hypnosis. People who have hypnotic dreams while in deep trance relate experiences that have much in common with lucid dreams. Hypnotic dreamers are almost always at least partly lucid in their dreams, and in the deeper states, like lucid dreamers, they experience imagery as real.

Deeply hypnotized subjects are able to exert remarkable control over many of their physiological functions: inhibiting allergic reactions, stopping bleeding, and inducing anaesthesia at will. Unfortunately, these dramatic responses are limited to the one person in ten or twenty capable of entering very deeply into hypnosis. Unlike lucid dreaming, this capability does not seem to be learnable. Thus, lucid dreaming could hold the same potential for self-regulation as deep-trance hypnosis, yet be applicable to a much greater proportion of the population.

Let us consider another example of the therapeutic use of imagery: Dr. Carl Simonton's work with cancer patients. Dr. Simonton and his colleagues found that patients with advanced cancer who practiced healing imagery in addition to taking standard radiation and chemotherapy treatments survived, on the average, twice as long as expected by national averages.[23] Unfortunately, we don't yet know how replicable these results are or how exactly it works. Still, they suggest some exciting possibilities.

Recent evidence supports the idea that the experimental reality, or vividness of mental imagery, determines how strongly it affects physiology.[24] Dreams, which everyone experiences every night, are also the most vivid form of mental imagery most people are likely to experience under normal circumstances. Dreams are so vivid that we have difficulty in telling them from waking reality. Therefore, they are also likely to be a source of highly effective healing imagery. Furthermore, laboratory studies at Stanford University and elsewhere have revealed a strong relationship between dreamed imagery and physiological responses. This fact indicates that in lucid dreams we may have an unparalleled opportunity for developing a high degree of self-control of our bodies which might prove useful for self-healing.

In 1985 I wrote:

> Since while dreaming we generate body images in the form of our dream bodies, why should we not be able to initiate self-healing processes by consciously envisioning our dream bodies as perfectly healthy during our lucid dreams? Further, if our dream bodies do not appear in a state of perfect health, we can heal them symbolically in the same manner. We know from our investigations that such things can be done. Here is a question for future lucid dream research to answer: "If we heal the dream body, to what extent will we also heal the physical body?"[25]

Five years later, the question remains as intriguing as ever and has yet to receive a definite answer. There are, however, intriguing anecdotes:

My findings are that healing is possible in lucid dreams. I had a lump in my breast which I took apart inside my body in a lucid dream. It was a beautiful, geodesic cathedral-like structure! A week later the lump was gone. (B.P., San Rafael, California)

About a year ago, I sprained my ankle. . . . It was very swollen and difficult to walk. In a dream I remember running . . . and suddenly I realized that I couldn't possibly be running with this ankle so I must be dreaming. At this point I began to come out of my dream, the pain of my ankle started to fade in, but then I reached for my ankle with my dream hands which caused me to tumble in my dream. As I held my ankle I felt a vibration similar to electricity. Amazed, I decided to throw lightning bolts around in my dream. That's all I remember of the dream, but I awoke with next to no pain in my swollen ankle and was able to walk on it with considerable ease. (C.P., Mount Prospect, Illinois)

Of course, these stories are *anecdotal*. We have no way of knowing whether lucid dreaming had anything to do with the reported improvements. B.P.'s lump *could* have gone away by itself anyway, and C.P.'s sprained ankle *might* have been on the threshold of healing just at that moment. Controlled scientific studies are the only certain way to determine the true potential of the healing dream.

12

Life is a Dream:
Intimations of a Wider
World

*I am standing quietly alone in a room when I become
aware that I am dreaming. After enjoying a few soft som-
ersaults in the air near the ceiling, I consider what to do
next. Shall I fly somewhere? Visit someone? Then I recall
my intention of seeking the meaning of life and decide to
pursue this task. Realizing I would prefer to be outdoors,
I leave the room and walk into the kitchen. My sister
appears to be engaged in some activity near the sink. I
pause to ask if she would like to go flying with me. She
declines the invitation, saying she is about to fix a cup of
tea. I tell her I will be right back, and feel mischievous
as I'm fully aware that I'm about to go off on an adventure.*

*Outside, the evening is clear and quiet with stars shin-
ing brightly. I float comfortably on my back, gazing up*

at the heavens. I notice the moon is not visible and assume it has already gone down. I'd like to see it, though, and figure that if I rise high enough I should be able to. Immediately I begin to ascend, still in the same position.

When I come to some power lines I hesitate and wonder how my body will react if I try to float through them. This concerns me only briefly as I say almost aloud, "Wait a minute, whose dream is this, anyway? This is no obstacle!" Having expressed this, I find I am now either beyond them or they have disappeared and I am beginning to rise a bit faster.

I decide at this point to visit the moon. I hold my hands out in front of me and fly upwards into the sky. Moving more and more rapidly, soon I sense a roundish shape appearing behind my hands. I lower my hands, expecting to see the moon. The shock of what I see is very dramatic and startling: It is not the moon at all, but quite clearly it is the planet Earth! It is an exquisitely lovely vision, a gem glowing in soft greens and blues with swirling whites against the sable sky.

Quickly replacing the sense of shock is a feeling of great elation and I jump up and down in space, clapping my hands and shouting joyfully. I've always wanted to be out here—I feel a thrilling rush and a sense of accomplishment.

I became so excited that I have to remind myself to calm down again, fully aware that if I lose my balance I will awaken. I shift my focus to my surroundings: I am floating in the midst of a vast, limitless darkness that is at the same time brilliant with countless stars, and very much alive. This aliveness is somehow almost audible: I feel I am "hearing" with my entire being, sensing the "deafening silence" as in a deep forest. This is an exquisitely wonderful place to be.

Now I am beginning to move away from the stars and Earth, which becomes smaller and smaller until it disappears. Soon I am seeing entire solar systems and gal-

axies, moving and spinning harmoniously, growing smaller and smaller as they, too, gradually fade into the distance. I hover in space totally amazed. There is a profound sense of eternal energy everywhere.

Again I remember the experiment and decide to try a question. I feel rather uncertain of how to put it and wish I had given more thought to formulating the question. But the moment seems most auspicious and I don't want to miss this opportunity, so I ask, "What's the meaning of the Universe?" This sounds too presumptuous so I rephrase the question, and ask, "May I know the meaning of the Universe?"

The answer comes in a wholly unexpected form. Something is emerging from the darkness. It looks like some kind of living molecular model or mathematical equation—an extremely complex, three-dimensional network of fine lines glowing like neon lights. It's unfolding itself, multiplying, constantly changing, filling up the Universe with increasingly complex structures and interrelationships.

This growing movement is not erratic but consistent and purposeful, rapid but at the same time unhurried, determined. When it has expanded beyond me, continuing to multiply, I think of returning to the ordinary world.

When almost back, I call out a very sincere "Thank you! Thank you!" to the Universe for the spectacular vision. I awake with wonder, excitement and delight, as well as a renewed and deeply moving respect for the Universe.

This experience left me with a renewed feeling of awe and respect for the nature and splendor and creative energy force of the Universe. It's as if I was seeing the invisible relationships connecting all things—the intimate molecular level superimposed over the vast and limitless Universe. This was indeed a powerfully moving and impressive event. It also led me to believe that in some way I, too, am a unique and essential part of whatever is

going on here—the Divine is within as well as without.
(P.K., San Francisco, California)

Knowing that I was dreaming, I found myself in an infinite void, no longer an "I" but a "We." This "We" was a sphere of pure light shining forth in the darkness. I was one of many centers of consciousness on the outer surface of this Sun of Being. We were an integrated collection of energy and consciousness and though we could work independently of each other it was as though we were one consciousness and worked in perfect harmony and balance.

I did not have a body or spirit. We were just energy and all-knowing consciousness. All opposites were perfectly complemented and cancelled out by each other.

I believe there was a tone vibrating through the galaxy but I can't remember it now. Later in the dream, I/We created a rectangle in the void—the door to life on earth. We created nature scenes in it and I moved forward into it and took a human form and experienced them. There were about ten scenes in all. All the while my consciousness was not separate and We all worked as one, though there were separate nodes of consciousness. I was very lucid as this all went on. (C.C., Whittier, California)

Over a year ago, I was researching Eastern religions, especially Buddhism, Jainism, and Hinduism. During that time, I had a lucid dream in which I experienced what I believe is called the "Dance of Shiva." I dreamed of a weather-beaten Hindu statue. As I looked at it, my entire field of vision began to break down. The scene resembled "snow" in a bad TV reception. I wondered during the dream if perhaps my retina had come loose from the optic nerve.

I then realized I was dreaming and that what I was perceiving was the primal energy underlying the Universe. I felt deeply interconnected and at one with every-

thing around me. I seemed to have rediscovered eternity. Either time had stopped or I had stepped beyond the arch of time. (T.D., Clarksville, Tennessee)

> The final phenomenon is the fullness of light. This light has appeared only while I dreamed lucidly, but it has not been brought about obviously by my own action. It has appeared while I was in darkness or in a significant room or while engaged in religious activity. It usually appears like the sun moving down from above my head until all I see is brilliant light. There remain no images. I become aware of the presence of God and feel spontaneous great joy. As long as I direct my attention to the light, I gradually lose awareness of my dreamed body.
>
> To lose awareness of myself and my dream images in the evident presence of God, is to experience transcendence of myself. This is the experience, whatever the explanation. Fullness of light, awareness of God, gradual loss of awareness of myself, joy (often called bliss), and uncontrollable devotion are phenomena mentioned commonly in mystical literature. These experiences of mine have proceeded only out of the context of lucid dreaming.[1]

"What endless questions vex the thought, of Whence and Whither, When and How?" wrote Sir Richard Burton in his *Kasidah*.[2] Since thought began, reflective individuals have asked countless variations on the question, "Why am I here?" They have received as many answers as there have been questioners, but the answers have seldom been put in words.

Likewise, when dreamworker Keelin asked in her lucid dream recounted above, "May I know the meaning of the Universe?" she was answered with an infinitely complicated living mathematical equation impossibly beyond her capacity to comprehend intellectually. One might take this answer as equivalent to "No, you may not!" However, the intellect may simply not be the proper organ with which to *perceive* the "meaning of life."

Peter Brent has described the problem in an article on Sufi teaching practices:

> We create what we become aware of, at least to some extent, by the sense we use to apprehend it. If you show a dog a book of philosophy, the dog will use its nose in order to decide what it is. It will have a series of categories—*food/not food, dog/not dog* and so on—that will serve as its criteria for judging the scents that are its primary data. It will as a result very soon lose interest in the book. That will not be because of a defect in its sense of smell, it will be because ability, instinct and experience force it to use the wrong sense for the task. In the same way, the manner in which we perceive the world may not be inadequate, given the senses we are employing; it may simply be irrelevant because we are employing the wrong senses.[3]

What *is* the proper sense with which to perceive the hidden meaning in life? Brent hints that it is a form of intuition and that its cultivation requires the direction of a teacher who already has the capacity. This fact may limit how far lucid dreaming can take you without guidance.

Nevertheless, lucid dreaming can give you a taste of the infinite, an intimation of a far wider world beyond the limits of ordinary reality. Whatever your views on spirituality and the nature of the self, you can use your lucid dreams to plumb the depths of your identity and explore the frontiers of your inner world.

A Vehicle for Exploring Reality

Tibetan teacher Tarthang Tulku has said:

> Dreams are a reservoir of knowledge and experience, yet they are often overlooked as a vehicle for exploring reality.[4]

For more than a thousand years, the Tibetan Buddhists have used lucid dreaming as a means of experiencing the illusory nature of personal reality and as one part of a set of practices said to lead to enlightenment and the discovery of the ultimate nature of the self.

The Sufis may also use lucid dreaming, or something like it, for spiritual purposes. The famous twelfth-century Spanish Sufi Muhiyuddin Ibn El-Arabi reportedly recommended that "a person must control his thoughts in a dream. The training of this alertness . . . will produce great benefits for the individual. Everyone should apply himself to the attainment of this ability of such great value."[5]

Tarthang Tulku explains the benefits of lucid dreaming as follows: "Experiences we gain from practices we do during our dream time can then be brought into our daytime experience. For example, we can learn to change the frightening images we see in our dreams into peaceful forms. Using the same process, we can transmute the negative emotions we feel during the daytime into increased awareness. Thus we can use our dream experiences to develop a more flexible life."[6]

"With continuing practice," Tulku continues, "we see less and less difference between the waking and the dream state. Our experiences in waking life become more vivid and varied, the result of a lighter and more refined awareness. . . . This kind of awareness, based on dream practice, can help create an inner balance. Awareness nourishes the mind in a way that nurtures the whole living organism. Awareness illuminates previously unseen facets of the mind, and lights the way for us to explore ever-new dimensions of reality.''[7]

According to *The Doctrine of the Dream State*, an ancient Tibetan manual of lucid dream yoga, the practice of certain dream control techniques lead to the capacity to dream anything imaginable.[8] Tulku makes a similar claim: ''Advanced yogis are able to do just about anything in their dreams. They can become dragons or mythical birds, become larger or smaller or disappear, go back into childhood and relive experiences, or even fly through space.''[9]

The wish-fulfillment possibilities of this degree of dream control may seem compelling, but Tibetan dream yogis set their sights far above the pursuit of any trivial pleasures. For them, the lucid dream represents ''a vehicle for exploring reality,'' an opportunity to experiment with and realize the subjective nature of the dream state and, by extension, *waking* experience as well. They regard such a realization as bearing the profoundest possible significance.

Realizing that our experience of reality is subjective, rather than direct and true, may have practical implications. According to Tulku, when we think of all of our experiences as being subjective, and therefore like a dream, ''the concepts and self-identities which have boxed us in begin to fall away. As our self-identity becomes less rigid, our problems become lighter. At the same time, a much deeper level of awareness develops.''[10] As a result, ''even the hardest things become enjoyable and easy. When you realize that everything is like a dream, you attain pure awareness. And the way to attain this awareness is to realize that all experience is like a dream.''[11]

A commentary on *The Doctrine of the Dream State* explains that long practice and much experience is necessary to understand dream yoga; both theory and experience is needed to complete the journey. Those who successfully follow the path of dream yoga to the end learn that:

1. DREAMS CAN BE CHANGED BY WILL

". . . matter, or form in its dimensional aspects, large or small, and its numerical aspects, of plurality and unity, is entirely subject to one's will when the mental powers have been efficiently developed by *yoga*."[12] As a result of diligent experimentation, the dream yogi learns that any dream can be transformed, by willing it so. Most lucid dreamers will already know this by experience. Also recall from our discussion in chapter 5 the powerful effect of expectation on dream content.

2. DREAMS ARE UNSTABLE

"A step further and he learns that form, in the dream-state, and all the multitudinous content of dreams, are merely playthings of mind, and, therefore as unstable as mirages."[13] Experienced lucid dreamers also will have observed this for themselves. Dreams are as realistic, but not as stable, as waking perceptions.

3. WAKING-STATE PERCEPTION IS AS UNREAL AS UNREAL DREAMS

"A further step leads him to the knowledge that the essential nature of form and of all things perceived by the senses in the waking-state are as equally unreal as their reflexes in the dream-state, both states alike being *sangsaric*," that is to say, illusory.[14] At this stage, the yogi's knowledge is a matter of theory, rather than experience. From chapter 5, you should remember that the dream state and waking state both use the same perceptual process to arrive at mental representations or models of the world. These models, whether of the dream or physical world, are only models. As such they are illusions, not the things they are representing, just as the map is not the territory, and the menu is not the meal.

4. THE GREAT REALIZATION: IT'S ALL A DREAM

"The final step leads to the Great Realization, that nothing within the *sangsara* [phenomenal world of space and time] is or can be other than unreal like dreams."[15] If we compare the mind to a television set, the Great Realization is understanding that nothing that appears on the screen can be anything other than an image, or an illusion. Simply having the idea, for example, "that the mind cannot contain anything but thoughts," is not the Great Realization, which is a matter of experience, not of theory.

In this light, "the Universal Creation . . . and every phenomenal thing therein" are seen to be "but the content of the Supreme Dream."[16] The dream yogi directly experiences this new perspective on reality.

5. UNION

"With the dawning of this Divine Wisdom, the microcosmic aspect of the Macrocosm becomes fully awakened; the dew-drop slips back into the Shining Sea, in *Nirvanic* Blissfulness and At-one-ment, possessed of All Possessions, Knower of the All-Knowledge, Creator of All Creations—the One Mind, Reality Itself."[17] Here, I take refuge with philosopher Ludwig Wittgenstein: "Whereof one cannot speak, thereof one must remain silent."

Plainly, this is not the sort of knowledge that is subject to public verification and scientific testing. However, this qualification is in no way intended to deny the possible value of mystical experiences, since there is no reason to believe that the limits of science are the limits of knowledge. Nor do we intend to imply that you should follow the ways of the Tibetan yogis in seeking your own knowledge of "Divine Wisdom." The methods and symbology of the Tibetan mystical schools were designed to function within the cultural context of Tibetan culture. If you are serious about pursuing your highest potential, we recommend that you find a guide or teacher who can speak to you in a language that *you* can understand.

Self-Knowledge

Nasrudin went into a bank to cash a check. The teller asked him if he could identify himself. "Yes, I can," Nasrudin replied, taking out a mirror with which he scrutinizes his features. "That's me, all right."[18]

Who we really are is not necessarily the same as who we believe ourselves to be. We are not who we think we are in our dreams (or indeed while awake). You can readily observe this fact for yourself in your next lucid dream. Ask yourself about the nature of each thing you find in your lucid dream. For example, you may be sitting at a *dream table*, with your feet on the *dream floor*. And yes, that's a *dream shoe*, on a *dream foot*, part of a *dream body*, so this must be a *dream me*! All you need to do is to reflect on your situation in a lucid dream and you see that the person you appear to be in the dream cannot be who you really are: it is only an image, a mental model of your self, or to use the Freudian term, your "ego."

Seeing that the ego cannot be who you really are makes it easier to stop identifying with it. Once you no longer identify with your ego, you are freer to change it. Simply recognizing that the ego is a simplified model of the self gives you a more accurate model of the self, and makes it more difficult for you to mistake the map for the territory.

If you can see your ego objectively in its proper role as the representation and servant of the self, you won't need to struggle with your ego. You cannot get rid of it in any case, nor would it be desirable to do so—the ego is necessary for effective functioning in the world. The fact that both ego and self say "I" is a source of confusion and misidentification. The well-informed ego says truly, "I am what I know myself to be." The self says merely, "I am." If I know that I am not my ego, I am detached enough to be objective about myself, as in the story in which a monk boasts to Nasrudin, "I am so detached that I never think of myself, only of others." Nasrudin replies, "Well, I am so objective that I can look at myself as if I *were* another person; so I can afford to think of myself."[19]

The less we identify with who we think we are, the more likely we are to discover who we really are. In this regard, the Sufi master Tariqavi wrote:

> When you have found yourself you can have knowledge. Until then you can only have opinions. Opinions are based on habit and what you conceive to be convenient.
>
> The study of the Way requires self-encounter along the way. You have not met yourself yet. The only advantage of meeting others in the meantime is that one of them may present you to yourself.
>
> Before you do that, you will possibly imagine that you have met yourself many times. But the truth is that when you do meet yourself, you come into a permanent endowment and bequest of knowledge that is like no other experience on earth.[20]

Before feeling the sincere desire to "meet yourself," you may find the fulfillment of your ego's wants and wishes far more compelling. This is natural, and it would probably be counterproductive and frustrating for you to try to pursue more sublime aspects of yourself when part of you is still crying for the satisfaction of drives and passions unsatiated in waking life.

Likewise, you should not seek transcendence as a means of escapism. Remember van Eeden's demon-dreams. You must first be willing to deal with whatever problems you may find on your personal level. But, after having resolved any problems within the dream, and after a sufficient amount of wish-fulfillment activity, you may feel the urge or need to seek possibilities beyond what you have known or conceived. You may seek to meet your Self.

Surrender

I suddenly became lucid in the dream as I was walking in the hallway of my high school. I was very glad to be lucid, and to be virtually as aware as in waking life. As usual, I wanted to get outside, into the light. Walking down the hallway, I came to the exit, but my attempt to open the door was thwarted by the hulk of a wrecked truck. Realizing it was only a dream, I managed to get through the door enough to grasp the vehicle with both hands and heave it to the side almost without effort.

Outside, the air was clean, the sky blue, the scene pastoral and brilliantly green. I ran through the grass and leaped into the air joyously. Soaring through the treetops, I became entangled in the branches, and had to hover while extricating myself. Finally above the limbs, I continued my flight to a few hundred feet high. While flying, I thought, "I've flown so many times before, maybe I'll try a floating meditation in the sky." Having decided on the attempt, I asked for help from the "Higher," saying aloud, "Highest Father-Mother, help me to get the most out of this experience!" I then rolled over backwards and ceased attempting to control my flight, without fear of falling. Immediately, I began to float through the sky, upside down, with my eyes closed, the sun beaming brilliantly down on me, filling my head with light. I felt like a feather floating lazily through the air. During about the five minutes of floating, I gently but firmly pushed thoughts out of my mind, as in my waking meditation practice. The less distracted I was by thoughts, the more intensely aware and genuinely joyous the experience became—what I can only describe as ecstasy. Gradually I became aware of my body in bed, and as I awoke I felt a lightness and well-being which is hard to describe. [21]

I enter a church and know that I am expected to speak. The congregation is singing hymn #33 from a red hymnal. While they go through the usual preliminary exercises, I decide to go outside to gather myself. I am worried and afraid because I don't know what I will say. I sit down in the grass and suddenly come up with a topic which feels right—''The Way of Surrender.''

At this point I look up in the eastern sky and see a large orb of white light many times the size of the moon. I realize that I'm dreaming. I yell out in joy knowing it is coming for me. As soon as I do, the Light withdraws into the sky as if it is awaiting a more appropriate response on my part. I know that I must turn my eyes away and trust. As I do, the Light descends. As it approaches, a woman's voice says, ''You've done well reflecting this Light within yourself. But now it must be turned outward.''

The air becomes charged and the ground is brilliantly lit. The top of my head begins to prickle and be warmed by the Light. I awaken. [22]

To go beyond the ego's model of the world, the lucid dreamer must relinquish control of the dream (''surrender'') to something beyond the ego. The concept of surrender is illustrated by the dreams above. Each of us probably has a different conception of this ''something beyond,'' the form of which depends on our upbringing, philosophy or exposure to mystical ideas.

A common theme, expressed in religious terms, is "Surrender to the Will of God." However, if you don't like or don't understand religious terminology, you may wish to express your desire in a different manner. In the context of what we have been discussing here, the phrase could easily be "I surrender control to my true self." Whatever you assume about the nature of your true self, surrendering control from who you think you are to who you truly are will be an improvement. Because it includes everything you know, whether consciously or unconsciously, the true self is capable of making wiser decisions than your ego.

Despite having surrendered ego-control of the direction of your dream, you must maintain your lucidity. If you do not, your ego's drives and expectations are likely to regain command. Furthermore, lucidity can help you to respond creatively and intuitively to the flow of the dream, and to remember that there is no need to hold back from new experiences because of fear of the unknown.

"The Highest" is a particularly satisfying formulation for the transcendent goal. No assumptions need be made about "The Highest" except that whatever it is, it is hierarchically speaking, prior to everything else, and also more valuable than anything else. The following two accounts provide some sense of what may happen when lucid dreamers seek "The Highest." In the first case, Scott Sparrow dreamed:

I am sitting in front of a small altar which has figurines upon it. At first, I see an ox. I look away momentarily, then look back, only to find that there is a figure of a dragon in its place. I begin to realize that I am dreaming. I turn my head away and affirm that when I look back, I will see the highest form possible. I slowly turn back and open my eyes. On the altar is the figure of a man in meditation. A tremendous wave of emotion and energy overwhelms me. I jump up and run outdoors in exhilaration. [23]

Sparrow comments that this dream showed him what the highest was to him, after which it could be consciously established as an ideal, to serve thereafter as a "veritable measuring device by which the inner experiences can be evaluated."[24] However, we need to remember that making an image into an idol, that is, a fixed idea or belief, can inhibit further growth.

Here is the second account, one of my most memorable and personally meaningful lucid dreams:

Late one morning several years ago, I found myself driving in my sports car down a dream road, delighted by the vibrantly beautiful scenery, and perfectly aware that I was dreaming. After driving a short distance further, I saw a very attractive hitchhiker on the side of the road just ahead. I hardly need to say that I felt strongly inclined to stop and pick her up. But I said to myself, "I've had that dream before. How about something new?" So I passed her by, resolving instead to seek "The Highest." As soon as I opened myself to guidance, my car took off into the air, flying rapidly upwards, until it fell behind, like the first stage of a rocket and I continued to fly higher into the clouds. I passed a cross on a steeple top, a star of David, and other religious symbols. As I rose still higher, beyond the clouds, I entered a space that seemed a limitless mystical realm: a vast emptiness that was overflowing with love, an unbounded space that felt somehow like home. My mood had lifted as high as I had flown, and I began to sing with ecstatic inspiration. The quality of my voice was truly amazing—it spanned the entire range from deepest bass to highest soprano. I felt as if I were embracing the entire cosmos in the resonance of my voice.[25]

This dream gave me a vastly expanded sense of identity. I felt as if I had discovered another form of being to which my ordinary sense of self stood in relation as a drop of water to the sea. Of course, I have no way of evaluating how close this vision comes to the ultimate nature of reality (if there is any such thing) and I say this in spite of the conviction of certainty that came with the experience.

As convincing as these experiences may be at the time, it is difficult to evaluate their ultimate validity. As George Gillespie has repeatedly emphasized, the fact that someone has a dream in which he experiences some transcendental reality, whether God, the Void, Nirvana, and so on, does not allow us to conclude that the dreamer actually experienced the transcendental reality.[26] To assume otherwise would be like expecting that if you dream you have won the lottery, you will wake up rich overnight. Therefore, it is probably sensible to maintain a healthy reserve of judgment in your explorations: remember they are dreams, and as such, can as easily represent delusion or truth. Neither believe nor disbelieve them, but keep their lessons in mind as showing you that there is more to life than you presently know. Psychologist Charles Tart has similarly recommended caution in interpreting the meaning of experiences:

Knowledge or experience of the psychic, meditation, lucid and ordinary dreams, altered states, mystical experiences, psychedelics: All of these can open our minds to new understandings, take us beyond our ordinary limits. They can also temporarily create the most convincing, "obviously" true, excitingly true, ecstatically true delusions. That is when we must practice developing our discrimination. Otherwise the too-open mind can be worse off than a closed but reasonably sane mind.[27]

Fariba Bogzaran conducted a study on what happens when people deliberately seek the Divine in lucid dreams. Her inquiry focused on the effect that people's prior conceptions of divinity and their approach to seeking it had on their actual dreamed experience of God. Some people conceive of God as a personal divinity—a wise old man, Christ, or all-encompassing Mother. Others see the Divine as a force in the universe, or some other intangible, nonpersonal power. Significantly, of the people in her study who succeeded in encountering an image of "The Highest" in lucid dreams, more than 80 percent of those who believed in a personal divinity found God in their dreams represented as a person. Also, more than 80 percent of those who believed in an impersonal divinity experienced the Divine as something other than a person.

The way people approach seeking the Divine also affects their experience. Bogzaran divided her subjects into two groups: those who actively sought God in their lucid dreams, and those who opened themselves up to whatever experience of the Divine might come to them. The difference in approach was evident in the way the dream seekers phrased their intentions. Active seekers tended to say that they planned to "seek the Highest" in their lucid dreams. Those who opened themselves, surrendering to Divine Will, as it were, expressed their intentions more as wishing to "experience the Divine," or to open themselves to the Divine. The passive, surrendering group seemed to have less expectations about the appearance of God, and experienced more unexpected outcomes than the active, seeking group. The "surrenderers" usually encountered some representation of divinity without looking for it; the "seekers" also usually found a God, often the one they expected to find.

This study shows that our preconceptions have a powerful effect on the experiences of God that we have in lucid dreams, at least when we are deliberately seeking such experiences. Does this mean that we do not really see God when we find divinity in lucid dreams? I don't think we can say. Divinity may have a different form for each individual, and our preconceptions may be simply the image we project upon "The Highest" when we see it. However, Bogzaran's results suggest that we may have a more profound experience of the Divine if we surrender control, if we don't try to force the experience by looking for God in the dream. Also, when seeking the Divine, you should take care in phrasing your intention, because this directly affects how you will behave in your lucid dreams as you seek an experience of God.[28]

EXERCISE: SEEKING THE HIGHEST

1. Pick an affirmation or question that captures your highest aspiration

Think about what is ultimately most important to you. Formulate a phrase in the form of an affirmation or question that best captures your highest aspirations. Make sure it is a question you genuinely want answered, or an affirmation that you can make without reservations. Some possibilities might be:

- "I seek God (or Truth, The Highest, the Divine, the Ultimate Mystery, etc)."
- "I want to meet my True Self."
- "Let me see the Beginning of All."
- "Who am I?"
- "I don't know my Heart's Desire. How can I find it?"
- "I have a duty to perform. What is it?"
- "Where did I come from, why am I here, and where am I going?"

(exercise continues)

- "What is the most important thing for me to know (or do) now (or next)?"
- "Guide me to Love and Light."
- "Let me remember my mission."
- "Let me be awakened."

Pick only one phrase at a time. Write down and memorize your affirmation or question.

2. Remind yourself before going to sleep

At bedtime, remind yourself of your affirmation or question and your intention to ask or affirm the phrase in your next lucid dream.

3. In your lucid dream, make your affirmation or ask your question

Once in a lucid dream, repeatedly state your affirmation or ask your question while going along with the flow of the dream. Remember what the phrase means to you. Open yourself to guidance from a higher source. Strive to be sensitive to where the dream wants to take you, and go with it. Detach as much as you can from preconceptions about what should happen, and you will be able to accept what is given to you.

Commentary

If you have trouble deciding what you want to seek, you may find it helpful to imagine that the Angel of Death has just come for you. "More time! More time!" you plead. "That's what everybody says," he replies, "but in fact you are allowed the traditional last wish. Most people waste it calling their priest or lawyer, or smoking a cigarette, so be careful. What do you want to do with your final dream?" Putting the question in this context certainly clears away the trivial, leaving what is of real importance to you.

Humanity is Asleep

In the twelfth century, the great Afghan Sufi Hakim Sanai wrote that "humanity is asleep, concerned only with what is useless, living in a wrong world.''[29] Nearly a thousand years later, the situation is little altered: humanity is still asleep. Some may find this hard to believe. You might suppose that if it were true, you ought to know it! However, if it were indeed true that while in the state we ordinarily call ''awake,'' we are virtually sleepwalking through life, it would be difficult for us to observe this fact directly. The one thing the sleepwalker doesn't see is that he is asleep.

Similarly, as we walk down the road of life, we almost always assume we are awake. Sleeping, we think, is inaction; *this* is action, so this is *waking*. We don't think of ourselves as being asleep, but then neither does the sleepwalker or the nonlucid dreamer. Indeed, a Sufi aphorism puts the matter pointedly:

O you who fear the difficulties of the road to annihilation—do not fear.
It is so easy, this road, that it may be travelled sleeping.[30]

Sometimes lucid dreamers become acutely aware of their usual sleeping state, as in the following experience of J. H. M. Whiteman, a South African mathematician:

After [attending a concert by a celebrated string quartet] . . . I remember going to bed with mind peacefully composed and full of a quiet joy. The dream during the night that followed was at the beginning quite irrational, though perhaps more keenly followed than usual. I seemed to move smoothly through a region of space where, presently, a vivid sense of cold flowed in on me and held my attention with a strange interest.

I believe that at that moment the dream became lucid. Then suddenly, . . . all that up to now had been wrapped in confusion instantly passed away, and a new space burst forth in vivid presence and utter reality, with perception free and pinpointed as never before; the darkness itself seemed alive. The thought that was then borne in upon me with inescapable conviction was this: "I have never been awake before."[31]

It's ordinarily very difficult to conceive how you might not yet be fully awake, unless you have had experiences like lucid dreams. But if you have, you can understand by thinking through this analogy: as ordinary dreaming is to lucid dreaming, so the ordinary "sleep-walking" state is to what we could call "the lucid waking" or "awakened-waking" state.

I'm not saying that lucid dreaming is the same thing as enlightenment, only that a comparison of the two levels of awareness in dreams can show us how there might be a level of understanding of our waking lives far beyond our present one.

Consider how muddled and confused most of us are when trying to comprehend the origin and purpose of our lives, and compare this confounded state of mind to that of the nonlucid dreamer trying to rationalize the bizarre events of the dream in the wrong terms. Our dream worlds make much more sense and offer many more possibilities when we realize we are dreaming. Thus, an analogous realization in our waking lives would lead to increased understanding of the context of our lives, and greater access to our potentials and creativity.

As I said above, I do not regard lucid dreaming as a complete path to enlightenment. Perhaps in the hands of the Tibetan Buddhists, with the right guidance, and combined with other necessary techniques, seekers could use lucid dreaming to take them to their spiritual goals. However, I see it primarily as a signpost pointing to the possibility of higher consciousness, a reminder that there is more to life than people are ordinarily aware of, and an inspiration to seek a guide who knows the way.

Idries Shah has vividly described our situation in the following story.

THE MEN AND THE BUTTERFLY

Once upon a time, on a hot summer's day, two tired men who were on a very long journey came to a riverside, where they stopped to rest. Moments later, the younger man had fallen asleep and—as the other watched—his mouth fell open. Can you believe it when I tell you that a little creature, to all appearances a beautiful miniature butterfly, then flew out from between his lips?

The insect swooped onto a small island in the river, where it alighted upon a flower and sucked nectar from its cup. Then it flew around the tiny domain (which must have seemed huge to an insect of that size) a number of times, as though enjoying the sunshine and the soft breeze. Soon it found another of its own kind and the two danced in the air, as if flirting with one another.

The first butterfly settled again on a gently swaying twig; and, after a moment or two, it joined a mass of large and small insects of several kinds which swarmed around the carcass of an animal lying in the lush green grass. . . . Several minutes passed.

Idly, the wakeful traveller threw a small stone into the water near the little island; and the waves which this created splashed the butterfly. At first it was almost knocked over; but then, with difficulty, it shook the droplets from its wings and rose into the air.

It flew, with wings beating at top speed, back towards the sleeper's mouth. But the other man now picked up a large leaf, and held it in front of his companion's face, to see what the little creature would do.

The butterfly dashed itself against this obstruction again and again, as if in panic: while the sleeping man started to writhe and groan.

The butterfly's tormentor dropped the leaf, and the creature darted, quick as a flash, into the open mouth. No sooner was it inside than the sleeper shuddered and sat up, wide awake.

He told his friend:

"I have just had a most unpleasant experience, a dreadful nightmare. I dreamt that I was living in a pleasant and secure castle, but became restless and decided to explore the outside world.

"In my dream I travelled by some magical means to a far country where all was joy and pleasure. I drank deep, for instance, from a cup of ambrosia, as much as I wanted. I met and danced with a woman of matchless beauty, and I disported myself in endless summer. I played and feasted with many good companions, people of all kinds and conditions, natures, ages and complexions. There were some sorrows, but these only served to emphasize the pleasures of this existence.

"This life went by for many years. Suddenly, and without warning, there was a catastrophe: huge tidal waves swept over the land. I was drenched and I very nearly drowned. I found myself hurtling back towards my castle, as if on wings; but when I reached the entrance gate I could not get in. A huge green door had been put up by a giant evil spirit. I threw myself against it again and again, but it did not yield.

"Suddenly, as I felt that I was about to die, I remembered a magic word which was reputed to dissolve enchantments. No sooner had I spoken it than the great green portal fell away, like a leaf in the wind, and I was able to enter my home again and to live thenceforth in safety. But I was so frightened I woke up."[32]

Shah comments: "NOW IT IS SAID that you, as you may have guessed, are the butterfly. The island is this world. The things which you like—and dislike—are therefore seldom what you think they are. Even when your time arrives to go (or when you think about it) you only find distortions of the facts, which is why this question cannot ordinarily be understood. But beyond 'the butterfly' is 'the sleeping man.' Behind both of these is the true Reality. Given the right opportunity, 'the butterfly' can learn about these things. About where it comes from; about the nature of the 'sleeping man.' And about what lies beyond these two.''[33]

Afterword

The Adventure Continues

Congratulations, Oneironauts!

You have learned a great deal about your dreaming mind, and you are on your way to becoming an expert oneironaut. If you have not yet succeeded at having lucid dreams after reading this book, and experimenting with the exercises and techniques—don't give up! How quickly you can learn this skill depends on a number of factors, such as what other matters are demanding your attention, or how well you remember your dreams. Nevertheless, perseverance will pay off.

Be sure to devote sufficient time to developing the basic skills necessary for practicing the induction techniques. If you are having poor success with the induction techniques, concentrate on the basic exercises and also practice the supplementary exercises in the appendix. Remember, a tall building will not stand on a weak foundation.

This book is not the final word on lucid dreaming. Our research continues, searching for better, easier ways to achieve lucidity. As described in chapter 3, we have developed a lucid dream induction device called the DreamLight™, and have found it can help people to have lucid dreams. This is true both for people who have never had lucid dreams before as well as those with more experience. We also continue our search to develop ways to apply lucid dreaming to the problems of life. For those of you who would like to learn more or to join us in exploring the world of lucid dreaming, I would like to introduce you to the Lucidity Institute.

The Lucidity Institute

The media interest in lucid dreaming, and the numbers of letters I received over the past decade, made it clear to me that others find the experience or prospect of being awake in their dreams as fascinating and compelling as I do. *Lucid Dreaming* and the present book are part of my response to the burgeoning public interest in lucid dreams.

With the invaluable assistance of Michael LaPointe, a management consultant and oneironaut who feels a duty to bring the benefits of lucid dreaming to the public, I have established the Lucidity Institute. The purpose of the Lucidity Institute is to promote research on the nature and potentials of consciousness, with an emphasis on lucid dreaming, and to apply the results of this research to the enhancement of human health and well-being.

The Lucidity Institute works to make the benefits of lucid dreaming available to as many people as possible, and this effort takes several forms. The DreamLight lucid dream induction device is available, so if you are interested in trying out the device, contact the Lucidity Institute at the address below. We have a membership society for people interested in participating in and helping to advance research on lucidity in dreams and waking life.

We conduct training programs and publish a quarterly newsletter, *NightLight*, that allows members to learn about, participate in, and support ongoing research on consciousness during sleep.

In each issue of *NightLight*, Lucidity Institute members are presented with experiments on lucid dreaming—different ways of inducing, studying, or using lucid dreams. The Lucidity Institute oneironauts report their results to the editors of *NightLight* who publish summaries of the results in subsequent issues. In addition, *NightLight* answers common questions about lucid dreaming, provides updates on the activities of the Lucidity Institute (workshops, technological developments, and networking ideas), and showcases examples of inspirational lucid dreams. *NightLight* helps oneironauts and researchers learn from each other.

I hope you will join us in the exciting adventure of exploring the world of lucid dreaming. For more information, contact:

> The Lucidity Institute
> Box 2364, Dept. B2
> Stanford, CA 94309
> (415) 851-0252

Appendix

Supplementary Exercises

Strengthening the Will

During after-dinner conversation with the prophets Ezekiel and Isaiah, William Blake asked, "Does a firm persuasion that a thing is so, make it so?" Isaiah replied: "All poets believe that it does, and in ages of imagination this firm persuasion removed mountains; but many are not capable of a firm persuasion of any thing."[1]

Many lucid dream induction procedures require the specific use of intention—the active mode of that elusive characteristic known as "will." Like other aspects of personality, will seems to be distributed unevenly through the population. Some people seem to accomplish things through sheer "force of will," while many people seem to "have no willpower." Fortunately, it appears that the will can be strengthened by the application of appropriate exercises.

Roberto Assagioli described methods for strengthening the will in his book *The Act of Will*.[2] The next exercise is a means of empowering by impressing upon yourself the value of your will.

EXERCISE:
UNDERSTANDING THE VALUE OF THE WILL

1. Think of the problems caused by lack of will.

Sit down with a pad of paper. Close your eyes and think about the possible *negative* consequences that might result from your present lack of will. If you smoke or drink or eat too much, if you can't bring yourself to claim something you deserve or protect yourself from injury, if you can't seem to do what you know is best for you, then dwell on the unpleasant consequences for a moment, and make sure you write each of them down as you think of them and contemplate them. Think of lost opportunities, or pain and aggravation inflicted on yourself and others. If these images invoke negative emotions, allow yourself to feel them. You don't have to write an essay or even a sentence. Simply make a list. After you have finished your list, read it over. As you read, resolve to change or avoid negative consequences. Derive some power from the repugnance of these images, and use that power to strengthen your resolution.

2. Think of the benefits of a strong will.

Now paint an equally vivid picture in your mind's eye, this time depicting all the *positive* consequences of building a stronger will. Just as in the first part of the exercise, first examine and contemplate each potential positive result of a stronger will, then write it down. Again, if you feel strong positive emotions as you contemplate the benefits that could be yours—the satisfaction, recognition, enjoyment, achievement—allow yourself to dwell on these emotions. Then focus on transforming your feelings into a powerful desire to develop the necessary will.

(exercise continues)

> **3. Create an image of yourself with a strong will.**
> Now see yourself *already possessing* a strong will, think-
> ing and acting the way you would think and act if your
> will was fully developed. Fantasize about the best of the
> possible worlds that would be within your reach with a
> highly developed will. See yourself as you could be. Let
> this "Ideal Model" of yourself, as Assagioli called it,
> power your intention to develop your will.

As with other organs and functions of our bodies and
minds, the will can be strengthened by exercise. To spe-
cifically strengthen a particular muscle group, we employ
exercises aimed at exercising just that group. In strengthening the will, likewise, it is useful to train the will in
isolation from other psychological functions.[3] This can
be done by performing "useless" exercises. William
James, the founder of American psychology, wrote that
you should "keep alive in yourself the faculty of making
efforts by means of little useless exercises every day."[4]
An example of this sort of exercise is one proposed by
Boyd Barrett in his book *Strength of Will and How to
Develop It*.[5] Every day, for seven days, the trainee should
stand on a chair for ten minutes, while trying to remain
contented. One man who practiced this exercise reported
after the third day's session, "Have had a sense of power
in performing this exercise imposed by myself on myself.
Joy and energy are experienced in willing. This exercise
'tones me up' morally, and awakens in me a sense of
nobility. . . ."[6]

You can make many daily activities and experiences
into exercises of the will. For example, you could make
an exercise of remaining serene in trying situations at
work, or retaining your patience when stuck in traffic.
Below, we provide a program for training your will.

EXERCISE: STRENGTHENING YOUR WILL

Below is a list of "useless" exercises:

- Move fifty paper clips from one box to another, one at a time, deliberately and slowly.
- Get up and down from a chair thirty times.
- Stand on a chair for five minutes.
- Repeat quietly, but aloud: "I *will* do *this*," while beating time for five minutes.
- Walk back and forth in a room, touching in turn a certain object on each side of the room (say, a vase on one side, and a window on the other) for five minutes.
- Get out of bed fifteen minutes earlier than necessary in the morning.
- Resist completely the impulse to complain for an entire day.
- Write 100 times, "I will write a useless exercise."
- Say hello to five people to whom you've never before spoken.
- Find a poem you like, about twenty lines, or 200 words long, and memorize it.

1. Start with one task from the list above

On the first day, select one of the tasks above, and do only that one. Focus on the task and your feelings as you perform it. Try to maintain a calm state of mind, free from impatience or speculation about the results of the exercise. When you are done, take notes on the thoughts and feelings you experienced. If you succeeded in completing the task, the next day go on to Step 2. If you failed to finish or do the task, try again with the same task the next day.

2. Add another task

After completing Step 1, select another task, and perform both it and the one you did in Step 1 on the same day. Again, maintain a placid frame of mind during the

(exercise continues)

tasks and take notes after you are done. Do these two tasks for two days (or until you successfully complete them on two days).

3. Add a third task
On the fourth day, add a third task. Do all three tasks for two more days. Continue to take notes for the rest of the exercise.

4. Drop one old task and pick up a new one
After completing three tasks on two days, drop one of the old tasks, and add a new one, so that you still have three tasks. Again, perform all three tasks on two days. Continue to drop one task and add a new one after two days with a set of three until you have succeeded with all of the tasks.

5. Experiment on your own
Continue the exercise under your own direction. You can make up your own tasks, and add as many as you like to your daily regimen. Don't give yourself too many, however, or you might get discouraged. Remember to try to feel contented as you perform the tasks—don't feel impatient, or eager for reward.

Exercises in Concentration and Visualization

Many of the lucidity induction procedures in this book involve visualization. For example, the dream lotus and flame exercise in chapter 4 requires that you be able to visualize a flame located in the center of a lotus flower and concentrate on it until you enter a dream. If you don't feel that you have the ability to visualize vividly enough, don't despair—your skill will improve if you practice. The following exercises are designed to strengthen your capacity to visualize mental images by adapting your visual perception of external objects to an internal ability to see imagery.

EXERCISE: CANDLE CONCENTRATION

1. Watch a candle flame
Place a burning candle in front of you. Seat yourself about three or four feet away from the candle so that you can see the flame easily. Look steadily at the flame. Do this for as long as you can, but not so long as to tire your eyes.

2. Rest when you need to
When you begin to feel eye strain, close your eyes and sit quietly for a while, picturing the flame before you. Practice this regularly, and you will soon increase your power to focus for indefinite periods of time.

(Adapted from Mishra.[7])

EXERCISE: VISUALIZATION TRAINING
Practice Part A once or twice a day for two or three days. Each session need not be longer than five minutes. Then move on to Part B.

PART A
1. Sit facing a simple object
Choose an object to gaze at, such as an apple, a rock, a candle, or a coffee cup. Choose something small, simple, and stationary. Put it a few feet away from you and sit comfortably.

2. Concentrate on looking at the object
With your eyes open, try to encompass the entire object with your vision. Try to soak in an overall visual impression, rather than concentrating on any specific fea-

(exercise continues)

ture of the object. Acknowledge distracting thoughts and perceptions and then just let them float away.

3. Close your eyes and observe the afterimage of the object

After a few minutes, close your eyes and watch the afterimage of the object until it fades. Then open your eyes and look intently at the object again. Repeat this several times; the afterimage should become more clear, vivid, and crisp each time. Don't strain to create the image. Let the clarity emerge as if of its own will.

PART B

1. Warm up by concentrating on an object in front of you

Warm up by repeating Part A several times.

2. Visualize the object hanging in space in front of you

With your eyes open, move your gaze away from the object and try to picture it directly in front of you, several feet away, floating at eye level. It might seem strange at first, but don't strain. Simply try to let the outlines of the image emerge in space. You might want to start by concentrating on the way you feel about the object rather than its detailed structure. Just accept that the object occupies the space where you are gazing, and pay attention to that feeling—that the image occupies the space because you intend it to. The sense of seeing an image will emerge from that awareness and feeling.

3. Visualize the object inside of you

When you can visualize the object in front of you, then repeat Step 2, except this time visualize it inside your body. Since some of the lucid dream induction techniques require visualizations of objects in the throat area, try to see the object in your throat. Then move it out again. Shift your visualization from external to internal positions again and again, until it is effortless.

(Adapted from Tulku.[8])

Notes

1: THE WORLD OF LUCID DREAMING

1. Principally Lynne Levitan and Robert Rich, under the sponsorship of Dr. William Dement.
2. T. Tulku, *Openness Mind* (Berkeley, Calif.: Dharma Publishing, 1978), 74.
3. G. S. Sparrow, *Lucid Dreaming: The Dawning of the Clear Night* (Virginia Beach: A.R.E. Press, 1976) 26–27.
4. I. Shah, *Seeker After Truth* (London: Octagon Press, 1982), 33.
5. W. James, *Principles of Psychology* (New York: Dover, 1891/1950).

2: PREPARATION FOR LEARNING LUCID DREAMING

1. S. Rama, R. Ballantine, and S. Ajaya, *Yoga and Psychotherapy* (Honesdale, Pa.: Himalayan Institute, 1976), 166.
2. P. D. Ouspensky, *A New Model of the Universe* (London: Routledge & Kegan Paul, 1931/1971), 244.
3. S. LaBerge, *Lucid Dreaming* (Los Angeles: J. P. Tarcher, 1985).
4. I. Shah, *The Way of the Sufi* (London: Octagon Press, 1968), 244.
5. For further discussion of dream journals, see G. Delaney, *Living Your Dreams* (New York: Harper & Row, 1988); A. Faraday, *The Dream Game* (New York: Harper & Row, 1974); P. Garfield, *Creative Dreaming* (New York: Ballantine, 1974); M. Ullman and N. Zimmerman, *Working with Dreams* (New York: Delacorte, 1979).

6. O. Fox, *Astral Projection* (New Hyde Park, N.Y.: University Books, 1962), 32–33.

7. See J. M. Williams, ed., *Applied Sport Psychology* (Palo Alto, Calif.: Mayfield Publishing, 1986).

8. E. A. Locke et al., "Goal Setting and Task Performance," *Psychological Bulletin* 90 (1981): 125–152.

9. D. Gould, "Goal Setting for Peak Performance," in *Applied Sport Psychology*, ed. J. M. Williams (Palo Alto, Calif.: Mayfield Publishing, 1986).

10. LaBerge, op. cit.

11. A. Worsley, "Personal Experiences in Lucid Dreaming," in *Conscious Mind, Sleeping Brain*, eds. J. Gackenbach and S. LaBerge (New York: Plenum, 1988), 321–42.

12. E. Jacobsen, *Progressive Relaxation* (Chicago: University of Chicago Press, 1958).

13. S. Rama, *Exercise Without Movement* (Honesdale, Pa.: Himalayan Institute, 1984).

14. Adapted from Rama.

3: WAKING UP IN THE DREAM WORLD

1. O. Fox, *Astral Projection* (New Hyde Park, N.Y.: University Books, 1962), 35–36.

2. P. Tholey, "Techniques for Inducing and Maintaining Lucid Dreams," *Perceptual and Motor Skills* 57 (1983): 79–90.

3. C. McCreery, *Psychical Phenomena and the Physical World* (London: Hamish Hamilton, 1973).

4. W. Y. Evans-Wentz, ed., *The Yoga of the Dream State* (New York: Julian Press, 1964).

5. Ibid.

6. Ibid.

7. Tholey, op. cit.

8. Ibid.

9. Ibid, 82.

10. Tholey, op. cit.

11. S. LaBerge, *Lucid Dreaming: An Exploratory Study of Consciousness During Sleep* (Ph.D. diss., Stanford University, 1980). (University Microfilms International No. 80–24, 691).

12. J. Harris, "Remembering to Do Things: A Forgotten Topic," in *Everyday Memory*, eds. J. Harris and P. Morris (London: Academic Press, 1984).

13. LaBerge, op. cit.

14. P. Garfield, "Psychological Concomitants of the Lucid Dream State," *Sleep Research* 4 (1975): 184.

15. P. Garfield, *Pathway to Ecstasy* (New York: Holt, Rinehart & Winston, 1979).

16. LaBerge, op. cit.

17. Tholey, op. cit.

18. C. Tart, "From Spontaneous Event to Lucidity: A Review of Attempts to Consciously Control Nocturnal Dreams," in *Conscious Mind, Sleeping Brain*, eds. J. Gackenbach and S. LaBerge (New York: Plenum, 1988), 99.

19. LaBerge, op. cit.

20. J. Dane, *An Empirical Evaluation of Two Techniques for Lucid Dream Induction* (Ph.D. diss., Georgia State University, 1984).

21. S. LaBerge, et al., " 'This Is a Dream': Induction of Lucid Dreams by Verbal Suggestion During REM Sleep," *Sleep Research* 10 (1981): 150.

22. W. Dement and E. Wolpert, "The Relation of Eye Movements, Body Motility, and External Stimuli to Dream Content," *Journal of Experimental Psychology* 55 (1958): 543–53.

23. R. Rich, "Lucid Dream Induction by Tactile Stimulation During REM Sleep" (Unpublished honors thesis, Department of Psychology, Stanford University, 1985).

24. S. LaBerge et al., "Induction of Lucid Dreaming by Light Stimulation During REM Sleep," *Sleep Research* 17 (1988): 104.

25. DreamLight™ is a registered trademark of the Lucidity Institute, Inc., Woodside, California.

26. S. LaBerge, unpublished data.

27. S. LaBerge, *Lucid Dreaming* (Los Angeles: J. P. Tarcher, 1985), 149.

28. S. LaBerge, "Induction of Lucid Dreams Including the Use of the DreamLight," *Lucidity Letter* 7 (1988): 15–22.

29. J. Gackenbach and J. Bosveld, *Control Your Dreams* (New York: Harper & Row, 1989), 36.

30. Ibid., 57.

31. S. LaBerge and R. Lind, "Varieties of Experience from Light-Induced Lucid Dreams," *Lucidity Letter* 6 (1987): 38–39.

4: FALLING ASLEEP CONSCIOUSLY

1. S. LaBerge, *Lucid Dreaming: An Exploratory Study of Consciousness During Sleep* (Ph.D. diss., Stanford University, 1980). (University Microfilms International No. 80–24, 691)

2. S. LaBerge, unpublished data.

3. Ibid.

4. S. LaBerge, *Lucid Dreaming*, (Los Angeles. J.P. Tarcher, 1985).

5. P. Tholey, "Techniques for Inducing and Maintaining Lucid Dreams," *Perceptual and Motor Skills* 57 (1983): 79–90.

6. D. L. Schacter, "The Hypnagogic State: A Critical Review of Its Literature," *Psychological Bulletin* 83 (1976): 452–481; P. Tholey, "Techniques for Inducing and Maintaining Lucid Dreams," *Perceptual and Motor Skills* 57 (1983): 79–90.

7. P. D. Ouspensky, *A New Model of the Universe* (London: Routledge & Kegan Paul, 1931/1971), 252.

8. Ibid., 244.

9. N. Rapport, "Pleasant Dreams!" *Psychiatric Quarterly* 22 (1948): 314.

10. Ibid., 313.

11. Tholey, op. cit., 83.

12. Ibid.

13. T. Tulku, *Hidden Mind of Freedom* (Berkeley, Calif.: Dharma Publishing, 1981), 87.

14. W. Y. Evans-Wentz, ed., *The Yoga of the Dream State* (New York: Julian Press, 1964).

15. R. deRopp, *The Master Game* (New York: Dell, 1968).

16. T. N. Hanh, *The Miracle of Mindfulness: A Manual on Meditation* (Boston: Beacon Press, 1975).

17. Evans-Wentz, op. cit.

18. Ibid.

19. T. Tulku, *Openness Mind* (Berkeley, Calif.: Dharma Publishing, 1978).

20. L. A. Govinda, *Foundations of Tibetan Mysticism* (London: Ryder & Co., 1969).

21. Tulku, op. cit.

22. LaBerge, *Lucid Dreaming: An Exploratory Study*, op. cit.

23. Ibid. See also S. LaBerge, *Lucid Dreaming* (Los Angeles: J. P. Tarcher, 1985).

24. Tholey, op. cit.

25. S. Rama, *Exercise Without Movement* (Honesdale, Pa.: Himalayan Institute, 1984).

26. Tholey, op. cit., 84.

27. LaBerge, *Lucid Dreaming*, op. cit.

28. Tholey, op. cit.

29. Rama, op. cit.

30. Tholey, op. cit., 85.

31. Ibid.

32. Ibid.

5: THE BUILDING OF DREAMS

1. G. J. Steinfield, "Concepts of Set and Availability and Their Relation to the Reorganization of Ambiguous Pictorial Stimuli," *Psychological Review* 74 (1967): 505–525.

2. F. C. Bartlett, *Remembering* (London: Cambridge University Press, 1932), 38.

3. B. R. Clifford and R. Bull, *The Psychology of Person Identification* (London: Routledge & Kegan Paul, 1978).

4. D. Rumelhart, quoted in D. Goleman, *Vital Lies, Simple Truths* (New York: Simon & Schuster, 1985), 76.

5. Rumelhart, op. cit., 77.

6. S. LaBerge, *Lucid Dreaming* (Los Angeles: J. P. Tarcher, 1985).

7. I. Shah. *The Sufis* (New York: Doubleday, 1964), 87.

8. P. D. Ouspensky, *A New Model of the Universe* (London: Routledge & Kegan Paul, 1931–1971), 281.

9. C. Green, *Lucid Dreams* (Oxford: Institute for Psychophysical Research, 1968), 85.

10. P. Garfield, *Creative Dreaming* (New York: Ballantine, 1974), 143.

6: PRINCIPLES AND PRACTICE OF LUCID DREAMING

1. L. Magallon, "Awake in the Dark: Imageless Lucid Dreaming," *Lucidity Letter* 6 (1987): 86–90.

2. H. von Moers-Messmer, "Traüme mit der gleichzeitigen Erkenntnis des Traumzustandes," *Archiv für Psychologie* 102 (1938): 291–318.

3. G. S. Sparrow, *Lucid Dreaming: Dawning of the Clear Light* (Virginia Beach: A.R.E. Press, 1976).

4. C. Castaneda, *Journey to Ixtlan* (New York: Simon & Schuster, 1972).

5. Sparrow, op. cit., 43.

6. A. Hobson, *The Dreaming Brain* (New York: Basic Books, 1988).

7. K. M. T. Hearne, *Lucid Dreams: An Electrophysiological and Psychological Study* (Unpublished Ph.D. diss., Liverpool University, 1978).

8. A., Worsley, Personal communication, 1982.

9. Sparrow, op. cit., 41.

10. S. LaBerge, *Lucid Dreaming: An Exploratory Study of Consciousness During Sleep* (Ph.D. diss., Stanford University, 1980). (University Microfilms International No. 80–24, 691).

11. A. Worsley, "Personal Experiences in Lucid Dreaming," in *Conscious Mind, Sleeping Brain* eds. J. Gackenbach and S. LaBerge (New York: Plenum, 1988), 321–342.

12. P. Tholey, "Techniques for Inducing and Maintaining Lucid Dreams," *Perceptual and Motor Skills* 57 (1983): 87.

13. F. Bogzaran, "Dream Marbling," *Ink & Gall: Marbling Journal* 2 (1988): 22.

14. Worsley, "Personal Experiences," op. cit.

15. Ibid., 327.

16. Tholey, op. cit., 79–90.

17. Ibid., 87.

18. Ibid., 88.

19. Worsley, "Personal Experiences" op. cit.

7: ADVENTURES AND EXPLORATIONS

1. H. Ellis, quoted in W. C. Dement, *Some Must Watch While Some Must Sleep* (San Francisco: Freeman & Co., 1972), 102.

2. K. Kelzer, *The Sun and the Shadow: My Experiment with Lucid Dreaming* (Virginia Beach, Va.: A.R.E. Press, 1987), 140–141.

3. R. Ornstein and D. Sobel, *Healthy Pleasures* (Reading, Mass.: Addison-Wesley, 1989).

4. P. Garfield, *Pathway to Ecstasy* (New York: Holt, Rinehart & Winston, 1979), 45.

5. F. Ungar, ed., *Goethe's World View* (New York: Frederick Ungar Publishing Co., 1983), 94.

6. J. Campbell, *The Hero With a Thousand Faces* (Princeton, N.J.: Princeton University Press, 1973).

7. Ibid., 30.

8: REHEARSAL FOR LIVING

1. C. A. Garfield and H. Z. Bennett, *Peak Performance: Mental Training Techniques of the World's Greatest Athletes* (Los Angeles: J. P. Tarcher, 1984).

2. R. S. Vealey, "Imagery Training for Performance Enhancement," in *Applied Sport Psychology*, ed. J. M. Williams (Palo Alto, Calif.: Mayfield Publishing, 1986), 209–234.

3. C. Corbin, "The Effects of Mental Practice on the Development of a Unique Motor Skill," *NCPEAM Proceedings* (1966); J. B. Oxendine, "Effect of Mental and Physical Practice on the Learning of Three Motor Skills," *Research Quarterly* 40 (1969): 755–763; A. Richardson, "Mental Practice: A Review and a Discussion, part I, *Research Quarterly* 38 (1967): 95–107; K. B. Start, "The Relationship between Intelligence and the Effect of Mental Practice on the Performance of a Mental Skill," *Research Quarterly* 31 (1960): 644–649; K. B. Start, "The Influence of Subjectively Assessed Games Ability on Gain in Motor Performance after Mental Practice," *Journal of Genetic Psychology* 67 (1962): 169–173.

4. Vealey, op. cit., 211–212.

5. R. M. Suinn, "Behavioral Rehearsal Training for Ski Racers," *Behavior Therapy* 3 (1980): 519.

6. M. Jouvet, "Neurophysiology of the States of Sleep," *Physiological Reviews* 47 (1967): 117–177.

7. Vealey, op. cit.

8. P. Tholey, "Applications of Lucid Dreaming in Sports." Unpublished manuscript.

9. Ibid.

10. Ibid.

11. Ibid.

12. A. Bandura, *Social Foundations of Thought and Action* (New York: Prentice Hall, 1986) 19.

13. Ibid., 19.

14. I. Shah, *Caravan of Dreams* (London: Octagon, 1966), 11.

9: CREATIVE PROBLEM SOLVING

1. R. Harman and H. Rheingold, *Higher Creativity* (Los Angeles: J. P. Tarcher, 1984).

2. C. Rogers, *On Becoming a Person* (Boston: Houghton Mifflin, 1961), 350.

3. O. Loewi, "An Autobiographical Sketch," *Perspectives in Biology and Medicine* 4 (1960): 17.

4. E. Green, A. Green, and D. Walters, "Biofeedback for Mind-Body Self-Regulation: Healing and Creativity," in *Fields Within Fields . . . Within Fields* (New York: Stulman, 1972), 144.

5. Rogers, op. cit.

6. F. Bogzaran, "Dream Marbling," *Ink & Gall: Marbling Journal* 2 (1988): 22.

7. R. L. Stevenson, "A Chapter on Dreams," in *Across the Plains* (New York: Charles Scribner's Sons, 1901), 247.

10: OVERCOMING NIGHTMARES

1. E. Hartmann, *The Nightmare* (New York: Basic Books, 1984).

2. S. LaBerge, L. Levitan, and W. C. Dement, "Lucid Dreaming: Physiological Correlates of Consciousness during REM Sleep," *Journal of Mind and Behavior* 7 (1986): 251–258.

3. S. Freud, "Introductory Lectures on Psychoanalysis," in *Standard Edition of the Complete Psychological Works of Sigmund Freud*, vol. 15 (London: Hogarth Press, 1916–17), 222.

4. Hartmann, op. cit.; A. Kales et al., "Nightmares: Clinical Characteristics of Personality Patterns," *American Journal of Psychiatry* 137 (1980): 1197–1201.

5. J. A. Gray, "Anxiety," *Human Nature* 1 (1978): 38–45.

6. C. Green, *Lucid Dreams* (London: Hamish Hamilton, 1968); S. LaBerge, *Lucid Dreaming* (Los Angeles: J. P. Tarcher, 1985).

7. I. Shah, *The Way of the Sufi* (London: Octagon Press, 1968), 79.

8. H. Saint-Denys, *Dreams and How to Guide Them* (London: Duckworth, 1982), 58–59.

9. P. Tholey, "A Model of Lucidity Training as a Means of Self-Healing and Psychological Growth," in *Conscious Mind, Sleeping Brain*, eds. J. Gackenbach and S. LaBerge (New York: Plenum, 1988), 263–287.

10. G. S. Sparrow, *Lucid Dreaming: Dawning of the Clear Light* (Virginia Beach: A.R.E. Press, 1976), 33.

11. See LaBerge, *Lucid Dreaming*, chapter 9, for a discussion of out-of-body experiences.

12. K. Stewart, "Dream Theory in Malaya," in *Altered States of Consciousness*, ed. C. Tart (New York: Doubleday, 1972), 161–170.

13. P. Garfield, *Creative Dreaming* (New York: Ballantine, 1974).

14. Tholey, op. cit.

15. Ibid., 265.

16. S. Kaplan-Williams, *The Jungian-Senoi Dreamwork Manual* (Berkeley, Calif.: Journey Press, 1985).

17. Tholey, op. cit.

18. Garfield, op. cit., 99–100.

19. Tholey, op. cit., 272.

20. C. McCreery, *Psychical Phenomena and the Physical World* (London: Hamish Hamilton, 1973), 102–104.

21. Kaplan-Williams, op. cit., 204.

22. J. H. Geer and I. Silverman, "Treatment of a Recurrent Nightmare by Behaviour Modification Procedures," *Journal of Abnormal Psychology* 72 (1967): 188–190.

23. I. Marks, "Rehearsal Relief of a Nightmare," *British Journal of Psychiatry* 135 (1978): 461–465.

24. N. Bishay, "Therapeutic Manipulation of Nightmares and the Management of Neuroses," *British Journal of Psychiatry* 147 (1985): 67–70.

25. M. Arnold-Forster, *Studies in Dreams* (New York: Macmillan, 1921).

26. P. Garfield, *Your Child's Dreams* (New York: Ballantine, 1984).

11: THE HEALING DREAM

1. E. Rossi, *Dreams and the Growth of Personality* (New York: Bruner/Mazel, 1972/1985).

2. Ibid., 142.

3. R. Rilke, *Letters to a Young Poet* (New York: Random House, 1984), 91–92. I am grateful to Gayle Delaney for first having drawn my attention to this reference.

4. F. van Eeden, "A Study of Dreams," *Proceedings of the Society for Psychical Research* 26 (1913): 439.

5. Ibid., 461.

6. Ibid.

7. P. Tholey, "A Model of Lucidity Training as a Means of Self-Healing and Psychological Growth," in *Conscious Mind, Sleeping Brain*, eds. J. Gackenbach and S. LaBerge (New York: Plenum, 1988, 263–287.)

8. G. S. Sparrow, *Lucid Dreaming: Dawning of the Clear Light* (Virginia Beach: A.R.E. Press, 1976), 31.

9. D. Pendlebury, *The Walled Garden of Truth* (New York: Dutton, 1976), 11.

10. G. Larsen, *Beyond the Far Side* (Kansas City: Andrews, McMeel & Parker, 1983).

11. I. Shah, *Caravan of Dreams* (London: Octagon, 1968), 132.

12. I. Shah, *The Way of the Sufi* (New York: Dutton, 1968), 104.

13. Tholey, op. cit.

14. Shah, op. cit., 110.
15. Tholey, op. cit.
16. E. Langer, *Mindfulness* (Menlo Park, Calif.: Addison-Wesley, 1989).
17. E. Langer, "Rethinking the Role of Thought in Social Interaction," in *New Directions in Attribution Research*, eds. H. Harvey, W. Ickes, and R. F. Kidd (Hillsdale, N.J.: Erlbaum, 1978), 50.
18. Langer, op. cit.
19. I. Shah, *Learning How to Learn* (San Francisco: Harper & Row, 1981), 50.
20. B. Strickland, "Internal-External Control Expectancies: From Contingency to Creativity," *American Psychologist* 44 (1989): 1–12.
21. S. LaBerge, *Lucid Dreaming* (Los Angeles: J. P. Tarcher, 1985), 153–154.
22. D. T. Jaffe and D. E. Bresler, "The Use of Guided Imagery as an Adjunct to Medical Diagnosis and Treatment," *Journal of Humanistic Psychology* 20 (1980): 45–59.
23. O. C. Simonton, S. Mathews-Simonton, and T. F. Sparks, "Psychological Intervention in the Treatment of Cancer," *Psychosomatics* 21 (1980): 226–233.
24. A. Richardson, "Strengthening the Theoretical Links between Imaged Stimuli and Physiological Responses," *Journal of Mental Imagery* 8 (1984): 113–126.
25. LaBerge, op. cit., 156.

12: LIFE IS A DREAM: INTIMATIONS OF A WIDER WORLD

1. G. Gillespie, "Ordinary Dreams, Lucid Dreams and Mystical Experience," *Lucidity Letter* 5 (1986): 31.
2. R. F. Burton, *The Kasidah of Hâjî Abdû El-Yezdî* (New York: Citadel Press, 1965), 13.
3. P. Brent, "Learning and Teaching," in *The World of the Sufi* (London: Octagon Press, 1979), 216.
4. T. Tulku, *Openness Mind* (Berkeley, Calif.: Dharma Press, 1978), 74.
5. I. Shah, *The Sufis* (New York: Doubleday, 1964), 141.
6. Tulku, op. cit., 77.
7. Ibid., 90.
8. W. Y. Evans-Wentz, ed., *The Yoga of the Dream State* (New York: Julian Press, 1964).
9. Tulku, op. cit., 76.
10. Ibid., 78.
11. Ibid., 86.
12. Evans-Wentz, op. cit., 221.
13. Ibid.
14. Ibid.
15. Ibid., 221–222.

16. Ibid., 222.

17. Ibid.

18. I. Shah, *The Subtleties of the Inimitable Mulla Nasrudin* (London: Octagon Press, 1983), 90.

19. Ibid., 54.

20. I. Shah, *Wisdom of the Idiots* (London: Octagon Press, 1971), 122–123.

21. D. Hewitt, Personal communication, 1990.

22. G. S. Sparrow, *Lucid Dreaming: Dawning of the Clear Light* (Virginia Beach, A.R.E. Press, 1976), 13.

23. Ibid., 50.

24. Ibid.

25. S. LaBerge, *Controlling Your Dreams* (audiotape) (Los Angeles: Audio Renaissance Tapes, 1987).

26. G. Gillespie, "Ordinary Dreams, Lucid Dreams and Mystical Experience," *Lucidity Letter* 5 (1986): 27–31; G. Gillespie, "Without a Guru: An Account of My Lucid Dreaming," in *Conscious Mind, Sleeping Brain*, eds. J. Gackenbach and S. LaBerge (New York: Plenum, 1988), 343–352.

27. C. T. Tart, *Open Mind, Discriminating Mind* (San Francisco: Harper & Row, 1989), xvi.

28. F. Bogzaran, Experiencing the Divine in the Lucid Dream State," *Lucidity Letter* 8 (1990): in press.

29. Shah, *The Sufis*, xxviii.

30. I. Shah, *The Way of the Sufi* (London: Octagon Press, 1968), 252.

31. J. H. M. Whiteman, *The Mystical Life* (London: Faber & Faber, 1961), 57.

32. A. Musa, *Letters and Lectures of Idries Shah* (London: Designist Communications, 1981), 18–20.

33. Ibid.

APPENDIX: SUPPLEMENTARY EXERCISES

1. W. Blake, *The Portable Blake* (New York: Viking Press, 1968), 256.

2. R. Assagioli, *The Act of Will* (New York: Viking Press, 1973).

3. Ibid.

4. W. James, quoted in Assagioli, op. cit., 40.

5. B. Barrett, quoted in Assagioli, op. cit., 39.

6. B. Barrett, *Strength of Will and How to Develop It* (New York, 1931).

7. R. Mishra, *Fundamentals of Yoga* (New York: Lancer Books, 1959).

8. T. Tulku, *Hidden Mind of Freedom* (Berkeley, Calif.: Dharma Publishing, 1981).

Index